T0305413

Urban Poverty in China

Urban Poverty in China

Fulong Wu

Professor, Cardiff University, UK

Chris Webster

Professor, Cardiff University, UK

Shenjing He

Associate Professor, Sun Yat-Sen University, China

Yuting Liu

Associate Professor, South China University of Technology, China

Edward Elgar

Cheltenham, UK • Northampton, MA, USA

Published by
Edward Elgar Publishing Limited
The Lypiatts
15 Lansdown Road
Cheltenham
Glos GL50 2JA
UK

Edward Elgar Publishing, Inc.
William Pratt House
9 Dewey Court
Northampton
Massachusetts 01060
USA

A catalogue record for this book
is available from the British Library

Library of Congress Control Number: 2009937764

Mixed Sources
Product group from well-managed
forests and other controlled sources
www.fsc.org Cert no. SA-COC-1565
© 1996 Forest Stewardship Council

FSC

ISBN 978 1 84720 969 6

Printed and bound by MPG Books Group, UK

Contents

Preface

This book originates from an ESRC[1]-DFID[2] funded project entitled 'Urban poverty and property rights changes in China'. The project allowed us to conduct social surveys in multiple cities, on a scale which is impossible for unfunded scholarly activity. So the support is duly acknowledged. Before we started the project, we had conducted various pilot studies that investigated China's urban poverty distribution and the nature of and variation in the country's impoverished neighbourhoods. Our interest in urban poverty originates from three different roots. The first is a theoretically-oriented quest to understand the emergent social spaces of the Chinese city. The second is a more practical concern about the plight of laid-off workers and migrant workers. The third is an interest in the links between the evolution of property rights, entitlements and poverty in the transitional economy. Through the course of this research, we began to appreciate the complexity of China's urban poverty. Rather than using borrowed terminology and concepts from the West or from other developing countries to describe the Chinese urban poor as *outcasts* and their places of living as *ghettos* or *slums*, we have sought to characterize the poor in ways that specifically acknowledge the institutional roots of poverty. Poverty groups are diverse and so are their places of residence. We thus attempt to link specific poverty profiles to the processes of poverty generation, in particular to institutional changes and the changes in property rights and entitlements that such institutional changes bring about. We analyse these matters at both the household and neighbourhood level.

During the writing of this book, the global credit crunch and associated financial and then real economy downturn has unfolded into a profound economic crisis. Of the perturbations in the world's economy since China's opening up, this one is unprecedented in terms of its global spread into emerging markets. Millions of rural migrant workers have suddenly lost their jobs, and the stress put on the urban labour market is enormous. It might even mean the end of China's current model of export-oriented accumulation. Much will depend on the degree to which the rate of growth in China's domestic demand can be stimulated. At the early stage of the crisis, there was much talk of a decoupling of emergent markets from the troubled economies of the advanced industrial states.

It is now quite apparent that the two parts of the global economy are too intrinsically coupled to prevent the spread of the problem. Whatever shape China's economy takes post-recovery, the processes and patterns of urban impoverishment identified in this book are likely to enter a new phase. Our research is by no means conclusive, therefore. But the trajectories of the livelihood of the poor in the future will inevitably be linked to the processes of economic and institutional change and socio-spatial reconfiguration that we discuss in some detail in this book. In this sense, the book lays down a benchmark for the future studies of China's urban poverty and socio-spatial change.

The book is very detailed. We have chosen to write it in this way so that it provides not only a rich storehouse of analytical insights but also a wealth of data that others might themselves use for their own analysis. The 25 poor neighbourhoods in six cities that we have surveyed are identified by name and location and described in some detail, making it possible for other researchers to undertake follow-up studies. The survey of 1803 households in these neighbourhoods is available as a digital dataset via the Economic and Social Data Service (ESDS) of the UK Data Archive (www.esds.ac.uk).

In addition to the financial support from ESRC and DFID, many people helped us with this project. We would especially like to thank those who live in the surveyed neighbourhoods for answering our questions and sharing their detailed life stories. Because of confidentiality, we cannot thank them in a more personal way. As for the many colleagues we have had the pleasure of working with over the last two and a half years, we thank the following in particular: Zhigang Li, Yuan Yuan, Xingzhong Wang, Ka Lin, Xiaotian Feng, Shuying Zang, Qiyan Wu, Gonghao Cui, Juan Sun, Fuhong Rui, Chaolin Gu, Shifei Zhang, Xingping Guan, and Xun Li. Many students of these colleagues were involved in data collection and we thank them collectively. Through the course of our research, Ya Ping Wang inspired us and shared many findings from his own scholarship. The copyrighted materials published in our earlier publication are duly acknowledged. Finally, we also wish to express thanks to Felicity Plester, commissioning editor at Edward Elgar, for her patience and efficient work as we have brought this publishing project to fruition.

NOTES

1. UK Economic and Social Research Council.
2. UK Department For International Development.

Acknowledgements

This book is supported by the ESRC-DFID funded project 'Urban poverty and property rights changes in China' (RES-167-25-0005).

The authors would like to thank the following for copyrighted materials:

SAGE Publications for Figures 4.11 and 4.12, in Wu, F. (2007), 'The poverty of transition: from industrial district to poor neighbourhood in the city of Nanjing, China', *Urban Studies*, **44**(13), 2673–94.

Blackwell Publishing Ltd for Table 4.2, in Wu, F. (2004), 'Urban poverty and marginalization under market transition: the case of Chinese cities', *International Journal of Urban and Regional Research*, **28**(2), 401–23.

Elsevier for Figures 4.1, 4.2 and 4.5, in Liu, Y.T. and F. Wu (2006), 'Urban poverty neighbourhoods: typology and spatial concentration under China's market transition – a case study of Nanjing', *Geoforum*, **37**(4), 610–26.

Dr Yuan Yuan for Figures 4.3 and 4.4, in Yuan, Y. and X.Q. Xu (2008), 'Geography of urban deprivation in transitional China: a case study of Guangzhou city', *Scientia Geographica Sinica*, **28**(4), 457–63.

Every effort has been made to trace all the copyright holders, but if any have been inadvertently overlooked the publishers will be pleased to make the necessary arrangements at the first opportunity.

Abbreviations and Chinese terms

CCP	Chinese Communist Party
COE	collectively owned enterprise, see also SOE
danwei	work unit of the state
dibao	Minimum Living Standard Support, MLSS
hukou	the 'household registration system'
LAL	Land Administration Law
lian zu fang	low-rent public housing
LQ	Location Quotient
MLSS	Minimum Living Standard Support, also known as *dibao*
RSC	Reemployment Service Centre
SOE	state-owned enterprise, see also COE
SOIE	state-owned industrial enterprise
sanwu	see 'Three Nos'
SSB	State Statistics Bureau
'Three Nos'	traditional urban poor, without relatives, without stable income, and without working capacity, also known as *sanwu*
TVEs	township and village enterprises
Urban villages	known as *chengzhongcun*, rural villages encroached by urban expansion

1. China's new urban poverty: an introduction

In this introductory chapter we depict the urban poverty problem in China. We aim to highlight that urban poverty is an emerging and complex phenomenon, which is driven by three broad processes: decline of the state-owned economy; changing welfare provision; and urbanization and rural-to-urban migration. We emphasize that urban poverty is intertwined with institutional legacies. That is, the urban poor do not comprise a homogenous social group. Their places of living also show great diversity.

Rapid economic growth in China has been accompanied by rising social inequality. China has changed from one of the most egalitarian countries to one with income inequality greater than most other developing countries in East Asia (UNCHS, 2001; Khan and Riskin, 2001). In the 1980s, the issue of poverty was mainly regarded as a problem affecting the backward western region, remote or ecologically fragile areas, and rural areas (Gustafsson and Zhong, 2000). Full employment under the socialist policy of an 'iron rice bowl' in the cities has meant that poverty was confined to rural areas. Only recently has poverty been recognized as an urban problem (UNDP, 2000: 7).

As a country with a socialist history, China is used to minimum social stratification, in particular in the cities, where full employment formed the basic right of social security (Khan and Riskin, 2001). The massive scale of urban poverty since the mid-1990s is quite different from the kinds of living hardships experienced in the former regime, which were caused mainly by physical disabilities. China is therefore facing what can be referred to as a new urban poverty.

Advanced market economies have experienced their own form of 'new' urban poverty; a by-product of economic restructuring, the transition to post-Fordist production; and the reconfiguration of the industrial structure, the labour market and social welfare (Mingione, 1996; UNCHS, 2001). The backdrop of this kind of new urban poverty is the widespread influence of globalization and subsequent re-orientation of the public policy towards market competitiveness (Mingione, 1996; Hamnett, 2001). China's new urban poverty shares some similar causes – economic restructuring and labour redundancy (Guan, 2001). The big difference is that this is occurring in the middle of industrialization through export-oriented manufacturing. China's economic restructuring and the associated differentiation of urban incomes, wages and fortunes involves not only de-industrialization but also a fundamental transformation of ownership from state to private sector.

The accelerating number of laid-off workers since 1995 began to reveal the problem of unemployment and poverty in the cities. The official unemployment rate was 3.1 per cent in 2001, but taking into account laid-off workers, the urban poor population could have been as high as 14 million, accounting for 3.6 per cent of the urban population (MoSS and SSB, 2001). The actual unemployment rate estimated by some scholars is much higher than the official one. In 1997 this may have been as high as 7.5 per cent (Hu, 1999: 35), while in 1998 it was estimated at 10.4 per cent (Li, 2002: 267). Solinger (2001) argued that because of the various forms of unemployment, it is difficult to reach a meaningful figure. In addition, there are millions of rural migrants who are not counted as official residents and are thus excluded from regular employment and services, and do not appear in official unemployment statistics. According to the *China Urban Development Report* (Liu and Pan, 2007), in 1995, the estimated unemployment rate was 4 per cent (including the estimated unregistered unemployment), and the registered unemployment rate was 2.9 per cent. By 2005 these figures had changed, respectively, to 5.8 per cent and 4.2 per cent, and by 2007, to 4.2 per cent and 4.0 per cent.

The new urban poverty is now officially recognized by the Chinese government. In a 2001 working report of the State Council, former Premier Zhu Rongji acknowledged the existence of urban poverty and 'marginal groups'. This marked the official recognition of a major new challenge for social policy in the country.

THE SIZE OF THE PROBLEM

Urban China had a very low absolute poverty rate. The World Bank suggests that the absolute rate of urban poverty has been continuing to decline since the 1980s (Table 1.1). Despite different benchmarks (see the note attached to the table), the rate of absolute poverty is rising. There is now a sizeable population of absolute poor in the cities, even without considering migrants. The numbers of absolute poor reached 20.6 million in 2002. The figure is measured according to the system of Minimum Living Standard Support (MLSS), known as *dibao*, literally, 'minimum security'. In 2008 there were, in total, 22.67 million MLSS recipients within 10.76

Table 1.1   *China's urban poverty line, the size of poor population and the absolute rate of poverty, 1981–2007*

Year	Poverty line (Yuan, per capita per year)	Size of poor population (million)	Number of laid-off workers in SOEs (million)	Absolute rate of poverty (%)
1981	171	3.9		1.9
1982	169	2.0		0.9
1983	178	1.4		0.6
1984	190	0.8		0.3
1985	215	0.9		0.4
1986	226	0.5		0.2
1987	247	0.6		0.2
1988	289	0.7		0.2
1989	304	0.9		0.3
1990	321	1.3		0.4
1995	2107	19.1		5.4
1998	2310	14.8	5.9	3.9
1999	2382	13.4	6.5	3.5
2000	1875	10.5	6.6	2.3
2001	2232	11.7	5.2	2.6
2002	2232	20.6	4.1	4.1
2003		22.5	2.6	4.3
2004	1824	22.1	1.5	4.1
2005	1872	22.3	0.6	4.0
2006	2040	22.4		3.9
2007	2184	22.7		3.8

Note: The absolute poverty rate is not comparable across different periods. The data from 1981 to 1990 is from World Bank (1993). The World Bank defines the international poverty line as expenditure of no more than US$1 per capita per day. The poverty line is defined through combining the expenditure on food, which satisfies the 2150 calories requirement for just enough nutrition for a normal person, and the expenditure on necessary services. The data from 1995 to 1999 was calculated in the same way by the National Statistical Bureau. The data for 2000 is from the calculation of Wang (2002), who works for the National Statistical Bureau. The data for 2001–2007 is the total number of the recipients of Minimum Living Standard Support.

Source: World Bank (1993); Wu and Huang (2007); Hong (2003: 133); Ministry of Civil Affairs (various years).

million households. In total, from January to June 2008, the expenditure on MLSS was 17.3 billion Yuan with an average value of 208 Yuan per capita per month (information obtained from the Department of MLSS, in 2008).

The poverty problem started to emerge after 1995. Before that, the poverty rate was low because the government had effective control over resource allocation, and could guarantee the basic living conditions for urban residents in the planned economy. First and foremost, there was an extensive system of rationing of the basic means of livelihood in the cities, which ensured that all urban residents had equal access to basic subsistence resources. Second, within the city, a full employment system was in place; the government was responsible for arranging jobs for all urban residents, making it impossible, in principle, for urban households to become jobless. Third, the income distribution was highly egalitarian (Riskin, 1987), effectively reducing the possibility of relative and absolute poverty induced by income inequalities. Fourth, inside the city there was a comprehensive social security and welfare system. The social welfare system, integrated with the workplace system, provided a wide range of social benefits, including medial care, education, housing and services. Households that were affiliated to state work units (so-called workplace people) were in an advantageous position in comparison with rural farmers, who had no institutionalized welfare provision at all. Fifth, the separation of urban and rural areas through the household registration system effectively constrained the inflow of rural–urban migrants. Because of this invisible wall, urban workers were shielded from competition from rural migrants (Knight and Song, 1999).

Because of these social and economic policies, Chinese cities effectively controlled urban poverty rates, despite having a low living standard similar to that of other developing countries. The few urban residents who were poor in the pre-reform period mainly consisted of a residual population such as self-employed small shop keepers and workers in street enterprises. They lived outside the formal state system. Within the state system, the system of 'low income and comprehensive welfare' was established in accordance with the socialist ideology. This ideology emphasizes social equality and justice through state control of the means of production. It assumed that government had the responsibility to provide comprehensive welfare and to protect the state's employees from slipping into deprivation. An entitlement to work was viewed as the basic right of all urban citizens – and this became established within the notion of a 'cradle to grave' welfare policy (Guan, 2001). As a result, although urban residents lived in material hardship consistent with the backward stage of the Chinese economy, they were not deprived of welfare entitlements. The state-owned sector provided medical care and recuperation, pensions, housing, children's education and adult job training. In this regime, the poor were those who had no stable income, working capacity, relatives or supporters; they lived in poor households of redundant, sick, disabled or elderly workers. These poor households were known as the 'Three Nos' (*sanwu*). Supported by the government, their relief was the responsibility of the Ministry of Civil Affairs, charged with allocating disaster support and designating five kinds of entitled households ('five guaranteed households', *wubaohu*, for example, veteran households). The ministry operated social welfare factories, social security residences and homes for the elderly.

Since the mid-1990s, the reform of the economic system has led to the widespread accumulation of wealth but also to increasing income and opportunity differences. In the cities, a sizeable social group of poor households has formed. In the last few years, the government has recognized this using various specific terms, including *di shouru qunti* (low-income groups), *ruoshi qunti* (weak social and economic groups) and *chengshi pinkun jumin* (urban poor residents).

The term 'urban poverty' did not feature in official documents until very recently. Besides the traditional urban poor ('Three Nos'), there are five new categories of urban poor population (see Table 1.2) and in 2007, the Ministry of Civil Affairs changed its categories of urban poor to reflect the diversity of the phenomenon (see Table 1.3). The first group in Table 1.2 is the so-called 'Three Nos' (*sanwu*) who have been in receipt of Ministry of Civil Affairs support before and after the reform. The second group are the poor unemployed, that is, households whose family members claim unemployment benefits and whose per capita household income is lower than the local poverty line. The third are the poor employees: laid-off workers and pensioners who, after receiving wages, basic living expenses subsidy, pensions or insurance, still have a per capita household income below the local poverty line. Early retirees belong to this group – former workers who retired in the early stage of the reforms and did not benefit from the various opportunities that arose in later stages of reform. The fourth group consists of residents in economic hardship because of illness and other reasons. Fifth are poor students of universities and colleges who are not able to pay tuition fees and living costs. Under the *hukou* system, enrolling in a university or a college gives rural students a chance to register as urban residents after graduation and they are therefore viewed as belonging to the urban poor. It was estimated that about 3 million poor students could not afford to pay their fees and living costs in 2002, and the proportion of poor students ranged from 20 to 50 per cent in different universities in China (Xinhua News Agency, 2002). Among these poverty groups, the first is equivalent to the traditional urban poor, while the second, third, fourth and fifth are the new urban poor.

In contrast to these categories are those used by Y.P. Wang (2004: 56–66), who classifies the urban poor into the traditional poor, unemployed and laid-off workers, pensioners, poor students, landless suburban

Table 1.2 The composition of the urban poor with official urban household registration (hukou) in 2002–2006

	2002		2003		2004		2005		2006	
	Total (million persons)	Proportion (%)	Total (million persons)	Proportion (%)	Total (million persons)	Proportion (%)	Total (million persons)	Proportion (%)	Total (million persons)	Proportion (%)
Sanwu renyuan (Three Nos)	0.92	4.45	1.00	4.45	0.95	4.31	0.96	4.30	0.93	4.15
Shiye renyuan (the unemployed)	3.58	17.35	4.09	18.20	4.23	19.18	4.10	18.35	4.21	18.79
Xiagang zhigong (laid-off workers)	5.55	26.86	5.18	23.05	4.69	21.27	4.3	19.25	3.50	15.63
Tuixiu renyuan (retirees)	0.90	4.36	0.91	4.05	0.73	3.31	0.61	2.73	0.53	2.37
Zaizhi zhigong (on-post workers*)	1.87	9.05	1.79	7.97	1.41	6.39	1.14	5.10	0.98	4.38
The family members of the laid-off, unemployed, retired, and on-post workers	7.83	37.93	9.49	42.23	10.03	45.49	11.22	50.22	12.25	54.69
Total	20.65	100.00	22.47	100.00	22.05	100.00	22.34	100.00	22.40	100.00

Note: * On-post workers are the working poor; that is, they are still physically working.

Source: Ministry of Civil Affairs (various years).

*Table 1.3   The composition of the urban poor with official household
             registration (*hukou*) in 2007*

	Total (million persons)	Proportion (%)
Dengji shiye renyuan (the registered unemployed)	6.27	27.6
Weidengji shiye renyuan (the unregistered unemployed)	3.64	16
Laonianren (the elderly)	2.98	13.1
Zaizhi zhigong (on-post workers)	0.94	4.1
Linghuo jiuye renyuan (temporary employers)	3.44	15.1
Poor students	3.64	14.2
Wei chengnianren (Under-age persons)	2.23	9.8
Total	22.72	100.00

Source: Ministry of Civil Affairs (various years).

farmers and rural migrants. This is a more inclusive designation that views as 'urban' all those residents who live in an urban area. In the analysis presented in this book, we take this more inclusive and realistic view, and in so doing paint a picture of urban poverty that is less optimistic than the official one.

The estimated size of the urban poor in China varies widely according to the definition chosen. Poverty is normally measured with reference to either expenditure or income required for meeting basic needs. It makes a significant difference whether the urban poverty line is applied as a measure of per capita income or expenditure (Hussain, 2003; Asian Development Bank, 2004). The Urban Household Survey Team of the State Statistical Bureau estimates that the lower bound of the urban poor population was between 10 and 15 million in 2002 (Wang, 2002). The All China Workers' Union conducted a survey of workers, including retired workers and workers with a living standard lower than the local average, and showed that the urban poor population was 15 million. If we include those who are supported by MLSS, the total population of urban poor might have been as high as 21.827 million in June 2003. On 12 November 2001, the State Council issued the 'Notice on strengthening MLSS in urban areas', which defines the urban poor as those who receive MLSS support. However, because the living standard of the MLSS is still very low, it has been argued that the real population of urban poor is larger

than the number of MLSS recipients. Zhu argued that MLSS underesti-
mates the numbers of urban poor, and gave an adjusted estimate which
was as high as 30.56 million (Zhu, 2002). The Asian Development Bank
(2004: 90) agreed that since not all those entitled to assistance will have
been recruited into the MLSS system, the actual numbers of urban poor
may well exceed the official urban poverty figure of 21 million. In fact, the
number of MLSS recipients has been growing considerably since 2001 but
has stabilized more recently.

Clearly, the definition of poverty and the measurement of poverty rates
is problematic; Cai (2003) estimated that the poverty rate in 2002 should
have been 7.7 per cent rather than the official 4.1 per cent. What can be
said, however, by way of summarizing the controversy, is that the urban
poor population in China is in the range of between 15 and 31 million, and
is approximately 4 to 8 per cent of the total urban population; this figure
only includes people with urban household registration (*hukou*).

In the remainder of this chapter we discuss three structural forces that
shape the landscape of China's new urban poverty (Wu and Huang, 2007).
The first structural force is the decline of the state-owned sector. Together
with economic restructuring, the decline of the state sector transformed
the labour market, which generated millions of redundant and laid-off
industrial workers. The second structural force is the transformation of
welfare provision, which reduced the welfare coverage and had the effect
of commoditizing social services. The changing mechanisms of welfare
provision have created a gap that has helped create the new poor –
including poor migrant workers. The third structural force is urbanization
and migration, which has moved rural poverty into the city. Similar to the
'urbanization of poverty' documented in other developing countries (UN-
Habitat, 2003), rural-to-urban migration has created millions of working
urban poor. With the relaxation of internal migration control, surplus
labour in agriculture flowed into the cities.

At the same time, the modernization and redevelopment of urban areas
reduced the reciprocal and informal ties that had developed over many
years within urban communities. Old areas have been systematically razed
to the ground and their communities dispersed, and in places, pockets
of old communities remain as underdeveloped and marginalized neighbourhoods that form the homes of the economically weakest. Although
segregation and isolation are still low in Chinese cities, new forms of
socio-spatial patterns have started to emerge, and market-led spatial re-
organization has begun to impose a challenge for socio-spatial cohesion.

Before economic reform, the urban governance of the Chinese state was
organized through the framework of state socialism, which emphasizes
redistribution. Social surplus was concentrated in the state apparatus and

then redistributed to the urban population. Although the 'redistributive state', a concept originally proposed by Szelenyi (1983) in Eastern Europe, was organized according to a hierarchy of the cadre and working classes, the state upheld an egalitarian ideology which led to a nominally equal income distribution in urban society. The urban poverty rate was very low, and there was no underclass. Such a low poverty rate was achieved in the context of a low overall living standard.

Since the reform, this ideology has changed. Deng Xiaoping explicitly proposed to 'let a few people become rich first' and to explore different models of income distribution. His pragmatism was captured by the slogan 'wading the river by groping stones'. After an initial equalizing effect, which tended to favour direct market producers rather than the privileged cadre class who had benefited in the socialist redistributive state (Nee, 1989), the differentiating process of wealth accumulation began in cities. This started to happen roughly from 1995. The mechanism of resource allocation was transformed by the creation of markets, which immediately started to have far-reaching implications for social stratification (Walder, 1996; Bian and Logan, 1996; Khan and Riskin, 2001).

DECLINE OF THE STATE-OWNED SECTOR AND ECONOMIC RESTRUCTURING

The ending of the administrative allocation of labour and planned industrial structure led to a large number of surplus workers being laid off by state-owned enterprises (SOEs) (Steinfeld, 1998; Blecher, 2002). In the process of enterprise reform, the SOEs began to abandon egalitarian wage distribution and the administratively based assignment of jobs. In particular, since the mid-1990s, the deepening of reform policies at the enterprise level revealed the endemic problem of hidden un- and under-employment and led to massive lay-offs (starting in 1995). The performance of SOEs had declined significantly, with the proportion of loss-making state-owned industrial enterprises (SOIEs) growing to 41.4 per cent by 1999. The share of SOEs' contribution to the total industrial output has also been decreasing. From 1995 to 2004, SOEs have cut jobs at an annual rate of 3.68 million, according to the *China Labour Statistical Yearbook 2005* (State Statistics Bureau, 2006: 188). From 1998 to 2005, a total of 33.18 million SOE employees were laid off. These job losses, together with an annual increase in the new labour force of 10 million, have exerted a downward pressure on urban wages and have fuelled the rate of unemployment. But according to Solinger (2002), these figures could be seriously understated.

Even for those who have kept their jobs, their income has not generally seen a comparable increase with the rising cost of living expenses. The problems and mismanagement of SOEs have led them into a difficult situation. Low profit rates, and even deficits, have reduced not only the direct income of workers but also their welfare benefits, which were usually allocated by the workplace. Many residents have experienced actual and real income reductions. For some workers, their per capita household income even dropped below the local poverty line, making them the working poor. On the other hand, SOEs have to undertake many welfare functions and support their retired workers and staff. The ratio of retirees to on-post workers in SOEs is excessively high. In this sense, individual enterprises faced what many welfare states are now facing – an over-burdensome welfare liability caused by an imbalance of retired state dependents and active workers. In the decades before the economic reforms began, China adopted a unified financial system in which the government collected all revenues from enterprises and re-allocated the expenditures to SOEs. Pensions were managed and distributed by the government, while the SOEs did not maintain pension funds. However, the reform of the economic system transferred the pensions to the SOEs. That is, the SOEs had to provide pensions to their workers. Therefore, for the SOEs that have many retired workers, the pension cost is high. This is different from the situation before economic reform when pension costs were simply borne by the government.

As non-working staff demand security and welfare support, the high rate of retirees in SOEs has become a burden for these enterprises, increasing the cost of employment. Compared with newly formed enterprises that recruit staff according to their actual need for labour rather than administrative commands, SOEs have to spend 46 per cent more on wages (Sun, 2002: 18). This has had a significant effect on their competitiveness and performance.

Welfare benefits from workplaces used to occupy a significant proportion of the income composition of Chinese urban residents. They were a direct source of living expenditure. According to a survey of 1000 laid-off workers in 2000 in Beijing, redundancy led to a 61.2 per cent decrease in income (Sun, 2002: 18). In recent years, the commodification of housing, education and medical care has increased household expenditure, because these costs were previously borne by employers. The restructuring of the welfare system moved many households into a position of income vulnerability, not only exacerbating poverty and poverty vulnerability levels but also further reducing human capital development of these families. For the first time in decades, poverty in China risks being differentially transmitted between generations. Wang (2000) showed that the policy of requiring sitting tenants to purchase their housing had the effect of straining the budgets of poor families, redirecting scarce liquidity from education and other pressing needs into the improvement of housing.

One effect of this was to reduce the purchasing power of urban residents. From the late 1990s to 2003, China entered a stage of continuous deflation. The lack of effective demand had a negative impact on job creation. Along with the commodification of the labour force, more lay-offs were generated, causing a deepening and extension of urban poverty. Economic deflation, job shrinkage and decreasing purchasing power lead to a vicious circle of poverty generation.

The fundamental reform of industrial structure drove many SOEs into bankruptcy. The industrial sectors that had lost their comparative advantage in the face of international competition were forced to downsize. This produced large numbers of redundant workers in a short period of time. The urban poor population tended to be concentrated in industrial sectors such as textiles, coal mining, timber, traditional light industries and machinery, and military industries. These sectors were the labour-intensive industries developed in the planned economy with little market competition. Some of them were heavy consumers of natural resources, or in the small and low-tech commercial, service and handicraft industries. Since the 1990s, new technology has favoured capital-intensive and knowledge-intensive industries, leaving income levels in traditional industries, labour-intensive industries and industrial sectors with higher levels of competition to decline. Compared with 1992, in 2006, finance and insurance, scientific research and technological services have seen the largest increases in income levels, respectively reaching 1361 and 1222 per cent. Compared to these, farming, forestry, agricultural husbandry and fishery industries and construction industries were ranked bottom, respectively with a 523 and 532 per cent increase (State Statistics Bureau, 2007). Ranked according to income level, in 1992, the two top sectors were production and supply of electricity, gas and water, and real estate, but in 2006 the top two had changed to scientific research and technological services, and finance and insurance. Manufacturing and construction industries have become the sectors with an inferior income. In 2006, in Beijing, the average wage for construction workers was as low as 30 per cent of that of finance and insurance sector workers. By 2007, in Shanghai, the average wage in manufacturing industries was 52 per cent of those in the finance and insurance sectors. In Chongqing, the average wage of construction workers only amounted to 45 per cent of that in the finance and insurance sectors (State Statistics Bureau, 2007).

The analysis of industrial restructuring gives a gloomy prospect

for poverty alleviation based on job generation, currently the dominant policy agenda. There are several reasons for this. First, employment opportunities have been reduced in the initial stages of WTO
entrance, although WTO membership may contribute to long-term
job creation. This is because structural unemployment is being created
by industrial restructuring. The state-protected capital-intensive and
technology-intensive sectors, such as automobile, machinery, metallurgy
and petrochemical industries, and the iron and steel industry, are faced
with new and intense pressure from international competition. In order
to survive, large-scale adjustment becomes inevitable, including mergers,
reduction of workforces and bankruptcy. By comparison, access to
the WTO has given more opportunities to China's traditional labour-
intensive sectors, such as clothing, textiles, building and food processing,
because of the reduction of trade barriers and export quotas. However,
the increase in employment might not benefit the current urban poor
population, because it takes time to form a sizeable production capacity,
and enterprises are unable to increase exports immediately. Moreover,
after two or three years, the age disadvantage of laid-off workers becomes
more apparent. Compared with the younger workforce and cheaper rural
migrants, the employability of the current urban poverty population is
becoming lower. Workers laid off from SOEs are therefore a residual
poverty group resulting from China's economic transition, and one that
appears to have a bleak future.

Second, and related, the demographic attributes of the current urban
poor population tend not to allow them to return to mainstream industries.
The advance in technological development is eliminating job positions in
traditional industries (Solinger, 2002). For example, the labour-intensive
manufacturing industries and the textile industries, which absorbed a large
number of workers, have begun to resort to new technologies to increase
efficiency. Low-skilled workers are no longer able to find stable jobs in
the new labour market. Jobs in the new industrial sectors are not for them
because they are more than 35 years old (most new industries require
applicants less than 35 years old) and have middle or low education levels
with low transferable job skills. Their skills have become outdated, while
the new jobs are in the sector of scientific and technological services, com-
puters, finance, trade and insurance, biotechnologies and so on, which
require employees to have higher education and special skills. So, the new
industries do not offer employment opportunities to the currently laid-off
workers. The result means that the new urban poor (in particular those
laid off and the unemployed) are excluded by economic restructuring.
Most of them have little hope of returning to the mainstream industrial
sectors and finding a stable source of income there. Sun (2002: 24) uses the

term 'broken social structure' to describe the exclusive nature of the job market. In such a circumstance, the new urban poor are in desperate need of social security. Unfortunately, the social welfare system itself is under transformation. The marginal social groups fall into a gap between the old and the new systems.

TRANSFORMATION OF WELFARE PROVISION

Before economic reform, state employees received comprehensive social welfare benefits. The social security system was basically guaranteed with employment, rights to welfare transfer payments being bundled into employment rights. Workers enjoyed social security without paying an insurance fee, and this was regarded as one indication of socialism's superiority to capitalism. But since the mid-1990s, with accelerating economic reforms, the model of 'occupational welfare plus social relief' was no longer able to cope with the increasing numbers of poor outside the work-unit system. A new population without workplace affiliation forced the state to reform the social security system. The development of a societal-based system was justified on efficiency grounds. It would be more cost-effective because the work-unit-based delivery system often saw unconstrained allocation of benefits. There was inadequate financial discipline within the system and an incentive to allocate an inordinate proportion of enterprise revenue to welfare expenditures (particularly housing), before returning the residual to higher levels of government.

Looking generally at the post-reform city, the following systematic transformations have had a profound effect on the position of poverty in urban life. First, the state no longer distributes subsidized living materials to urban workers. In the past a low-price rationing system ensured cross subsidy between rural and urban sectors in favour of the latter. Food and all commodities are now only available at market prices. Second, the state no longer assigns jobs. Instead, residents have to seek job opportunities in the labour market. Third, instead of prescribing a high level of social security, the state sets a low minimum standard with relatively wide coverage. Fourth, the state has transformed workplace-based welfare provision into a 'social provision model'. Workplaces no longer provide medical care, housing, education and other social services. The new system emphasizes joint contributions from the state, enterprises and individuals, and makes individuals partially responsible for ensuring their security. All of these institutional shifts reduce the burden of the state in welfare provision.

In principle the new regime is MLSS. Shanghai was the first city to

*Table 1.4   Minimum Living Standard Support in cities and provincial
          capitals*

	Date of establishment	Standard before 1999 (Yuan)	Standard in 2007 (Yuan)
Beijing	Jul. 1996	200	328
Tianjin	Jan. 1998	185	330
Shijiazhuang	Jan. 1996	140	173
Taiyuan	Jul. 1997	120	216
Huhehaote	Jan. 1997	110	189
Shenyang	Mar. 1995	150	245
Changchun	Jul. 1996	130	225
Harbin	Apr. 1997	140	233
Shanghai	Jun. 1993	215	350
Nanjing	Aug. 1996	140	281
Hangzhou	Jan. 1997	165	287
Hefei	Jul. 1996	150	234
Fuzhou	Jan. 1995	170	201
Nanchang	Jan. 1997	100	197
Jinan	Jul. 1996	140	249
Zhengzhou	Aug. 1996	120	234
Wuhan	Mar. 1996	150	219
Changsha	Jul. 1997	130	198
Guangzhou	Jul. 1995	240	321
Nanning	Sep. 1995	150	190
Haikou	Jan. 1995	170	293
Chengdu	Jul. 1997	120	214
Chongqing	Jul. 1996	130	178
Guiyang	Jan. 1998	120	188
Kunming	Jul. 1996	140	201
Lasa	Jan. 1997	130	230
Xi'an	Jan. 1998	105	188
Lanzhou	Jan. 1998	120	211
Xining	Aug. 1997	120	178
Yinchuang	Jan. 1998	100	200
Wulumuqi	Jan. 1998	120	156

Source: Originally from the Ministry of Civil Affairs, cited in Cai (2003: 63); Ministry of
Civil Affairs (various years).

establish a MLSS, and by the end of 1998, 581 cities had followed its
example (Table 1.4). In September 1999, the State Council issued 'The
regulation of MLSS to urban residents', which designates who is qualified
for assistance. This specifies that non-agricultural registered households

Table 1.5 *The quantity of the recipients of Minimum Living Standard Support from 1998 to 2007*

	Total number of recipients (million)	Growth rate of the recipients (%)	Total amount of financial support (billion Yuan)
1998	1.84	109.4	0.70
1999	2.66	44.4	1.55
2000	4.03	51.4	2.72
2001	11.71	190.8	4.20
2002	20.65	76.4	11.26
2003	22.47	8.8	15.10
2004	22.05	-1.9	17.27
2005	22.34	1.3	19.19
2006	22.40	0.3	22.42
2007	22.72	1.4	27.74

Source: Ministry of Civil Affairs (various years).

that have a per capita household income lower than a locally set poverty line can receive a subsidy to make up the difference. Those who are classified as belonging to the 'Three-Nos' are eligible for the full living allowance set by the local minimum living standard. By 1999, all 668 cities and 1638 counties had established a MLSS system. The minimum living standard is regularly reviewed to take account of local variation in real living costs indicated by a representative basket of goods. From 1 October 1999, minimum living standards have been raised by 30 per cent on average across cities and counties.

According to the Ministry of Civil Affairs, in 2006 about 38.8 per cent of MLSS recipients were actually poor employees of state-owned enterprises or collectively owned enterprises. Only 4.2 per cent were made up by the traditional poor (the 'Three-Nos'). This starkly illustrates the changing nature of urban poverty (Table 1.2). By 2007, the number of MLSS recipients had increased to 22.72 million (Table 1.5).

There are a number of problems associated with the implementation of these policies. Hussain (2003: 25–8) noted the problems with MLSS: limited coverage, loopholes in the diagnosis of urban poverty, insufficient benefits, difficulty in balancing poverty alleviation and maintaining the incentive to work, the lack of financing, and inadequate administrative structure. These are elaborated below.

First, although the number of MLSS recipients has increased significantly since 2000, its coverage is still too limited, and some poor families are not receiving adequate support. MLSS formed 4.8 per cent of all urban residents in 2001. Recognizing the problem, in 2002 the principle of '*yingbao jinbao*' ('all qualified should be guaranteed') was put forward to expand coverage. The number of MLSS recipients increased to 20.65 million. The amount disbursed escalated to 10.5 billion Yuan, of which central government contributed 4.6 billion, accounting for 44 per cent, and local governments contributed 5.9 billion, accounting for 56 per cent (Tang, 2003). However, its coverage is still too limited, accounting for only 3.8 per cent of all urban residents by the end of 2007 (Table 1.5).

Many households are unable to enter the scheme because of the strict control of the benefit line. For example, some cities stipulate that those who are of working age (for males, aged 16–60 and for females, 16–55) are excluded, regardless of their actual employment status. Other cities exclude those who are still attached to workplaces, regardless of whether or not they receive wages. Those who still have a contractual relationship with their workplace even without wages are regarded as ineligible because the unpaid wages are treated as the debt of the workplace. Some cities specify that those who possess electrical household appliances such as a TV and refrigerator are not eligible for MLSS. Some neighbourhood committees exclude those who frequently eat meat. Some local governments exclude staff and workers of enterprises that belong to central government. Residents living outside the designated towns of the county (which is the lowest level of urban settlement according to China's administrative hierarchy) are not considered eligible because they are not urban residents. Local governments have adopted various exclusionary practices known as the '12 excluded categories' and the '16 types of disqualification' (Tang, 2003). Although these practices are not formally permitted, they reflect a mentality that treats MLSS as a last resort welfare safety net. The MLSS is clearly a measure to address absolute poverty. This sets it apart from the kind of universal social welfare systems in developed economies, in which minimum living standards tend to be set to prevent relative poverty. In China, the concern is to prevent people from becoming truly destitute and starving.

Second, and developing the last point, MLSS adopts a *low standard* that only covers limited items. The 'Regulation of urban MLSS' promulgated in 1999 specifies that 'the line of urban minimum living is determined with reference to a basket of basic expenditure on clothing, food, accommodation, water, electricity, gas or coal, as well as the cost of children's compulsory education'. However, the standard excludes medical care, middle and higher education, legal and other costs. For poor households in China, illness is a major cause of financial difficulty. When unexpected disastrous life events occur, a poor household or one vulnerable to poverty is often driven into hardship which cannot be dealt with without outside help.

Poor and vulnerable residents, as members of society (as opposed to being subsistence dwellers), have needs other than basic physical survival. They are in need of employment, children's education, housing and medical care. MLSS covers the very basic needs and excludes the need for development. It does not help poor families afford increasing education costs, and this has the effect of reducing human capital investment.

In addition to its design faults, the MLSS as operated in a specific city is sometimes less than adequate because it is not fully implemented. Because of the lack of a concrete operating scheme, the principles proposed in MLSS are often not fully realized. While some implementation regulations call for service fee exemptions or discounts for example, in reality the reduction of charges is not fully carried out because the commodification of service provision often strengthens the interest of service providers, who are unwilling to give financial concessions. In Beijing, only 3.4 per cent of poor households received tuition fee discounts; 9 per cent had rent reductions; and 10.8 per cent had a discount on sanitary charges (Yin, 2002: 47–51). These figures suggest that fee exemptions are selectively implemented. For small items such as the sanitary charge, the rate of exemption is higher, while for the large items such as tuition fees, the exemption rate is relatively low. This pattern clearly suggests that service providers have an incentive not to make the legally required concessions.

For these reasons, as well as the low level of the poverty line, the per capita financial support from MLSS is very limited (Table 1.6). Exacerbating this is the way that the subsidy provided by MLSS is determined – set according to the difference between the legally set minimum living standard and 'actual' household income. Very often, 'actual' income is not measured, but is estimated by the officials in charge of evaluating the qualifications of potential recipients. It may be presumed that incomes tend to be overestimated if officials have capacity constraints to follow in their allocations. The low levels of transfer payments that result under the MLSS scheme very often do not give residents sufficient support in overcoming their poverty situation. They may be spared starvation and homelessness but the financial package does not guarantee a return to mainstream society.

Third, MLSS as a key part of China's new social security package provides help of *last resort* for the poor. At present, the system of social security consists of three major security lines: the minimum living allowance for laid-off workers (including pension); unemployment and old age pension; and the minimum living standard scheme. The first two lines have major loopholes. For example, in Beijing more than 60 per cent of poor households did not have any medical insurance or insurance against serious illness in 2001. About 86.1 per cent of eligible households did not

Table 1.6   *Average per capita monthly subsidies of MLSS in the cities
              directly under the jurisdiction of the central government and
              selected provinces, 2007*

Cities/provinces	Average subsidies per capita monthly (Yuan)	Total recipients (million persons)	Finance subsidies (million Yuan)
National	102	22.72	27472.05
Beijing	267	0.15	476.88
Shanghai	205	0.34	844.25
Zhejiang	184	0.09	194.47
Jiangsu	118	0.45	621.28
Chongqing	104	0.83	1042.36
Hebei	90	0.89	936.24
Henan	84	1.41	1383.03
Heilongjiang	96	1.46	1660.11
Inner Mongolia	129	0.80	1162.43
Hunan	93	1.39	1503.93

Source: Ministry of Civil Affairs (various years) (http://www.mca.gov.cn), accessed
4 November 2008.

receive unemployment insurance; 72.1 per cent did not receive elderly
pension insurance; 74.6 per cent did not receive minimum wages; and 9.9
per cent did not receive minimum living support (Yin, 2002: 48). This is
because, in the transition period, the social security system mainly consists
of social insurances, secured by the payment of a premium. There are three
major types of insurance that are currently implemented: elderly pension
insurance, unemployment insurance and medical insurance. However,
these types of insurance require premiums from individuals and emphasize the individuals' responsibility in social security. Poor households
who struggle to survive cannot afford the insurance premium and as a
consequence, social insurance has become meaningless to them.

Finally, despite progress with MLSS, there is *a negative side-effect* that
should be mentioned. Because the MLSS is intentionally configured at
the minimum survival level, a side-effect is that it keeps a pool of low-
income households surviving at the 'edge of poverty'. The rationale of
maintaining a low standard is justified in several ways. First, in the overall
environment of market reorientation, the redistributive policy is often
not compatible with local governments' ambition to maintain economic
competitiveness. This aligns with concerns about the pitfalls of Western
welfare state models, which encourage welfare dependency. Second, the

low level of support given is justified pragmatically: the urban poor have accumulated in cities and regions with poor economic performance and a history of heavy industrialization, and local governments cannot afford to set the MLSS bar any higher. Third, because of the country's size, there is inevitably a large number of urban households living near the poverty line, and raising the line even a little will generate large increases in the number of official urban poor and in the financial liability of supporting them (Hussain, 2003: 30).

The approach to social policy reform in China has been to commodify the provision of welfare. There have been various experiments in using social insurance to provide social security. The design of social welfare policy is based on the assumption of continuing economic growth and expansion of the labour market. Thus, social insurance is used to prevent urban poverty. The new social security system is designed for those who are currently working rather than those who have been laid off and excluded from job participation. The emergence of large numbers of laid-off workers driven by economic restructuring has challenged this basic assumption. Although the new MLSS system has been set up to cope with the poorest population, the overall transformation of welfare provision is similar to welfare retrenchment under the post-Keynesian workfare state in the West (Musterd and Ostendorf, 1998). Welfare retrenchment in advanced market economies refers to the reduction of welfare expenditure and conversion from welfare to workfare (Peck, 2001). Similarly in China, the entitlement based on work-unit affiliation has now been transformed to a service supplied on the basis of the ability to contribute to employment insurance. A significant number of poor households have lost their entitlement but have not qualified for MLSS because of the extremely stringent screening process. Welfare retrenchment is a result of a disjuncture between old service and new provision, as the reduction of coverage of welfare is not made up by the expansion of new social security coverage.

URBANIZATION, MIGRATION AND URBAN REDEVELOPMENT

Since the 1980s Chinese cities have grown steadily due to the influx of rural-to-urban migrants. In 1989, the number of rural migrants was 30 million. In 1993, the number increased to 62 million. Then by the end of 2005, rural migrants rapidly increased to around 200 million (The Investigating Group of Chinese Migrant Workers' Problems, 2006).

For rural migrants, access to urban services is hindered by the household registration system (*hukou*). The *hukou* system was introduced as an 'invisible wall' dividing China institutionally into urban and rural sectors (Chan, 1994; Chan and Zhang, 1999). The initial purpose of this institutional arrangement was to prevent workers from migrating from rural areas and to guarantee scarce non-agricultural employment and related welfare to urban residents. This was essentially directed at supporting the heavy industry-oriented strategy under the planned economy (Cai et al., 2002). Until the early 1980s, the adoption of the household responsibility system in rural areas and the liberalization of agricultural production resulted in surplus labourers in rural areas and an increase in their mobility. Later, the relaxation of the *hukou* system, the abolition of state-controlled food rationing, and the introduction of contract workers further loosened the restrictions over labour mobility between regions and sectors. With the attraction of more development opportunities and better living conditions, a huge number of rural workers migrated to urban areas to seek employment and make a living.

Although the Chinese government has relaxed its control over population mobility, the *hukou* system in urban areas remains essentially unchanged (Y.P. Wang, 2004). There are still many obstacles for migrants created by the *hukou* system. For example, even if rural workers can find jobs within the industrial sectors that they are allowed to enter, they are still at risk of being dispelled by security officers in the name of maintaining social order. Their employment rights are by no means unambiguously defined and protected. Furthermore, because of their rural *hukou*, rural migrants face considerable hardship in the cities as they are denied access to good jobs and to urban entitlements (Ma, 2002; Solinger, 1999). A dual labour market has been created by the present *hukou* system and the urban–rural pattern of divided management. To alleviate employment pressure, quotas have been set by most cities to limit the employment of workers who do not possess urban *hukou* (Lee, 2001). Rural migrants are excluded from some formal and steady occupations. In Beijing, for example, rural migrants were not allowed to take up jobs in some high-profile areas such as finance and insurance in 2001. Without access to these jobs, rural migrants tend to take the hard, dangerous and dirty physical and labour-intensive jobs (Y.P. Wang, 2004). While the central government has strengthened the legal benefits of migrants in cities recently, the situation is not optimistic. Against this background, it is very difficult to develop a uniform and open labour market. Consequently, the employment of rural migrants is typically informal, low-quality and unstable, which has directly resulted in their low income and poor living standards. Rural migrants mainly work in highly labour-intensive, temporary, insecure and low-income jobs, such as building, portering, waste collecting, hawking, peddling and domestic service. As a result of occupational exclusion and restriction, rural migrants tend to receive lower incomes.

In addition, under the present *hukou* system, the urban and rural populations are clearly divided, and it is extremely difficult to transfer one's rural registration to an urban one (Y.P. Wang, 2004). Although rural migrants effectively work and live in urban areas, they are still treated as outsiders. The movement of rural workers into urban areas follows economic rationales, yet they have not obtained reasonable institutional rights to live in urban areas and are denied access to crucial urban entitlements due to their rural *hukou* status.

Clearly marginalized by the *hukou* system, rural migrants in the cities face several kinds of hardship. First, though peasant workers have entered urban areas, their homes are still in rural areas. For those who commute daily or periodically, they face high commuting costs, as well as suffering inconvenience to themselves and their families. Second, if their families move to the urban area with them, they face significant extra costs for housing and education. Rural migrant households often find themselves isolated because of limited access to urban social services and lack of social ties. All of these negative factors have turned many rural migrants into a marginal group characterized by unstable employment and living conditions. This is a group that earns the simplest of livings through the hardest of work, and a group that suffers discrimination everywhere just because of its status.

The institutional and economic marginalization of rural migrants and the other groups of urban poor is graphically framed and exacerbated by the physical manifestations of modernization and transition: urban redevelopment. Urban redevelopment is spatially selective, leaving out those poor areas with high population density. In these left-over places, population invasion and succession by migrants has occurred. Some inner urban areas are 'downgraded' to places in which rural migrants concentrate. Most important of these are the 'villages within the city' (*chengzhong-cun*); these areas are created through informal housing development in former rural villages that have been encroached and surrounded by city development.

Figure 1.1 shows the different route of marginalization. For the workers in SOEs and COEs, they are marginalized by the introduction of a labour market after all inclusive welfare was dismantled. For farmers, rapid urbanization has driven them into the cities. They become rural migrants and face institutional and social exclusion. The evolving urban poverty issue is thus more than a simple outcome of market development. It is a complex interaction between the institution and market mechanism.

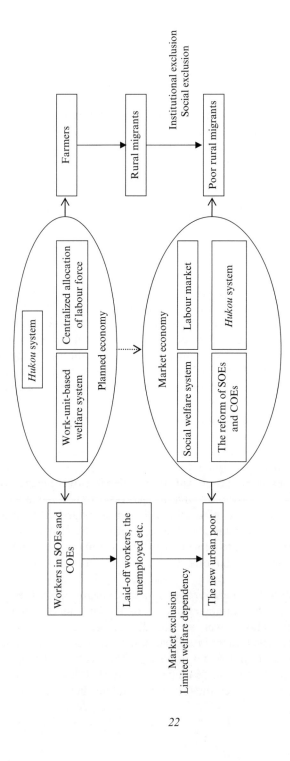

Farmers → Rural migrants → Poor rural migrants

Institutional exclusion
Social exclusion

Hukou system

Work-unit-based welfare system | Centralized allocation of labour force

Planned economy

Market economy

Social welfare system | Labour market

The reform of SOEs and COEs | *Hukou* system

Workers in SOEs and COEs → Laid-off workers, the unemployed etc. → The new urban poor

Market exclusion
Limited welfare dependency

Source: Liu et al. (2008).

Figure 1.1   Different routes of poverty experience of China's new urban poor

22

FRAGMENTED POVERTY GROUPS

The new urban poverty population is not a homogenous social group (Wu and Huang, 2007). Rather, poverty groups are produced by different institutional processes and are affected in different ways by the institutional changes according to their position within the state system (known as *tizhi*, or institution, the most important factor determining the level of welfare provision in the planned economy system). The system represented the state's organization of the labour reproduction process. The foundation of the institution is based on numerous work units (*danwei*), including government organizations, SOEs, collectively owned enterprises (COEs), hospitals and public organizations. People working in the state system received a wider range of welfare benefits than did those outside the system, including free housing, free medical care and education. The system was part of the state machinery that not only facilitated accumulation of resources but also provided public goods to its members. Housing, education, health services and so on were a cost of production within the *danwei*, ensuring the unit's ability to sustain itself over time. It was perfectly reasonable therefore to exclude outsiders from accessing these 'club-good' welfare benefits. A fundamental reason why the new urban poor are not homogenous is because they had different relations with the state system. Some were 'within the state system' (*ti zhi nei*), while others were 'outside the state system' (*ti zhi wai*) before economic reform. Economic restructuring and the transformation of welfare provision have exerted different impacts on these social groups.

The 'Insiders of the System'

The new urban poor who were inside the system include laid-off workers, unemployed workers, the low-skill working poor and retirees. They contributed to the SOEs, through which they had received lifelong social security from the government. While their wages were low in the planned economy, they were promised comprehensive welfare benefits in the event of retirement, illness or other disastrous life events. However, along with the restructuring of the economy and reform of SOEs, the performance of their workplaces declined, and so did their welfare benefits. The reform of housing, education and medical care has required individuals to make a greater financial contribution, which has changed the structure of their living expenses and increased uncertainty in consumption. Meanwhile, the re-employment programme has been confronted with the incapacity of administrative departments, lack of funds and the disadvantaged position of laid-off workers in the labour market (Solinger,

2002; Lee and Warner, 2004), and is unlikely to immediately improve the condition of the poverty group. At the end of 2002, only 55.6 per cent of the registered unemployed had received unemployment benefits. In addition the average annual income per capita of unemployed households was only 2774 Yuan, which is equivalent to only 22.3 per cent of the urban average of 12422 Yuan (State Statistics Bureau, 2004: 33, 135–6, 345). The income of re-employed workers is generally lower than their previous wages.

Social security reform has sometimes exacerbated the situation of poor households. In the old system, the government did not require them to pay various insurance premiums but promised lifelong security as a right. Now working households must pay premiums for insurance against emergency needs.

In 1998, China abolished in-kind housing benefit. However, for poor households, no rental subsidies have been offered, while the stock of social rental housing has decreased. Recently, the Ministry of Construction has promoted social rental housing (*lian zu fang*). But the amount of social rental housing for the poor is limited. In 1998, the central government anticipated that 15 per cent of low-income families would rent social housing from the municipal government. But by 2003, the practice of social housing was still at an experimental stage. By the end of 2002, the municipal authority of Beijing paid rent allowances to only 998 households (Y.P. Wang, 2004: 138).

The reform of education includes reduction of government subsidies, which has significantly increased the households' actual expenses for education. In Beijing, the tuition fee for a high school student is about 4000 Yuan per year, while in 2002 the average annual income for non-working staff was only 2774 Yuan. Poor households cannot afford the cost of education, which forces them to consider reducing their children's years of schooling.

Medical care reform is another example of a significant cost increase (Duckett, 2004: 155–73). Up to 2002, 94 million residents had joined the medical insurance programme, accounting for 63.9 per cent of total staff and workers (State Statistics Bureau, 2004: 543–4). Among them, 24.74 million retirees had joined medical insurance, accounting for 58.6 per cent of total retirees. However, even those who have joined medical care insurance sometimes do not receive full reimbursement of medical costs because their enterprises have gone bankrupt and cannot pay their contribution to the insurance premium. As a result, reimbursement is delayed. Meanwhile, the cost of medical care has increased significantly over the years (Duckett, 2004). In 2000, a visit to the local surgery cost, on average, 86 Yuan, a six-fold increase from 1990. In contrast, the real income of poor households has decreased. In this circumstance, illness has become a major factor in driving poor households into deep poverty and tipping vulnerable households into poverty.

The 'Outsiders of the System'

Outsiders include those who are self-employed and those who have never been inside the state system, even in the socialist era. A large number of self-employed individual workers have appeared after economic reform. They do not have work-unit affiliation and thus are outside the state system. In the 1980s, they were engaged in small and informal sectors, forming a social stratum that benefited from the emergence of markets. However, since the 1990s, many cities have begun to demolish simple stores and kiosk shops and to ban the use of the pedestrian pavement for trade. Petty traders and hawkers lost their trading places and were forced to abandon their businesses. The regulation of small businesses has become more stringent, with various fees and fines imposed on them, which effectively reduced the profitability of self-employed businesses. On the other hand, market competition has become intense, and some private businesses have accumulated enough capital to transform their small shops or workshops into small retail enterprises and firms. But it has become more and more difficult for the individual self-employed to initiate new businesses and to survive market competition. Most of the self-employed belong to the informal sector. Because of a lack of skills and necessary capacity, they cannot find a job in the formal labour market. The informal sector has never been covered by social security, even in the socialist era. The individual workers are vulnerable because declining health, illness or a sudden change in life course can knock them into poverty.

Besides self-employed individuals, a large number of employees who work in the private sector, township and village enterprises, joint ventures, and various non-governmental organizations are in the formal labour market but without work-unit affiliation. Although they are working in these enterprises or organizations, there is no dependent relationship between the workplace and employees. Their working contract could be terminated at any time. The wage level of these private sector employees may not be low, and indeed may even be relatively high compared with state workers; however, they have no workplace benefits in the form of housing allocation or state pension. Because China is now experiencing peak labour supply, with an annual increase in the working population of over 10 million, supply exceeds demand in many sectors of the labour market. The private sector, especially at the low end of the labour market, thus cuts wages and offers no fringe benefits. Employers do not even contribute their share to the social security programme and their workers therefore remain outside any social security system.

The outsiders of the state system are already in a marginal position because of their low educational attainment. Such a marginal position has become even more peripheral, with the new social security being designed mainly for the working population (and to some extent for newly laid-off workers while they are in a programme of re-employment). The programme of re-employment, which is now ended, pushed those laid-off workers into unemployment. Some began to work in the informal sector. For those who were outside the system, although they benefited from the expansion of the informal labour market initially, economic restructuring has released more workers into the informal labour market and some of this initial advantage has been lost.

To sum up, economic restructuring forced a significant number of workers to leave the state system and at the same time squeezed the informal labour market. The transformation of welfare provision by commodifying housing, education and health care adds new burdens to the poor who have not been deemed eligible for the MLSS. The poverty groups are thus fragmented by their previous status and the advantage or otherwise that this gives them in the new system.

SUMMARY

Market-oriented reforms in China over the past 30 years have simultaneously led to the accumulation of wealth and the deprivation of livelihood. In particular, since the 1990s, a large population of urban poor has emerged in Chinese cities. This chapter described some of the institutional processes that have led to poverty generation. We attempt to explain why in a country with a history of relatively low wealth inequalities and income differentiation, massive urban poverty has been generated during a period of rapid economic growth.

In the planned economy, urban hardship was limited to the 'Three Nos'. Unemployment and poverty were regarded as the social problems of capitalism. The full-employment policy and integrated social security within the workplace ensured a low incidence of poverty. Since economic reforms, the egalitarian ideology has been replaced by 'allowing the few to get rich first'. In particular, since the 1990s, social stratification has increased across various dimensions (Tang and Parish, 2000). The institutional reforms and industrial policies have aimed at promoting economic growth and the 'optimal' allocation of resources, for example, closing down 'sunset industries', laying off redundant workers, increasing economic incentives, differentiating income, and allowing the owners of capital to derive private profit from investment. All these policies are 'double-edged', because they stimulate economic efficiency but at the expense of social equity losses. Those who are marginalized by the market-oriented reforms, have for various reasons, and not surprisingly, fallen behind in wealth accumulation. Many have fallen into poverty.

By tracing the institutional process of urban poverty generation, we can see that the 'new' urban poverty is not entirely new. In fact, the creation of new urban poverty is tied up with the social differentiation existing in the pre-reform regime and exacerbated by the new market transition. Unlike the traditional urban poor, caused by individual incapacity, the new poverty is generated by the disjunctive social entitlement in the process of economic restructuring and welfare retrenchment. De-industrialization and the demise of SOEs have generated a significant number of laid-off workers, forming the core of the new urban poor. The majority of the new urban poor population have little hope of returning to mainstream of society. Their demographic attributes, such as low education levels, already constrained them to the periphery of the state system in the socialist era and further led to their marginalization in the market transition. They have borne the cost of economic restructuring without receiving adequate support under the new social security policy. For those who were 'outsiders' of the state system in the socialist era, the market reform has generated new negative externalities, making their survival more difficult. They were subject to the disadvantaged condition under state-centred industrialization and are now further marginalized by market-oriented transformation.

For the 'insiders' of the state system, the lifelong security and privileged welfare provision, in comparison with deprived rural farmers who produced the social surplus for industrialization, have been eroded by economic restructuring, the decline in the state-owned sector and welfare provision gaps. While the state has established a countermeasure, namely MLSS, to large-scale redundancy, the limitations of MLSS are significant.

The new social security aims to 'rationalize' the cost structure by emphasizing the role of 'social insurance' and personal contributions to insurance premiums. While it might be effective for the working population, for those who survive at the margin of poverty, such a reform of social policy is becoming increasingly irrelevant. Their modest income is barely enough for physical survival, let alone for coping with the rising cost associated with the privatization of housing, medical care and education. The increasing gap between rich and poor, and the emergence of impoverished and deprived neighbourhoods should give cause for concern for the social sustainability of Chinese cities. The unemployed and laid-off workers, together with other marginal groups, are in desperate need of social security, but are confronted with gaps in a changing pattern of welfare provision through which they can so easily plunge. The transition of social welfare is either a direct cause of their poverty or exacerbates their underprivileged condition. They have lost the right to lifelong social security, conferred as an unwritten contract between the worker and the state in the old system, without gaining replacement entitlements to welfare provision. Therefore, for at least a significant proportion of the newly impoverished, without the hope of returning to the mainstream labour market, redistributive policies associated with citizenship are imperative. The implication is that, while generating more employment opportunities is still important, it must be realized that the pressure of employment will not be eased (Chen, 2000: 170; Lee and Warner, 2004), at least in the short term. Economic restructuring led to the disappearance of jobs. However, it is only part of the broad dynamics of social marginalization, which is generating an impoverished urban population. The other important factor is the legacy institution from the pre-reform era, namely the *hukou* system. We will elaborate this institution-based discrimination in the chapters that follow.

Various institutional reconfigurations, to form a regulatory regime that is more market-compatible, seem to be working against the marginal population. Social marginalization works in a similar way to that in advanced capitalist economies, which have been described as in transition from a 'welfare' to 'workfare' regime. However in China at the present time, the welfare safety net that the government can put in place is pitifully minimalistic and is aimed only at preventing absolute poverty. The lack of capacity (or willingness) to develop a universal social security system that guards against relative poverty and that gives sufficient support to keep impoverished households functioning within the urban system means that poverty has grown along with income differentiation. Local governments are more willing to use vast earnings from land in infrastructure investment. Income differentiation in itself is an inevitable and necessary condition of economic growth. Preventing the households at the lowest end of that distribution from becoming destitute and from the position of not being able to invest in the future of their children is avoidable.

Paradoxically the social policy reforms have often exacerbated poverty, and the new social security system must therefore be extended to go beyond allowing the poor to survive on the margins of poverty. While there has been a significant expansion in social security coverage, the overall rationale follows a welfare retrenchment in that the state work-units-based full welfare entitlement has been abandoned along with workers' job contracts, and this has been replaced by a new uniform safety net set at a destitution-avoiding minimal standard. The current minimum living standard programme keeps the poor on the edge of survival without adequately protecting their capacity to invest and develop their human capital. China's new urban poverty is emerging in the context of rapid economic growth and overall enhancement of living standards.

The structure of this book is as follows. After this introductory chapter, Chapter 2 analyses poverty incidences and the determinants of poverty rates among different social groups and neighbourhoods. We pay particular attention to the concentration of poverty, in both social and spatial terms. Chapter 3 further describes a detailed poverty experience of different social groups. We draw the material from our interviews in low-income neighbourhoods to paint a picture of their livelihood and trajectory of poverty experience. Chapter 4 focuses on impoverished neighbourhoods and tries to understand how poverty is generated in specific areas and how the poverty experience is contingent upon the neighbourhoods' position in urban development. We provide detailed documentation of our surveyed neighbourhoods and their transition. Then, in Chapter 5 we explore poverty dynamics, especially with reference to property rights changes. We quantify the implication of entitlement failure in education, health care and housing. In particular, we examine landless farmers and the mechanism that marginalizes them into the new urban poor. In conclusion we aim to give a broad picture of poverty incidence and distribution in low-income neighbourhoods in Chinese cities but also focus on specific poverty experiences and trace their root cause.

2.   Poverty incidence and determinants

In this chapter we begin to examine poverty incidence and its determinants. Through our surveyed data, we aim to reveal how poverty rates are unevenly distributed among different social groups and different living places. This will be followed by more detailed analyses of respectively poor groups in Chapter 3 and impoverished neighbourhoods in Chapter 4.

The problem of urban poverty has been widely recognized in China and has attracted extensive research and policy studies (for example, Guan, 2000; Tang, 2003; Cai, 2003; Chen et al 2006; Hussain, 2003; Hong, 2003; Y.P. Wang, 2004; F. Wu, 2004; Li and Sato, 2006; Solinger, 2006). However, the measurement of urban poverty, that is the number of urban poor, is still not very clear. Data unavailability was once a major constraint for poverty studies in China. With micro-data such as household survey data becoming available, greater progress has been made, however. A different set of problems have emerged as a result: different data sources suggest very different poverty rates. Using official national statistics, the urban poverty rate seems not to be a problem and is, in fact, on the decline.

There are two major official sources of urban household data. The first one is the household survey data conducted by the Chinese Income Distribution Project Team at the Institute of Economics, the Chinese Academy of Social Sciences (CASS), in cooperation with several foreign research institutes. The three large-scale CASS household surveys in 1988 (9009 urban households), 1995 (6931 urban households) and 1999 (4471 urban households and 790 rural migrant households) are the largest household surveys administered in both rural and urban areas across the country (Li and Sato, 2006). The second source is the Urban Household Survey (UHS), administered by the State Statistics Bureau through its provincial and local survey network. The Chinese UHS, begun in 1956, was suspended during the Cultural Revolution from 1966 to 1976 and resumed in 1980. The survey covers 30 provinces, 146 sample cities, and more than 80 counties. Based on the UHS data, the World Bank provides urban poverty estimates, using a poverty line of $32.74 per month. On this basis, the World Bank reports relatively low estimated poverty rates. Between 1978 and 1993, only a few years were registered with an absolute poverty rate exceeding 1 per cent. The rate changed from 0.83 per cent in 1992 to 0.98 per cent in 1998 (Fang et al., 2002: 436), and to 0.27 per cent in 2004 (World Bank, 2007). Absolute poverty is extremely low in urban areas, partly because the subsistence level adopted for measuring it is relatively low and partly because urban dwellers earn relatively high wages and receive food subsidies compared to rural dwellers. Table 2.1 gives various estimates of poverty rates in China. All of this data indicates a relatively low and declining poverty problem.

Other studies based on CASS data and UHS data also suggest an optimistic trend of declining poverty rates during China's market reforms from the late 1980s to the current time (Appleton and Song, 2007; Fang et al., 2002; Gustafsson and Li, 2001; 2004; Gustafsson and Zhong, 2000; Li and Sato, 2006). Analysing the CASS data, Appleton and Song (2007) found that the rising unemployment rate from 1995 to 2002 did not lead to a rise in poverty rate. They used a very 'generous' $2 PPP a day poverty line, almost double the official poverty line, and showed that the poverty rate declined from 7.33 per cent in 1988, to 7.00 per cent in 1995, 3.66 per cent in 1999 and 2.08 per cent in 2002. On their poverty incidence chart for the same period, the $1 PPP a day poverty line gives an even more negligible poverty rate, which is well below 1 per cent. These results present a very optimistic picture of declining poverty. Appleton and Song even argued that the new urban poverty is a 'myth' and that there is no evidence to suggest that absolute poverty rose during China's reforms. Their conclusion was that urban poverty generally does not exist in Chinese cities. Unemployment, they admitted, may be a source of disadvantage but not a direct cause of absolute poverty. Using the same data, Gustafsson and Zhong (2000), Gustafsson and Li (2001) and Li and Sato (2006) studied the changing incidence and distribution of poverty and reached similar conclusions.

Using the 1992 to 1998 UHS data, Fang et al. (2002) reported that the urban poverty rate measured by $1 a day changed from 2.09 per cent in 1992 to 2.06 per cent in 1998, and measured by $2 a day, changed from 13.74 per cent in 1992 to 8.86 per cent in 1998. Their findings are generally similar to those of Appleton and Song (2007), but with a higher poverty rate estimated. Furthermore, they found that for the bottom 10 per cent of the population, an increase in expenditure on health care, education and housing has outpaced income growth, leaving the poor with less real income to cope with the risk of falling into a poverty trap. This finding clearly shows that the efficiency gains from introducing a market-based system of rewarding labour have been associated with worsening income distribution. The gains from growth have not significantly or sufficiently trickled down to the lowest income strata, in spite of an apparently declining urban poverty rate.

Table 2.1 China's urban poverty rates since the 1980s

	$1 a day	$1.5 a day	Official poverty line	World Bank	$1 a day 'new poverty line'	$2 a day	2150 calories by SSB	Asian Development Bank (on data of SSB)	Poor headcount (million)	Poor headcount (million)
	(a)	(b)	(c)	(d)	(e)	(f)	(g)	(h)	(i)	(j)
1981				2.00	6.01				3.9	
1985				0.28	1.08				0.9	
1987				0.93	1.62	7.33 (1988)			0.6	
1991	2.09			1.28	1.66			5.8	1.3	14.2
1992	2.73	13.74	2.48	0.83	1.13			4.5		11.3
1994	1.65	13.18	2.90	0.86	1.19			5.7		15.3
1995	1.69	10.27	1.68	0.61	0.85	7.00	5.4	4.4	19.1	12.4
1996	2.00	8.41	1.76	0.46	0.61			4.2		11.8
1997	2.06	9.21	2.44	0.53	0.70			4.1		11.7
1998		8.86	2.13	0.98	1.16		3.9	4.1 (4.73)	14.8	11.9
1999				0.46	0.57	3.66	3.5	3.1	13.4	10.0
2000					0.63		2.3	3.4	10.5	10.5
2001					0.50		2.6		11.7	
2002				0.32	0.54	2.08	4.1		20.6	
2004				0.27						

Notes:

(a)–(c) From Feng et al. (2002); official poverty line is cited in Fang et al. (2002) as the city-specific official lines in China Development Report 1998.

(d) World Bank poverty rate is from *PovcalNet* sponsored by the World Bank, at $32.74 per month.

(e) From Ravallion and Chen (2007), the new poverty line is 1200 Yuan per capita per year in 2002, constant prices used; this is about $1 a day.

(f) From Appleton and Song (2007), based on the respective CASS data.

(g), (i) From Wu and Huang (2007), this is a 2150 calories requirement for 1995 to 1999 SSB data; 2000 data from Wang (2002) who works for SSB; 2001 and 2002 data are based on MLSS recipients.

(h) From ADB (2004), the data for the year 1998 in the bracket is from Hussain (2003).

(i) From Wu and Huang (2007), the data is not comparable across different periods: from 1981 to 1990 data is from the World Bank (1993); from 1991 to 1999 it is based on SSB data; 2000 is from Wu (2004); and 2001–2002 data are MLSS recipients.

(j) From ADB (2004) and Hussain (2003).

Source: Wang (2002); Hussain (2003); Hong (2003); Fang et al. (2002); ADB (2004); Wu and Huang (2007); Ravallion and Chen (2007); Appleton and Song (2007); World Bank (2007).

33

On the other hand, detailed studies of individual cities, neighbourhoods or social groups reveal a serious situation of poverty in Chinese cities (Solinger, 2002, 2006; Yao, 2004; M. Wang, 2004; Y.P. Wang, 2004, 2005; Chen *et al.*, 2006; Liu and Wu, 2006a, 2006b; Wu and Huang, 2007; Wu, 2007). Individual researchers have organized their own surveys to study the urban poor, for example a household survey of low income communities in Shenyang and Chongqing by Wang (2005); a household survey in Nanjing by Liu and Wu (2006a, 2006b); and a survey in a neighbourhood of Nanjing by Wu (2007). Wang (2005) reported over half the households being under the $1 a day poverty measure in two different types of low-income communities: poor traditional pre-1949 residential areas, and run-down post-1949 residential areas that have been home to state-owned industrial enterprises. Yao (2004: 184) reported that in Tianjin and Guangzhou the poverty rate among unemployed households varied between 34.5 per cent and 46.4 per cent, while the poverty rate from official data was between 0.9 per cent and 3.7 per cent. Obviously, there is a significant discrepancy in surveyed and official poverty rates. The latter clearly masks the poverty situation of specific groups of people living in specific places. It implies that there is significant variation in poverty rates around the mean and that that variation is not randomly distributed but systematically distributed across social groups and spaces. An understanding of urban poverty is not complete, therefore, without an analysis of the concentration of poverty and poverty vulnerability in certain social groups and in low-income neighbourhoods.

Asking the question: 'which are the vulnerable groups?', Meng et al. (2006), for example, find that large households and households with more non-working members are more likely to be poor. They reason that the change from the old implicit price subsidies based on household size, to an explicit income subsidy based on employment, has worsened the position of large families. Besides demographic features such as this, vulnerability is also caused by marginalization and social exclusion (B.Q. Li, 2006). Published studies indicate two major vulnerable social groups: laid-off workers and migrant workers.

First, Solinger (2002, 2006) notes that laid-off workers are becoming a 'new urban underclass' in China. Retrenched workers become trapped in poverty because their middle age and low skills and education cause an obstacle to returning to the job market. Giles et al. (2006) provide evidence of the impact of industrial restructuring on urban households. Laid-off workers face social exclusion because they belong to a particular social group of state industrial workers and it is difficult for them to return to mainstream economic production. Y.P. Wang (2004) also notes the competition between unemployed workers and more energetic rural migrants.

The unemployed workers are clearly disadvantaged in terms of quality of labour. They do not suit the needs of industrial development and need costly training programmes to make them re-employable. Whether this marginalized and vulnerable group is also disadvantaged by exclusion that operates independently of labour quality, is less clear.

Second, rural migrants face an institutionalized form of social exclusion: they are discriminated against by the lack of urban citizenship (Solinger, 1999). B.Q. Li (2006), for example, studies rural migrants' access to welfare provision and demonstrates that they are excluded from the formal provisions of the state. Their welfare provision is partially covered by employers' contributions and partially by the informal social network, but this leaves a significant gap.

Migrants and laid-off workers are clearly both marginal groups but their vulnerability to poverty has different causes. One is disadvantaged by institutional constraints, by the rules of urban governance; the other by human capital deficit and a cruel accident of history.

Rural migrants have become synonymous with the urban poor (Y.P. Wang, 2004; B.Q. Li, 2006; ADB, 2004). Table 2.2 reproduces estimates of the Asian Development Bank (ADB) that show that the migrant poverty rate in the city is much higher than that of locals. In the city of Jinan in 1999, the migrant poverty rate was as high as 39.3 per cent, while the poverty rate of locals was 11.0 per cent. The respective rates were 29.0 per cent and 9.0 per cent in Nanjing; 15.1 per cent and 6.3 per cent in Wuhan; and 15.0 per cent and 9.2 per cent in Guangzhou. In subsequent sections of this book we ask if this pattern still stands and whether there is a spatial

Table 2.2   Variation and comparison of urban poverty rates between migrants and locals, 1999 (percentage)

City	Locals	Migrants
Shenzhen	0.0	16.9
Jinan	11.0	39.3
Tianjin	3.5	11.9
Shanghai	5.8	18.3
Nanjing	9.5	29.0
Wuhan	6.3	15.1
Beijing	4.6	10.3
Guangzhou	9.2	15.0
Harbin	7.1	7.6
Xi'an	27.5	17.9

Source: Extracted from ADB (2004: 93).

dimension to it, considering that there are significant variations across different neighbourhoods.

Neighbourhood level studies reveal some interesting patterns. Wu (2007) examined a poor neighbourhood that was developed under state organized industrialization. Because of their active job participation, migrants actually earned higher incomes than the poorest urban residents. This was because migrants tolerated harsh working conditions. They became a self-exploiting group of working poor in the sense that they are willing to accept a marginal standard of living for the sake of monetary income and a foothold in the city. Having said that, they were not the poorest group in the poor neighbourhood studied by Wu (2007). So far, very few studies have compared these two vulnerable groups (the unemployed and migrant workers) within the context of poverty concentrations (poor neighbourhoods). Their poverty levels have not been compared directly in this sense.

Examining different types of poor neighbourhood permits us to ask questions about the relative sources of vulnerability facing the two groups. To what extent is their vulnerability to poverty a result of human capital factors, institutional factors and neighbourhood factors?

Spatially, there are three types of poor neighbourhood (F. Wu, 2004; Liu and Wu, 2006b; see also Chapter 4): inner-city dilapidated neighbourhoods, degraded workers' villages (concentrated areas of industrial workers), and rural migrants' enclaves. These places are concentrations of different vulnerable groups. Old urban neighbourhoods are mixed residences of low-income urban households and migrants; workers' villages often become concentrations of laid-off workers because of large-scale de-industrialization in the context of worker villages that have developed around single large employers (many of them rather like company towns). Rural migrants concentrate in the villages in the city where local farmers use their housing plots to develop multi-floor and high-density private rental accommodation. F. Wu (2004) noted that all of these neighbourhoods are produced by a combination of legacies from socialist development (for example neglected old inner-city neighbourhoods are there because the state invested in new industrial areas) and new impacts of market transition (for example redundancy in concentrated industrial areas). In a sense, these neighbourhoods can also be considered as residual/neglected spaces in post-reform China. Work-unit compounds are unsustainable spaces created by the defunct socialist production process. Pre-1949 old urban neighbourhoods were left unattended during the socialist industrialization period because of the low priority attached to consumption-oriented investment outside of work units. Urban villages are particular products of the rapid urbanization process and they are temporarily overlooked by the city government because of their property rights structure.

Studies of poor neighbourhoods suggest that there is an issue of poverty concentration in Chinese cities. Let us take Guangzhou and Nanjing as examples. More detailed neighbourhood-level analysis will be given in Chapter 4. In terms of intra-urban distribution of the urban poor, both Guangzhou and Nanjing data present similar patterns. The concentration is relatively modest. Measured by the official poverty line, Nanjing has a location quotient (LQ) of Minimum Living Standard Support (MLSS) recipients' concentration in street-office areas that ranges from 0.2 to 2.7 (Liu and Wu, 2006b), with poverty rates ranging from 3.18 per cent to 6.24 per cent (Chen et al., 2006). The data for Guangzhou shows a variation of LQ from 0.1 to 2.6 (Yuan and Xu, 2008). The poor street-office areas are largely in the traditional industrial areas of the inner suburbs and in the dilapidated inner urban areas. They represent different types of poverty. Poverty near industrial areas is caused by industrial redundancy policy and enterprise reform, while near the old city centre it is the persistent poverty from denied industrial investment and decades of filtering in the housing market (and before the market, the housing allocation system), in which low-paid members of poor work units and workers not in work units gravitated to the areas of poorest quality housing. However, studies based on official figures have tended to neglect rural migrants and the urbanized villages on city fringes where they live. In the research reported in this book, we have conducted the first systematic analysis of poor neighbourhoods to include rural migrants and urban villages alongside the official urban poor.

To sum up, there are discrepancies in poverty rates, depending upon whether the data is drawn from national statistics or from case studies of individual cities or neighbourhoods. Another drawback of existing studies is that few studies use recent data. The latest national survey data (2002 UHS data) is now dated. Based on a large-scale household survey conducted in 25 poor neighbourhoods in six major Chinese cities in 2007, our research reveals realistic poverty rates within those areas. It is aimed at developing the most detailed understanding yet of poverty concentration and the morphology of urban poverty in China at a sub-municipal level. In contrast to city-wide or national studies of poverty rates, our approach uses an 'extreme-case sampling' approach to investigate the problem. Our focus is solidly on understanding the morphology of urban poverty rather than to estimate city-wide urban poverty rates. We have therefore sought out the poorest neighbourhoods in our six survey cities with a view to understanding the poverty rates in the most concentrated areas of poverty; understanding the variation in poverty between different kinds of poor neighbourhood; and understanding the different poverty experiences of the different social groups living within those neighbourhoods.

SURVEY METHOD AND DATA

Given the complexity of the issue and the size of the Chinese urban population, we undertook a large-scale household survey in six cities from December 2006 to June 2007. The survey was conducted with the help of collabourators in local universities. The cities are distributed in the coastal, central and western regions, and include Xi'an, Guangzhou, Nanjing, Wuhan, Harbin and Kunming. Xi'an is an industrial city in the north-western region and the capital city of a comparatively underdeveloped hinterland. Guangzhou represents south coast cities that have experienced a high level of marketization and openness. Nanjing represents a developed coastal city which is a provincial capital with a strong industrial base. Wuhan is a city in the central region with a concentration of socialist-era heavy industries. It suffers from economic restructuring but is relatively better positioned in the process than some other cities such as our fifth city, Harbin. Harbin is an industrial city in the north-eastern region with severe de-industrialization problems. Kunming is in the underdeveloped south-western region, and has a relatively low level of industrialization.

Table 2.3 shows the profiles of these cities in terms of city size, industrial structure and levels of unemployment. Judging from GDP per capita and average disposable income, Guangzhou is the most developed city; Nanjing comes second; while Xi'an and Kunming are the least well-off cities. Guangzhou has a highly developed tertiary industry, Nanjing retains a strong industrial base, and Harbin still has a high proportion of secondary industry. In terms of official poverty and unemployment rates, Wuhan has the highest percentage of MLSS recipients and the highest proportion of unemployed, while Guangzhou is the least poor of all six cities. Their poverty performance is clearly highly related to their industrial structure. Industrial restructuring, for example, has created a large volume of retrenched workers in Wuhan – a national base of heavy industries, while Guangzhou is less affected since secondary industry was not a dominant industry in the city.

Selecting four of the poorest neighbourhoods in each of these different cities gives us a unique and powerful lens through which to study the patterns and dynamics of urban poverty concentration and differentiation. The selected neighbourhoods are not representative of their respective cities in a statistical sense and we do not therefore attempt to make generalizations about the differences between the six cities. Strictly speaking,

Table 2.3 Basic information on six cities surveyed (2006)

City	Population (million)	GDP per capita (Yuan)	Average disposable income (Yuan)	Average housing area (m²)	Added value of the primary industry (%)	Added value of the secondary industry (%)	Added value of the tertiary industry (%)	Percentage of MLSS recipients (%)	Official unemployed rate (%)
Harbin	9.803	21,374	11,230	27.8	7.9	43.0	49.1	2.03	3.5
Nanjing	6.072	39,379	17,538	28.6	3.0	49.5	47.5	1.25	3.3
Wuhan	8.188	29,890	12,360	26.9	4.5	46.1	49.4	3.02	4.5
Kunming	5.143	19,663	10,766	29.9	6.8	46.7	46.5	1.61	3.0
Xi'an	7.531	17,794	10,905	28.9	4.9	42.4	52.7	2.08	4.3
Guangzhou	7.607	58,500	19,851	29.3	2.4	39.9	57.7	0.63	2.1

Source: State Statistics Bureau (2007).

what we have done is to take case studies that are broadly, but not statistically, representative of the poorest neighbourhoods in each of the cities. Sampling households systematically within these gives us a population of household who live in some of the poorest neighbourhoods in these cities. We can generalize to this population and make comparisons between the residents of the 24 neighbourhoods, noting city and neighbourhood type as independent factors in explaining variations in household poverty.

Specifically, we designed a two-stage sampling method. First, we tried to identify neighbourhoods with the lowest social stratum in the city. The study covers not only central districts but also peripheral urban districts that include both permanent urban residents and rural migrants. To include migrants, we purposely include so-called 'urban villages'. We used different approaches to identify low-income neighbourhoods with different population compositions. For neighbourhoods of predominantly permanent urban residents, we referred to official statistical data. The Civil Affairs Bureau, which is responsible for identifying MLSS recipients, maintains yearly-based statistics at the street-office level. The rate of MLSS can be used to assess the poverty situation of permanent social groups. Therefore, low-income neighbourhoods are defined as those that exceeded a certain statistical threshold of MLSS recipients. We selected the places with the highest concentration of MLSS recipients where possible. For neighbourhoods of predominantly non-permanent residents (migrants), there are no official statistics about poverty levels. We used the fifth population census (2000) to identify migrant distributions. Through consulting local officials and key informants, we selected the lowest-income neighbourhoods among these areas of high migrant concentration. The selection of permanent residents' low-income neighbourhoods was also validated through consultation with key informants. We also visited alternative sites to compare their built environments to assess which appeared to be the most disadvantaged in terms of housing and environmental quality.

By combining MLSS data, local expert knowledge and our own research, we selected our four poorest neighbourhoods in each city. In the case of Guangzhou, five neighbourhoods were selected. The sampling area was the residents' committee area, which is smaller than a sub-district area, and is a neighbourhood more naturally defined by streets and building blocks. The size of the neighbourhoods is about the same in each city. Seventy-five copies of questionnaires were allocated to each of the 24 neighbourhoods (in the case of Guangzhou, 60 copies to 5 neighbourhoods). For five of the cities, we selected one workers' village (concentrated industrial area); one inner older neighbourhood; and two urban villages. For Harbin, because there are very few urban villages, two workers' areas, one inner city neighbourhood, and only one urban village were selected. The result is a cross-regional purposive selection of the poorest urban neighbourhoods with various population compositions.

For the second stage, in each neighbourhood selected, households were chosen for interview based on a random start of an address and a fixed spatial sampling interval (for example every twentieth address). The use of an address-based approach rather than an official registration list is for two reasons. First, we would like to include migrants (and other temporary residents in these places, for whom the official list is not available). Second, the address-based approach can generally ensure an adequate degree of randomness and representativeness. We devised a standard sampling schedule to deal with different types of built environment. For example, for work-unit compounds or multiple households sharing the same address, we select the first household on the left after entering a building. This approach has been commonly used in surveys of Chinese cities (for example Fan, 2002; W.P. Wu, 2004; Wang, 2005; Li and Li, 2006). In this way, we not only collected information about poor households, but also information about non-poor households, which makes possible an analysis of poverty incidence and profile in the different types of low-income neighbourhood. Questionnaires were distributed to household heads. Questions include socioeconomic information pertaining to household heads and their household, including *hukou* status, income and expenditure, education, employment history, housing status, neighbourhood interactions, commuting and relocation experiences, and so on. During the survey, investigators undertook face-to-face interviews to complete the questionnaires. If the selected respondent refused to answer or was unable to, the investigator went to the next household. That is, the failed interview was dropped from the sample. On average, 60 to 75 effective questionnaires were collected in each neighbourhood, yielding 300 questionnaires in each city. In total, we collected 1809 completed questionnaires in 25 neighbourhoods.

The survey is literally a sample of the bottom stratum of neighbourhoods and their households in each city. The limitation of this sample is that it cannot be used to estimate overall urban poverty rates at the city scale. But because they all belong to the bottom layer, it is still of value to compare neighbourhoods across the cities. This makes for a unique database in contemporary urban China studies.

The distribution of samples is shown in Table 2.4. They are cross-tabulated according to the status of household head and neighbourhood type. Because within each neighbourhood, the sample is systematically drawn on the basis of addresses, it is possible to take these as representing the social composition of different neighbourhoods. In general, migrant

Table 2.4   Distribution of samples among different household types and neighbourhoods

Household head status	Urban villages		Inner old neighbourhoods		Workers' villages		Sub-total	
Working local	139	17%	129	25%	137	26%	405	22%
Unemployed	73	9%	178	35%	163	32%	414	23%
Retired	33	4%	114	22%	188	36%	335	18%
Migrant	551	69%	81	16%	23	5%	655	36%
Sub-total	796	100%	502	100%	511	100%	1809	100%

households account for 36 per cent of the total combined sample. Urban households with unemployed heads in these neighbourhoods reach a level of 23 per cent. Working locals account for 22 per cent. The remaining 19 per cent are retirees. As expected, most migrants are concentrated in urban villages. In these villages, 69 per cent of surveyed households belong to the migrant status, while in contrast the percentage of migrant families in workers' villages is as low as 5 per cent. There is, as expected, a relatively high level of unemployed households in old neighbourhoods, reaching 35 per cent of the surveyed households there. The percentage of working urban households is lower in urban villages than in old urban neighbourhoods and in workers' villages. There is a very low rate of unemployed urban households in city villages, only accounting for 9 per cent of the sample. Even lower is the percentage of retired urban households in urban villages. In workers' villages, however, they account for 36 per cent of the households there. This figure is high, partially because the sampled workers' villages were established in the early stage of industrialization. Many workers who were initially recruited into these workplaces are now retired.

A location quotient is used to measure relative concentration or dispersal of different social groups in these neighbourhoods (see Table 2.5). For working urban households, they are under-represented in urban villages. The majority of people are actually economically active in these villages, but most of them are rural migrants. There is also under-representation of unemployed urban households in these villages. Working urban households mainly live in workers' villages, while unemployed households concentrate in inner urban neighbourhoods, giving a location quotient well above 1. Rural migrants are concentrated in urban villages, giving a very high location quotient value (1.91). In contrast, migrant households find it difficult to settle in workers' villages, due largely to the underdeveloped rental market in former work-unit housing estates. Measured in terms

Table 2.5   Location quotient for different social groups in various neighbourhoods

Household head status	Urban villages	Inner old neighbourhoods	Workers' villages
Working	0.78	1.15	1.19
Unemployed	0.40	1.55	1.39
Retired	0.22	1.23	1.99
Migrant	1.91	0.45	0.12
Sub-total	1.0	1.0	1.0

of location quotient, there is clear under-representation of migrants in workers' villages.

POVERTY INCIDENCE

Studies in Poverty Concentration

Intensified economic reforms in the public sector since the 1990s and large-scale rural–urban migration have broken the social and spatial patterns that became established in cities during the planned economy period (Liu and Wu, 2006a; Wang, 2005; F. Wu, 2004). Residential differentiation has naturally emerged, as people with similar income or socioeconomic status have started to concentrate in certain neighbourhoods (Wang, 2005). As a result, low-income neighbourhoods have appeared. The emergence of poverty concentration symbolizes the rise of a new urban socio-spatial order in Chinese cities and calls for a programme of sustained in-depth research. The depth of the problem is such that Chinese cities are in great danger of moving in the direction of the highly segregated cities of Latin America (Gilbert, 1997), with a large informal sector living in slums and ghettos.

There is a well established body of literature on poverty concentration in Western cities, especially American cities. As Walks (2001) argues, the social ecology of the post-Fordist global city is characterized by increasing social complexity and differentiation among, between and within neighbourhoods. In spatial terms, the ghetto as an extreme form of residential segregation emerged and then dispersed widely in highly industrialized countries, particular in large American cities (Friedrichs and Blasius, 2003; McCulloch, 2001; Orfield, 1998; Small and Newman, 2001). Marcuse (1996) pointed out that the increasing ghettoization was one of the particular spatial characteristics of the post-Fordist city. The spatial concentration of poverty has come to threaten the health of entire metropolises, and exacerbates a wide variety of social pathologies (Wilson, 1987; 1996). The concentration of a given amount of poverty is arguably unhealthy for society. This is so for a number of reasons including the danger of compounding poverty with social exclusion as groups of people and neighbourhoods become labelled and discriminated against. It is also unhealthy because it separates the poor from other income groups, which is socially divisive and limits opportunities for social mobility and functional economic integration between income groups. There are not many arguments in favour of poverty concentration. One might be the economies of scale and scope that build up in the provision of services to the poor. So the poor may be better provided for if they are living in large concentrations rather than dispersed. But not many scholars would give much weight to this compared to the negative results of poverty concentration.

There are also plenty of studies on the profound social and political processes behind the spatial concentration of poverty and linking this with more general explanations of poverty. The prevailing interpretation of the new urban poverty considers it to be an outcome of global economic restructuring, changes in the welfare state, and changes in social structure (Morris, 1993; Neef, 1992; Sassen, 1991; Wacquant, 1993; Walks, 2001; Wessel, 2000; Wilson, 1987). Wilson (1987, 1996) in his seminal work raises concerns about 'concentrated poverty' in the US. He argues that concentration of the poor in urban ghettos develops a social pathology. Poor African-Americans are isolated from the mainstream and develop a culture of poverty. In *The Truly Disadvantaged*, Wilson (1987) discusses poverty concentration in the inner cities; and in *When Work Disappears* (1996), he discusses the impact of de-industrialization on poverty concentration. Although Wilson's work points to the importance of structural factors (de-industrialization) and class-specific features (racial segregation), the impact of his work on the policy literature represents what might be viewed as a new *spatial turn* in poverty studies (Crump, 2002: 583).

Wilson's work in the 1980s (Wilson, 1987) helped develop the tradition of studying the geographic impacts of job loss, middle-class out-migration, and social pathology (Crump, 2002). As an example of this tradition, Jencks and Mayer (1990) describe social consequences of living in poverty neighbourhoods. They provided an early comprehensive treatment on the mechanism of neighbourhood effects. These have now been expanded to include many other aspects such as neighbourhood reputation, model learning, socialization, and resident perceptions of deviance (Friedrichs et al., 2003). Jencks (1992) makes a focused analysis of the idea of social pathology in the inner city. Marcuse (1996) relates ghettoization with the spatial order of the post-Fordist city.

In the US, Jargowsky (1997) conducted detailed census-based analysis on the spread of high-poverty areas. He provides the most systematic research on high-poverty neighbourhoods, defined as those with poverty rates of at least 40 per cent. He documents the remarkable spread of poverty neighbourhoods and shows that the predominant dimension in the USA is racial. He classified high poverty areas into ghettos (black high-poverty neighbourhoods), 'barrios' (Latino areas), and 'slums' (similar white areas). His research reveals how the impact of structural changes in the economy is mediated through places in addition to the overall effect of de-industrialization as depicted in Wilson (1987). Because of a spatial mismatch, the de-concentration of employment reduces the probability of finding employment: economic changes adversely affect inner city areas where poor ethnic groups reside. More recently, Wacquant (2008) provides an ethnographic account of Chicago's black ghetto and Paris's de-industrializing *banlieue*. Arguing against the notion of 'underclass', he insists that the joint withdrawal of market and state has led to urban abandonment.

The post-Fordist economy and an employment regime characterized by a precarious labour market and the curtailment of employment for life have caused very large numbers of uneducated or unskilled workers to be excluded in Western cities (Gans, 1993). The new urban poor therefore have limited welfare security (Silver, 1993; White, 1998) and weakened social support networks (Mingione, 1996; Musterd and Ostendorf, 1998). In general, the new urban poverty is regarded as a complex phenomenon caused by economic disadvantage and social exclusion (Mingione, 1993). Exclusion from the world of regular employment and from mainstream society is the main feature of the new urban poor in Western society. Specifically, the spatial concentration of poverty becomes both an outcome and a part of the restricted life chances of the urban poor (van Kempen, 1994).

The proliferation of studies on poverty measurement and causation improves our understanding of China's new urban poor. Similar to the prevailing explanation in the West, the emerging new poverty in China is believed to be the result of economic restructuring, the retrenchment of redundant labour and social exclusion, for example institutional discrimination against rural migrants (Liu et al., 2008; Lu and Song, 2006; Shen, 2002; Solinger, 2006; Y.P. Wang, 2004; F. Wu, 2004; 2007). Nevertheless, until now, what we know about China's poor neighbourhoods and social groups is still very limited, especially the variations in the patterns and causes of poverty within these neighbourhoods and groups. Moreover, studies combining or contrasting poverty groups and poor neighbourhoods are still lacking. Studies of the spatial concentration of poverty, that is low-income neighbourhoods, and the social concentration of poverty, that is poverty groups, are separated. It is not clear how poverty rates vary within and between groups and what contributes to such variation. Therefore, one of the important goals of this book is to study the uneven distribution of urban poverty in different low-income neighbourhoods and social groups, especially disadvantageous social groups. By poverty concentration, we mean socio-spatial concentration, that is concentration measured by the proportion (poverty rate), the intensity of poverty (poverty gap) and the inequality of poverty (weighted poverty gap) in different neighbourhoods and different social groups. In an attempt to get as full a picture as possible in investigating these, we calculate average income per capita for migrant households, including not only household members living in the city, but also immediate relatives staying in home towns, such as parents and children.

Poverty Line and Poverty Measures

Since the second half of the 1990s, a number of Chinese organizations, including the State Statistics Bureau (SSB), the Ministry of Civil Affairs (MOCA), and the Institute of Forecasting of the Chinese Academy of Sciences, have calculated an urban poverty line. However, a standard framework for calculation is lacking and there is no widely accepted poverty line for the whole country (Hussain, 2003). The national poverty lines are only used for estimating the number of the urban poor by those organizations engaged in generating the statistics. Without an official poverty line, the de facto line used in many policy discussions and studies adopts the measurement used for MLSS, which is based on 'cost of basic needs'. This is essentially a measure of absolute poverty: a calories-based food basket measure using a threshold of about 2100 calories per person per day. Since the pattern of consumption, average income per capita and food prices vary substantially across localities, each city sets its own poverty line for MLSS to provide social relief and assistance to poor urban households. As well as being more practical it is also more reasonable to use local MLSS thresholds rather than a uniform poverty line to measure poverty rate, although the latter might have some advantages in terms of other dimensions of comparability. In our sampled cities, the MLSS line ranges from 200 Yuan to 330 Yuan per capita per month. Guangzhou has the highest poverty line, while Xi'an and Kunming have the lowest. The other three cities have similar poverty lines. This is a very tough poverty measure, very near to $1 PPP a day. It is a social security measure designed merely to keep people from falling into destitution and starving.

A traditional measure for poverty incidence is counting the number of people below the poverty line, that is the headcount measure. However, this takes no account of poverty intensity and inequality among poor households (He et al., 2008). Our study applies the FGT (Foster, Greer, Thorbeck) index, one of the most popular and robust poverty measures, introduced by Foster, Greer and Thorbecke (1984) to measure various dimensions of poverty. The formula used is:

$$P_\alpha = 1/n \sum_{i=1}^{q} ((Z - I_i)/Z)^\alpha$$

where n = total population, q = the number of poor, Z is the poverty line, and I_i is the average income of the ith household ($i = 1, 2, \ldots, q$). When $\alpha = 0$, the index is the standard headcount ratio, defined as the fraction of the population below the poverty line Z. One limitation of the headcount ratio is that it does not take into account the degree of poverty for those falling below the poverty line. When $\alpha = 1$, the index becomes the poverty gap measure, which takes into consideration the total shortfall of individual income below the poverty line. However, for the poverty gap index, transfers among the poor will not change the value of the measure. To overcome this problem, we can set $\alpha > 1$. In so doing, we get an index of weighted poverty gap, which is sensitive to transfers among the poor. Among the distribution-sensitive FGT measures, the most frequently used is $\alpha=2$ (Foster et al., 1984).

To measure poverty based on respondents' perception and to assess the poverty profile in a different way, a subjective poverty line approach was developed by economists in the Netherlands, and then applied in several European countries (e.g. van Praag et al., 1982), the United States (e.g. Colasanto et al., 1984), and some developing countries (e.g. Pradhan and Ravallion, 2000). This approach has also been applied in China by Gustafsson et al. (2006) to measure respondents' perception of income adequacy. The subjective poverty line methodology often asks what the minimum monetary amounts are that people consider necessary to support their families, and then sets a poverty line based on these figures.

In our study, we do not ask a minimum income question in order to set a subjective poverty line. Rather, we seek to understand the sense of deprivation/perception of poverty by simply asking whether or not respondents consider their families poor. Based on the results, we calculate the percentage of respondents who consider themselves to be poor in each social group. A higher percentage suggests a stronger sense of deprivation within households in the social group. Although this indicator might suffer from potential bias, since different people have different definitions of poverty according to their life experiences, it provides useful information

with which to understand respondents' perception of deprivation. We
compare this with their actual situation. To capture gaps between absolute, relative (perceived) and official (de facto) poverty rates implied by
policy thresholds, we compare the percentage of MLSS recipients, headcount poverty rates and self-classified (subjective) poverty rates.

Poverty Incidence by Neighbourhood and Group

We first look at poverty measures in the six sampled cities. Results are
shown in Table 2.6. P_0 is the headcount measure of poverty incidence for
different groups, P_1 shows the poverty gap, that is the intensity of poverty,
within each group, while P_2 is the weighted poverty gap, that is the inequality of poverty. P_p represents the percentage of respondents who have the
sense of deprivation in each group. P_m stands for MLSS coverage rate.

Both the poverty rate and the MLSS coverage rate in the six cities are
quite different from those figures shown in Table 2.3. As we have stated
earlier, these selected neighbourhoods do not necessarily represent the
average situation of those cities in which they are located, since they
represent the lowest stratum in each city. These figures are much higher
than those suggested by other scholars. For instance, a study by S. Li
(2006) using the 1999 CASS data suggests that the urban poverty rate was
between 5 per cent and 6 per cent in the whole country. Setting a relative
poverty line at 50 per cent of median income, Wong (1995) found that 12
per cent of Guangzhou's population fell below the poverty line in 1993,
while 13 per cent of Shanghai's population were poor in 1996 (Wong,

Table 2.6   Poverty measures in six cities

City	No. of cases	Poverty line (Yuan/ month)	FTG indices			P_m	P_p
			P_0	P_1*100	P_2*100		
Guangzhou	304	330	22.7	6.29	2.65	2.3	17.8
Harbin	300	245	25.0	6.15	2.74	11.7	34.3
Kunming	300	210	22.3	5.60	2.89	9.7	23.7
Nanjing	300	260	9.7	1.09	0.46	6.3	10.4
Wuhan	305	248	16.4	3.08	1.32	8.2	13.8
Xian	300	200	38.3	6.10	2.98	21.3	32.2
Whole sample	1809	n/a	22.4	4.72	2.17	9.9	22.0

Note: P_0 = Poverty rate; P_1 = Poverty gap; P_2 = Weighted poverty gap; P_p = poverty
perception, P_m = MLSS coverage rate.

1997). With only a comparatively small portion of unemployed/ laid-off workers and rural migrants included, the CASS data under-represents poverty and suggests a rather conservative figure. As a matter of fact, tens of thousands of unemployed/laid-off workers and rural migrants have emerged in the Chinese city since the late 1990s, and have substantially added to the growing number of new urban poor. None of the above figures represents an up-to-date or accurate picture on poverty incidence in urban China. Our figures are current and include rural migrants. Despite the possible distortion caused by respondents' understated income, we have sufficient reason to believe that these measurements reflect the actual situation.

By calculating the FTG indices, percentage of self-perception of poverty, MLSS coverage rate, and location quotient (LQ) indices, we have compared poverty measures and their concentration among different neighbourhoods and groups. We first compare three types of neighbourhood, namely urban villages, old inner city neighbourhoods, and workers' villages. Poverty measures adopted are the same as in Table 2.6. Meanwhile, LQ indices of five poverty measures are calculated, as shown in Table 2.7.

Among three types of poor neighbourhood, old urban neighbourhoods have the highest poverty rate, poverty gap and weighted poverty gap. This suggests that the poverty intensity, that is the total shortfall of income below the poverty line, is the highest in this kind of poverty cluster; and the degree of inequality of poverty, that is the gap between the poorest and the least poor, is the highest.

When we look at MLSS coverage rate and poverty perception, old inner city urban neighbourhoods, again, have the highest MLSS coverage rate and the highest percentage of self-perceived poverty.

In contrast, urban villages have the lowest MLSS coverage rate and the lowest self-perceived poverty rate. For both old urban neighbourhoods and workers' villages, the percentage of poverty perception is higher than their actual poverty rate, while for urban villages, the percentage of poverty perception is comparatively lower than the actual poverty rate. The LQ indices suggest that poverty concentration is over-represented in old inner city neighbourhoods, where all the five poverty measures are the highest. The poverty rate in urban villages is slightly higher than the average level, while the poverty gap and weighted poverty gap are very close to the average level. Poverty perception and MLSS coverage rate are also extremely low in this type of neighbourhood. This suggests that while people in urban villages have fewer entitlements to state welfare provision, they are more positive about their lives.

Overall, compared to the other two neighbourhood types, workers' villages have a lower level of poverty concentration, while their MLSS

Table 2.7 *Poverty measures and their concentration (categorized by neighbourhood)*

| | % | FTG indices | | | P_m | P_p | LQ_0 | LQ_1 | LQ_2 | LQ_m | LQ_p |
		P_0	P_1*100	P_2*100							
Old inner city urban neighbourhood	27.8	29.3	6.04	2.88	16.1	31.3	1.31	1.28	1.33	1.63	1.42
Workers' village	28.2	22.3	3.45	1.33	13.3	19.8	1.00	0.73	0.61	1.34	0.90
Urban villages	44.0	18.1	4.70	2.26	3.8	17.6	0.81	1.00	1.04	0.38	0.80
Whole sample	100	22.4	4.72	2.17	9.9	22.0	1.00	1.00	1.00	1.00	1.00

Note: LQ_0 = location quotient for poverty rate; LQ_1 = location quotient for poverty gap; LQ_2 = location quotient for weighted poverty gap; LQ_m = location quotient for MLSS coverage rate; LQ_p = location quotient for percentage of poverty perception.

coverage rate is comparatively high. This indicates unequal access to welfare entitlements.

Our subjects are also categorized into different groups by *hukou* status; age, educational attainment and occupation of household head; and housing tenure. We analyse each of these attributes in turn. We first look at the variation of poverty concentration between working urban residents, laid-off/unemployed urban residents, retirees and rural migrants (Table 2.8). In the laid-off/ unemployed group, we include people who are currently laid-off/unemployed and people who used to be laid-off and who have now managed to find a formal or informal job.

It is quite obvious that laid-off/unemployed urban residents are the poorest in terms of poverty rate, poverty gap, weighted poverty gap, and poverty perception. This group also has the highest MLSS coverage rate, which means that it has the greatest access to state welfare. Working urban residents have the lowest poverty incidence. Retirees are also better off in comparison. Interestingly, rural migrants are not the poorest when compared with laid-off/unemployed urban residents, and their MLSS coverage rate is very low. While, in general, migrants are ineligible for MLSS, a few managed to enter the system because of variation in local practice. Although the urban laid-off/unemployed and rural migrants have been recognized as two major poverty groups in Chinese cities, which group is the poorer has hitherto been unknown. Conventionally, rural migrants are considered poorer than urban residents, as they are widely understood to be disadvantaged by the institutionally defined urban–rural dichotomy (Lu and Song, 2006; Shen, 2002; Wang, 2005). However, our study reveals that rural migrants are not necessarily the poorest group in the city. On the contrary, laid-off/unemployed urban residents have the highest level of poverty concentration, while migrants have less poverty concentration than the average level, although the levels of poverty intensity and inequality in this group are slightly higher than the average level. The reason mainly lies in the fact that most migrants are economically active, while laid-off/unemployed urban residents are not. Rural migrants also have a much lower level of deprivation perception when compared with laid-off/unemployed urban residents. This may be explained by different expectations of life and attitudes towards their present living conditions. Rural migrants tend to make stronger comparisons with their former (or intermittent) rural situation and with their anticipated future than do more established urban groups. So they do not identify themselves as poor as frequently as members of the urban class who have fallen into misfortune. By contrast, established urban residents who have lost their jobs as a result of mass unemployment have three comparators to make them feel miserable: their previous position of greater well-being; their lack of hope

Table 2.8 *Poverty measures and their concentration (categorized by hukou group)*

	%	FTG indices			P_m	P_p	LQ_0	LQ_1	LQ_2	LQ_m	LQ_p
		P_0	P_1*100	P_2*100							
Working	22.4	11.4	1.74	0.61	4.4	11.6	0.51	0.37	0.28	0.44	0.53
Laid-off/unemployed	22.9	44.2	8.47	3.98	30.4	43.5	1.97	1.79	1.83	3.07	1.98
Retired	18.5	15.8	2.52	1.07	7.8	13.7	0.71	0.53	0.49	0.79	0.62
Rural migrant	36.2	18.8	5.31	2.56	1.4	19.1	0.84	1.13	1.18	0.14	0.87

in the future; and the threat of migrants who generally work harder even under worse conditions and thus are more competitive in securing jobs.

We next compare poverty measures and concentration in different age groups (Table 2.9). Household heads between 40 and 60 years old have the highest level of poverty concentration. This finding further confirms that what the Chinese call the '40s and 50s' are the most vulnerable population in the post-reform era, suffering the most from SOE reform and retrenchment (Solinger, 2002; Y.P. Wang, 2004). Household heads above 60 and those under 40 have a lower level of poverty concentration than average. Household heads over 60 are mostly pensioners and have a lower poverty incidence because of a higher level of access to transfer payments (and to some extent a lower level of outgoings). Household heads under 40 are comparatively better off, since this group tends to be more economically active.

We also compare cases categorized by household heads' educational attainment (Table 2.10). Educational attainment is inversely correlated with poverty concentration. The comparison shows that the poverty rate of the secondary school group is lower than the primary school group. More importantly, the poverty gap and weighted poverty gap are also much lower in the secondary school educated group. In the higher education group, all five poverty measures are at a very low level.

Table 2.11 compares poverty measures and their concentration among groups with different occupations. Compared with other groups, the manager/director group is much better off. The poverty rate in this group is in fact zero. In spite of this, some people still have a sense of deprivation. The professional/civil servant group has a lower poverty rate than the skilled worker/technician group. However, the former has a higher poverty gap and higher weighted poverty gap than the latter. Poverty perception is also slightly stronger in the former group. Nevertheless, the latter group has a higher MLSS coverage rate. This could be explained by the fact that skilled workers and technicians working in SOEs normally have better access to state welfare provision. The self-employed/small business owner group has a slightly higher poverty rate, and a much higher poverty gap and weighted poverty gap than the skilled worker group. The MLSS coverage rate for self-employed/small business owners is lower than the skilled worker/technician group, while poverty perception is slightly stronger in the former than the latter. The contrast between skilled workers and manual workers is quite striking. The poverty rate among the latter is nearly three times that of the former, while the poverty gap and weighted poverty gap are much higher in the latter group. Accordingly, the MLSS coverage rate and poverty perception for the latter group are also nearly three times that of the former group.

Table 2.9 *Poverty measures and their concentration (categorized by household head age)*

	%	P_0	FTG indices		P_m	P_p	LQ_0	LQ_1	LQ_2	LQ_m	LQ_p
			P_1*100	P_2*100							
Under 40	38.1	13.6	3.40	1.42	2.6	13.8	0.61	0.72	0.65	0.26	0.63
40–60	45.6	29.9	5.93	2.82	15.5	30.2	1.33	1.26	1.30	1.57	1.37
Above 60	16.4	22.0	4.37	2.12	11.1	18.2	0.98	0.93	0.98	1.12	0.83

Table 2.10 *Poverty measures and their concentration (categorized by household head educational attainment)*

	%	P_0	FTG indices		P_m	P_p	LQ_0	LQ_1	LQ_2	LQ_m	LQ_p
			P_1*100	P_2*100							
Primary school and under	20.5	30.2	7.64	3.60	11.1	31.5	1.35	1.62	1.66	1.12	1.43
Secondary school	70.6	22.5	4.36	1.99	10.6	21.5	1.00	0.92	0.92	1.07	0.98
Higher education (college and above)	8.9	3.7	0.77	0.33	1.2	4.3	0.17	0.16	0.15	0.12	0.20

Table 2.11 *Poverty measures and their concentration (categorized by household head occupation)*

	%	FTG indices			P_m	P_p	LQ_0	LQ_1	LQ_2	LQ_m	LQ_p
		P_0	P_1*100	P_2*100							
Manager/director	5.4	0	n/a	n/a	0	6.1	0	n/a	n/a	0	0.28
Professional/civil servant	7.7	7.9	1.78	0.61	1.4	10.9	0.35	0.38	0.28	0.14	0.50
Skilled worker/technician	7.8	9.9	1.40	0.41	4.3	9.2	0.44	0.30	0.19	0.43	0.42
Self-employed/small business owner	18.9	10.9	2.05	0.86	3.8	10.0	0.49	0.43	0.40	0.38	0.45
Manual worker/social service worker	22.7	27.6	5.02	1.79	10.7	29.6	1.23	1.06	0.82	1.08	1.35
Informal job	37.6	33.5	7.84	4.06	16.6	30.7	1.50	1.66	1.87	1.68	1.40

These results show a deep division between manual workers and skilled workers. The informal job group is the poorest. Not only is the poverty rate much higher than in other groups, but also the poverty intensity and inequality are extremely high. This group also has a higher percentage of MLSS recipients and stronger poverty perception than other groups. Overall, poverty concentration is over-represented in the manual worker/ social service worker group and in the informal job group.

Finally, cases are compared across different housing groups (see Table 2.12). Inherited housing and public rental housing are two groups with the highest poverty concentration, followed by self-built housing and subsidized/welfare housing, and then privatized public housing and private rental groups. Finally the commodity housing group, not surprisingly, has the lowest level of poverty concentration. In these poor neighbourhoods, commodity housing schemes are rare. But occasionally through redevelopment, some commodity housing projects were built. Although the self-built housing group does not have the highest poverty rate, the poverty gap and weighted poverty gap within this group are the highest. The inherited housing group and public rental group have a very similar poverty measures. This suggests that these two housing groups have a very similar population composition. Public rental housing, inherited housing, and subsidized/welfare housing are three groups with the highest MLSS coverage rate, which means that people living in these houses have more access to state welfare. On the other hand, private rental housing and self-built housing (mainly for self-use through extensions) groups have least access to state welfare, despite their high poverty concentrations. Although the commodity housing group is comparatively better off in terms of absolute poverty measures, interestingly the percentage of poverty perception in this group is comparable to the private rental housing and privatized public housing groups. This may suggest that commodity housing owners compare themselves with the affluent homebuyers and feel the burden of a mortgage and the costs related to homeownership. Comparatively they thus have a sense of deprivation.

POVERTY DETERMINANTS

Poverty by Different Groups and Neighbourhoods

We have run logistic regression models to analyse the association between poverty generation and various explanatory variables. The advantage of multivariate analysis is to exclude the contribution of confounding factors, and to isolate the explanatory power of each variable. The dependent

Table 2.12 Poverty measures and their concentration (categorized by housing tenure)

	%	FTG indices			P_m	P_p	LQ_0	LQ_1	LQ_2	LQ_m	LQ_p
		P_0	P_1*100	P_2*100							
Private rental	35.4	16.8	4.00	1.68	3.9	18.9	0.75	0.85	0.77	0.39	0.86
Public rental	10.3	34.2	6.04	2.48	21.4	30.5	1.53	1.28	1.14	2.16	1.39
Self-built housing	13.4	28.4	8.79	4.79	6.6	25.1	1.27	1.86	2.21	0.67	1.14
Inherited housing	7.7	34.5	6.38	3.18	21.6	35.3	1.54	1.35	1.47	2.18	1.60
Privatized public housing	21.9	17.6	3.01	1.33	9.3	17.4	0.79	0.64	0.61	0.94	0.79
Subsidized/welfare housing	8.1	27.9	3.28	1.44	20.4	21.1	1.25	0.69	0.66	2.06	0.96
Commodity housing	3.0	9.1	2.92	0.98	1.8	18.2	0.41	0.62	0.45	0.18	0.83

variable is poverty status: 1 represents poor, while 0 represents non-poor. Thirteen explanatory variables are included in this model, of which six variables, that is city, neighbourhood, group, housing tenure, occupation and employer type, are set as dummy variables. We therefore create a composite reference: rural migrant living in private rental housing in an urban village in Kunming, and having an informal job. In short: informal rural migrant worker in private rental urban village housing in Kunming. The results are shown in Table 2.13.

With reference to the synthetic comparator, similar respondents from Xi'an have a higher probability of being poor, while respondents from Nanjing and Wuhan are less likely to be poor. Guangzhou and Harbin dummy variables do not show statistical significance. As for the neighbourhood variable, with all other important measurable attributes held constant, living in either a dilapidated old neighbourhood or a workers' village gives a household a significantly higher probability of being poor. For the group variable, the regression model shows that the laid-off/unemployed group is significantly associated with poor status, while the retired group is connected with non-poor status.

Table 2.13 also shows the association between demographic characteristics and poverty status. Household size, household head's school years, and household head's party membership are three variables significantly related to poverty generation. A larger household size indicates a higher probability of being poor; fewer schooling years gives a higher poverty incidence; while being a member of the Chinese Communist Party (CCP) gives a lower probability of being poor. This suggests that being a party member still gives income-earning advantages and/or better access to welfare provision. Household head's age shows no significant correlation with poverty status. With other predictors controlled for, the explanatory power of age has been weakened.

The model shows the association between different types of housing tenure and poverty status. With reference to an informal rural migrant worker in a private rental urban village house in Kunming, only those living in public rental housing and privatized public housing are significantly associated with non-poor status. For the rural migrant comparator, public housing benefits significantly decrease the probability of being poor.

For the variable 'household head occupation', excluding the jobs of manual worker or social service worker, all other occupations are significantly associated with non-poor status, when compared with the synthetic comparator. This is mainly because being a manual worker or social service worker usually means working longer hours and getting low pay. Some of these workers have become the working poor. Among all of

Table 2.13   Logistic regression model of poverty determinants (whole sample)

	B	SE
City (reference: Kunming)		
Xi'an	.528**	.224
Guangzhou	.336	.235
Nanjing	−.864***	.273
Wuhan	−.486**	.245
Harbin	.075	.238
Neighbourhood (reference: urban villages)		
Dilapidated old neighbourhood	.371*	.196
Workers' village	.449*	.245
Group (reference: rural migrant)		
Urban working	.152	.251
Urban laid-off/unemployed	.907***	.234
Retired	−.697**	.334
Demographic characteristics		
Household size	.116***	.033
Household head age	.008	.007
Household head years of schooling	−.083***	.022
Household head party membership	−.540**	.239
Housing tenure (reference: private rental housing)		
Public rental	.540**	.262
Self-built housing	−.001	.225
Inherited housing	.057	.275
Privatized public housing	−.560**	.262
Subsidized/welfare housing	.059	.287
Commodity housing	−.694	.539
Household head occupation (reference: informal job and others)		
Manager/director	−2.879***	1.042
Professional/civil servant	−.837**	.421
Skilled worker/ technician	−.810**	.387
Self-employed/small business owner	−1.469***	.271
Manual worker/social service worker	.104	.254
Employer type (reference: others)		
Public sector (CCP organization education, research, health care etc.)	−.632*	.335
SOE/CEO	−.543**	.224
Private enterprise	−.684***	.256
Joint venture/foreign enterprise	−1.834**	.783
Working experience		
Weekly working hour	−.002	.003

Table 2.13   (continued)

	B	SE
SOE/CEO working experience	−.061	.176
Job changing	−.128*	.077
Constant	−.589	.484
Chi-square	405.748***	
−2 Log likelihood	1514.716	
Cases	1809	

Notes: * p < 0.1; **p < 0.05; ***p < 0.01. B = coefficient; SE = standard error.

these occupations, being a manager or director has the strongest effect in decreasing the probability of being poor, followed by being self-employed or a small business owner, professional/civil servant, and skilled worker/ technician. When we look at the variable 'employer type', all employer types are associated with less probability of being poor compared with the same reference. Of all these employer types, 'joint venture/foreign enterprise' has the strongest effect in decreasing the probability of being poor.

We also examined the association between poverty status and three indicators of household head's working experience: weekly working hours, experience of working in SOE/COE, and number of job changes. Only the number of job changes shows a significant connection with non-poor status. The other two variables are not statistically significant. For the rural migrant comparator, changing jobs can actually decrease the probability of being poor. This suggests that the chance of getting reasonable pay/a stable job increases after several attempts.

Overall, the model in Table 2.13 identifies a number of determinants of poverty incidence. Most hypothesized explanatory variables are statistically significant.

To compare poverty determinants in different neighbourhoods, we ran a logistic regression model for each type of neighbourhood. Dependent variable and independent variables remain the same, except that the 'neighbourhood' variable and the 'city' variable are removed, since the number of cases in each sub-group is too small to compare the variation between cities. The composite reference is informal sector rural migrant worker in private rental housing. Results are shown in Table 2.14.

In urban villages, retiree status shows significant correlation with non-poor status, with reference to the synthetic comparator. However, in both the old neighbourhood and workers' village models, the laid-off/ unemployed group is significantly related to poverty status. This suggests

Table 2.14 Logistic regression models of poverty determinants (by neighbourhood)

	Urban villages		Dilapidated old neighbourhood		Workers' village	
	B	SE	B	SE	B	SE
Group (reference: rural migrant)						
Working	.038	.371	.689	.487	.753	.837
Laid-off/unemployed	.338	.357	1.373***	.482	2.206***	.805
Retired	-2.034***	.781	-.752	.649	1.342	.898
Demographic characteristics						
Household size	.108***	.040	.124*	.064	.395***	.086
Household head age	.008	.011	.020	.014	-.021	.016
Household head years of schooling	-.106***	.036	-.102***	.039	-.023	.044
Household head party membership	.183	.446	.274	.472	-1.164***	.378
Housing tenure (reference: private rental housing)						
Public rental	1.032**	.505	-.291	.427	.258	.558
Self-built housing	.132	.285	.396	.503	-1.241	1.489
Inherited housing	.433	.474	.006	.436	-20.628	11433.018
Privatized public housing	.353	.631	-.970*	.521	-1.027**	.478
Subsidized/welfare housing	.675	.664	-.692	.553	-.004	.527
Commodity housing	.702	.882	-.749	.912	-2.698**	1.189
Household head occupation (reference: informal job and others)						
Manager/director	-19.938	5621.711	-2.118*	1.166	-18.789	6482.395
Professional/civil servant	-1.930**	.760	-1.473*	.869	.429	.816
Skilled worker/technician	-1.272**	.637	-1.132	.762	.155	.778

Table 2.14 (continued)

	Urban villages		Dilapidated old neighbourhood		Workers' village	
	B	SE	B	SE	B	SE
Self-employed/small business owner	-1.534***	.371	-1.746***	.457	-22.447	6763.814
Manual worker/social service worker	-.279	.454	.162	.426	.421	.550
Employer type (reference: others)						
Public sector (CCP organization education, research, health care etc.)	.413	.579	-2.118***	.740	-1.659***	.584
SOE/CEO	-.265	.409	-.724*	.406	-1.175***	.410
Private enterprise	-.265	.422	-.849*	.453	-1.223**	.550
Joint venture/foreign enterprise	-18.703	6982.109	-2.139*	1.143	-2.823**	1.394
Working experience						
Weekly working hour	.000	.004	.003	.005	-.006	.008
SOE/CEO working experience	-.130	.269	-.081	.301	-.677*	.392
Job change	.045	.096	-.106	.136	-.498**	.210
Constant	-.697	.710	-.745	.881	.455	1.207
Chi-square	121.185***		149.908***		163.886***	
-2 Log likelihood	628.027		457.176		378.080	
Cases	796		502		511	

Notes: B = coefficient; SE= standard error. * p < 0.1; ** p <0.05; *** p < 0.01.

62

that in urban villages, retirees are relatively better off, while in both old neighbourhoods and workers' villages, the laid-off/unemployed are worse off, when compared to informal rural migrant worker in private rental housing.

The association between poverty incidence and demographic characteristics also varies in different neighbourhoods. In the urban village and old neighbourhoods models, household size and household head's schooling years are both significantly associated with poverty status. In both models, a large household size is associated with a higher probability of being poor, while more schooling years means a lower probability of poverty. However, in workers' villages, household size and household head's party membership are important indicators of poverty. Being a party member significantly decreases the chance of being poor in workers' villages. This is presumably due to a greater scope and scale of non-market material benefits and influence in neighbourhoods built around state-owned enterprises – and a greater legacy of these in the reform era.

Looking at housing tenure, in urban villages, when compared with informal sector rural migrant worker in private rental housing, only those living in public rental housing are significantly associated with a poorer status. Private rental is the dominant housing tenure in urban villages, and public rental housing only exists there in the few cases where small-scale SOEs/COEs have acquired housing from the village collective and allocated it to their employees. These employees are comparatively disadvantaged by virtue of the small scale of enterprises they work in or worked in and by the mass lay-offs during SOE/COE reforms. In old neighbourhoods, living in privatized public housing is the only factor to reduce the probability of being poor. Similarly, in workers' villages, living in privatized public housing (or in commodity housing) significantly reduces the probability of being poor. Access to privatized public housing and commodity housing is clearly reserved for the better off.

Next, consider the predictive ability of household head's occupation. In urban villages, professional/civil servants, skilled worker/technicians, and self-employed/small business owners are three types of occupation that are significantly associated with non-poor status, compared with an informal sector worker (rural migrant worker in private rental housing). Managers/directors and manual workers/social service workers are not significantly associated with poverty status. This result is influenced by the fact that only a very small proportion of respondents in urban village are managers/directors. Also, as mentioned earlier, being a manual worker/social service worker does not necessarily make a person better off when compared to an informal rural migrant worker. In old neighbourhoods, a household head being a manager/director, professional/civil servant, skilled worker/

technician, or self-employed/small business owner significantly reduces the probability of being poor. Among these occupations, being self-employed or a small business owner has the strongest effect in decreasing the poverty probability. In workers' villages, none of these occupational categories show significant association with poverty status. This is for two reasons: first, a great proportion of respondents in workers' villages are economically inactive; second, those who are economically active mainly work in the informal sector.

For respondents in urban villages, employer type and working experience do not significantly affect poverty status compared to the informal sector comparator. In the old urban neighbourhoods model, all employer types give a lower probability of being poor compared with the informal sector baseline. Nevertheless, the working experience variables have no statistical significance in determining respondents' poverty status. In workers' villages, again, all employer types are associated with less probability of being poor compared to informal sector working (for a rural migrant for example). This confirms previous finding that being economically active is of great significance in avoiding poverty in workers' villages. In terms of working experience, those who had SOE/COE working experience and those who changed their jobs more frequently are less likely to be poor in workers' villages. This suggests that people who used to work for SOEs/COEs have had better access to work-unit and state welfare provision. This also further provides evidence that actively looking for job opportunities can help laid-off workers in workers' village survive poverty.

Overall, as an enclave of former SOE employees, workers' villages still have a strong relationship with the state system. For instance, household head's party membership, living in subsidized/welfare housing, having SOE/COE working experience, are all associated with lower probability of being poor. Moreover, being economically active is very important for residents in a workers' village to avoid falling into poverty.

In comparison, urban villages and dilapidated old neighbourhoods show more connection with the market economy, since respondents in these two types of neighbourhood have been exposed to the mechanism of market remuneration to a greater extent. For instance, more schooling years (household head) is a safeguard against poverty in these neighbourhoods.

We also examine the variation of poverty determinants between different social groups, namely the working group, the laid-off/unemployed group, retirees' group and rural migrants' group. Table 2.15 shows the results of a logistic regression model developed for each group. The dependent variable and explanatory variables are similar to those in Table 2.14, except that the 'group' variable is replaced by the 'neighbourhood' variable. The

Table 2.15 Logistic regression models of poverty determinants (by group)

	Working		Laid-off/unemployed		Retired		Migrant	
	B	SE	B	SE	B	SE	B	SE
Neighbourhood (reference: urban village)								
Dilapidated old neighbourhood	.573	.480	.686*	.375	1.022	.860	.394	.332
Workers' village	.437	.594	.465	.424	1.336	.909	.004	.749
Demographic characteristics								
Household size	.408***	.124	.055	.072	.136***	.052	.211***	.062
Household head age	.026	.021	-.004	.014	-.008	.016	.004	.012
Household head years of schooling	-.013	.067	-.107**	.043	-.030	.041	-.146***	.042
Household head party membership	-.282	.582	-1.085**	.454	-.179	.374	-.149	.627
Housing tenure (reference: private rental housing)								
Public rental	-.097	.639	.300	.445	-1.415**	.718	.905	.624
Self-built housing	.624	.638	-.712	.476	-1.542*	.900	.734**	.321
Inherited housing	.105	.672	.184	.442	-2.046**	.936	.900	.672
Privatized public housing	-.913	.672	-.431	.437	-2.108***	.683	-.439	.909
Subsidized/welfare housing	-.385	.711	.406	.500	-1.557**	.772	.700	.739
Commodity housing	-18.589	7370.042	-.780	.997	-2.661**	1.213	1.475	.984
Household head occupation (reference: informal job and others)								
Manager/director	-.892	1.874	-20.332	15514.750	n/a	n/a	-19.768	7074.468
Professional/civil servant	.385	1.597	-1.629	1.132	n/a	n/a	-1.672**	.786
Skilled worker/ technician	.334	1.607	-.967	.761	n/a	n/a	-.961	.715

Table 2.15 (continued)

	Working		Laid-off/unemployed		Retired		Migrant	
	B	SE	B	SE	B	SE	B	SE
Self-employed/small business owner	-1.970	1.293	-1.916***	.547	n/a	n/a	-1.586***	.369
Manual worker/social service worker	1.503	1.511	.221	.429	n/a	n/a	-.107	.456
Employer type (reference: others)								
Public sector (CCP organization education, research, health care etc.)	-1.954*	1.155	-1.184*	.621	n/a	n/a	-.153	.687
SOE/CEO	-2.298**	1.024	-.831***	.313	n/a	n/a	-.446	.539
Private enterprise	-1.881*	.991	-1.132**	.472	n/a	n/a	-.126	.434
Joint venture/foreign enterprise	-2.856*	1.485	-1.236	1.333	n/a	n/a	-19.551	9069.510
Working experience								
Weekly working hour	.017*	.010	-.009	.005	n/a	n/a	.002	.004
SOE/CEO working experience	.021	.430	.193	.298	-.241	.509	-.435	.338
Job change	-.165	.220	-.252**	.127	-.501	.435	.103	.103
Constant	-3.821**	1.909	1.619	1.034	-.009	1.721	-1.112	.796
Chi-square	57.003***		112.004***		25.725***		106.079***	
-2 Log likelihood	225.315		455.175		266.856		526.647	
Cases	405		414		335		655	

Notes: B = coefficient; SE = standard error. * p < 0.1; ** p < 0.05; *** p < 0.01.

synthetic comparator is slightly different from the previous models. For three of the models, the comparator profile is a household head living in private rental urban village housing and having an informal job. In the regression model for retirees, three independent variables related to household head's employment, that is occupation, employer type and weekly working hours, are not applicable and thus removed. Therefore the composite reference for the retirees' group is living in private rental urban village housing. As mentioned earlier, a proportion of the laid-off/unemployed are still economically active. These employment-related variables are therefore kept in the model for the laid-off/unemployed.

We first look at the neighbourhood variable. With all other variables controlled for, only in the laid-off/unemployed group is there significant variation of poverty with neighbourhoods. 'Laid-off/unemployed' household heads working in the informal sector in old neighbourhoods are more likely to be poor when compared with those living in urban villages. Looking at demographic characteristics, for this group, only household size shows significant connection with poverty incidence. Large household size significantly increases the probability of being poor among the laid-off workers. For the laid-off/unemployed group, household head's schooling years and party membership are also significantly connected with poverty incidence. Longer schooling years and being a party member significantly reduce the risk of being poor for laid-off/unemployed urban residents. The absolute value of the coefficient of party membership is relatively high, which suggests that being a party member has a very strong effect in decreasing the probability of poverty. For retirees, none of these variables show statistical significance. For rural migrants, both household size and household head's schooling years are associated with poverty incidence. Smaller household size and longer schooling years suggest lower probability of being poor in this group.

In terms of housing tenure, for the working group and the laid-off/unemployed group, none of the housing types show significant connection with poverty status, with reference to those living in private rental urban village housing and having an informal job. On the other hand, for retirees, all types of housing tenure are connected with lower poverty probability, when compared with the same reference. This suggests that retirees living in private rental urban village housing are the most disadvantaged. For urban migrants, self-built housing is significantly related to poor status. This is mainly because self-built housing is illegal in principle and is therefore under strict control by the city government and vulnerable to demolition. Only those migrants who cannot afford other forms of housing would choose to live in self-build housing.

Only in the laid-off/unemployed group and rural migrants group, does household head's occupation show statistical significance. Compared with those living in private rental urban village housing and having an informal job, self-employed/small business owners are significantly associated with non-poor status in the laid-off/unemployed group. Being a professional/ civil servant and being a self-employed/small business owner suggest lower probability of being poor in the rural migrants group. When we look at household head's employer type, for the working group, all employer types show significant association with non-poor status, with reference to informal sector employment. Joint venture/foreign enterprises have the strongest effect in decreasing the probability of being poor. For the laid-off/unemployed group, working in the public sector, SOE/COE and private enterprises, give a lower probability of being poor. Among these employer types, private enterprise has the strongest effect in reducing the poverty risk. Joint venture/foreign enterprises do not show statistical significance, because the percentage of this group is comparatively low. For migrants, employer types do not significantly affect poverty generation. This is mainly because most migrants can only get low-profile jobs. It therefore does not seem to matter which type of employers they work for.

In terms of working experience, for both retirees and migrants, these variables do not show significant influence on poverty incidence. For the working group, interestingly, longer working hours indicate higher probability of being poor. This suggests that people working long hours are most likely to have a low-profile job and suffer from low wage and a low benefit package, thus becoming the working poor. For the laid-off/unemployed group, more job changes suggests less chance of being poor. Again, this suggests that the laid-off/unemployed can find ways of surviving through changing jobs.

The Effect of Concentration on Poverty Incidence

In this study we have shown the uneven distribution of poverty rates in different social groups and neighbourhoods. Clearly, some social groups and some neighbourhoods have much higher poverty rates than others. A particular social group within a particular neighbourhood could be even worse, since they are suffering from multiple disadvantages and vulnerabilities. Table 2.16 shows the cross-tabulated results of poverty distribution. As the above analyses have shown, unemployment is, not surprisingly, a major dimension of social deprivation. This dimension intersects with the geography of poverty, generating the most marginal social space, that is unemployed urban households in old neighbourhoods. The poverty rate for unemployed urban households in old neighbourhoods can be as high as 50.6 per cent, while working urban households in

Table 2.16   Uneven distribution of poverty rates (percentages)

Household head status	Urban villages	Inner old neighbourhoods	Workers' village	Sub-total
Working local	9.4	15.5	8.8	11.4
Unemployed	34.2	50.6	41.7	44.2
Retired	9.1	16.7	16.5	15.8
Migrant	18.5	22.2	13.0	18.8
Sub-total	18.1	29.3	22.3	22.4

workers' villages is the least poor group, with a modest poverty rate of 8.8 per cent. As the results in the table suggest, the combination of unemployment and old urban neighbourhood creates the least optimal conditions, and thus represents the highest poverty concentration.

To further understand the effect of poverty concentration on poverty incidence, Table 2.17 provides the results of logistic regression of the probability of being poor over a set of explanatory variables. The independent variables are slightly different from Tables 2.13, 2.14 and 2.15, since this model mainly aims to identify the impoverishing effect of social groups and neighbourhoods. And these social groups and neighbourhoods have a different degree of poverty concentration, as shown above. The reference profile is a rural migrant in an urban village. Thus the exponentiated coefficient of these two variables indicates the odds ratio of becoming poor, respectively compared with the reference group. Years of schooling of the head of household and party membership reduce the likelihood of poverty, while the number of dependent children increases it. With these factors controlled for, living in an old neighbourhood raises the chance of being poor 1.56 times (exponentiated coefficient) compared to living in an urban village. Unemployed urban household status raises the chance of being poor by 3.2 times that of rural migrants.

Next, the joint effect of neighbourhood and social group is tested through interaction of these two categorical variables. Results are shown in Table 2.18. The three significant control variables act in the direction expected. Compared to rural migrants in city villages, working urban households in old neighbourhoods and workers' villages do not have a significantly greater chance of being poor. That is, working status is perhaps an ultimate protection from falling into poverty. Retired households present very similar features to the working households. For unemployed urban households, however, living in old urban neighbourhoods raises the chance of being poor by 4.77 times, and in workers' village by 3.8 times. These figures pinpoint specific neighbourhood effects for specific

Table 2.17   Group effects of neighbourhood types and social groups on the likelihood of falling into poverty (y=1 if the household is under poverty line)

	B	SE
Household head age	.008	.005
Household head schooling year	−.101***	.019
Household head party membership	−.513**	.220
Household size	.042	.041
Number of dependent children	.259***	.091
Neighbourhood types (reference: 'urban villages')		
Old urban neighbourhoods	.442***	.171
Workers' villages	.261	.190
Social group (reference: rural migrants)		
Working urban households	−.386*	.216
Unemployed urban households	1.166***	.188
Retired urban households	−.460*	.257
Constant	−1.391***	.321
−2 log likelihood	1709.778	
Sample size	1809	
ρ^2	.168	

Notes: * $p < 0.1$; ** $p < 0.05$; *** $p < 0.01$. B = coefficient; SE = standard error.

social groups. That is, the effect of old urban neighbourhoods works more on unemployed households than the working population. While someone living in an old neighbourhood is more likely to be poor, being unemployed in an old neighbourhood is even more impoverishing.

To quantify the effect of neighbourhood, we introduce the average poverty rate as a measure of the depth of poverty in neighbourhoods. Table 2.19 represents the effect of neighbourhood poverty rate on the total sample, and different social groups. This test is therefore different from the previous one. The previous models test the existence of neighbourhood types on probability of falling into poverty. This test specifies the effect of percentage points in the poverty rate on the probability of being poor.

For the total sample, even when the major socioeconomic attributes are controlled for, the neighbourhood poverty rate still presents a significant effect on the households' probability of falling into poverty. That is, holding age, year of schooling, party membership, household size, number of dependent children, and the number of unemployed in the family the same, living in poverty neighbourhoods enhances the chance of becoming

Table 2.18   Joint effects of neighbourhood type and social group on the likelihood of falling into poverty

	B	SE
Household head age	.009*	.005
Household head schooling year	−.101***	.019
Household head party membership	−.556**	.219
Household size	.040	.041
Number of dependent children	.255***	.090
Joint effect		
Reference: rural migrants * 'urban villages'		
Working urban households by old urban neighbourhood	.066	.265
Working urban households by workers' villages	−.452	.323
Unemployed urban households by old urban neighbourhood	1.562***	.185
Unemployed urban households by workers' villages	1.334***	.193
Retired urban households by old urban neighbourhoods	−.296	.299
Retired urban households by workers' villages	−.145	.255
Constant	−1.307***	.320
−2 log likelihood	1723.097	
Sample size	1809	
ρ^2	.158	

Notes: * p < 0.1; ** p < 0.05; *** p < 0.01. B = coefficient; SE = standard error.

poor. For every 1 per cent increase in the poverty rate, the chance of living in poverty increased by 4.4 per cent for all households, that is exp(B) = 1.044.

For each social group, the effect of the controlling factors is different. Unemployed urban households behave in a similar way to migrants, while retired urban households share similar features with working urban households. The meaning of 'retirement' suggests there is some continuation between the individuals and their employers, because they exit 'normally' from their workplaces. For unemployed urban households, schooling tends to protect them from poverty. The same is true of rural migrants. Party membership only presents a significant advantage in unemployed urban households. This is because there are few party members among

Table 2.19 Effects of neighbourhood poverty rate on the likelihood of falling into poverty (total sample and by different social groups)

	Total sample		Working urban households		Unemployed urban households		Retired urban households		Rural migrants	
	B	SE	B	SE	B	SE	B	SE	B	SE
Household head age	.008*	.005	.027	.019	.009	.014	.004	.016	.001	.006
Household head schooling year	-.077***	.019	-.040	.061	-.140***	.041	-.011	.041	-.148***	.037
Household head party membership	-.778***	.231	-.594	.525	-1.298***	.458	-.333	.369	-.078	.584
Household size	-.134**	.052	-.156	.174	-.049	.112	-.143	.130	-.032	.088
Number of dependent children	.291***	.096	.382	.306	.074	.211	.446	.286	.386***	.139
Number of unemployed	.712***	.072	.885***	.216	.553***	.145	.420**	.192	.599***	.114
Neighbourhood poverty rate	.043***	.004	.033***	.012	.051***	.008	.030***	.011	.045***	.008
Constant	-2.490***	.355	-3.867***	1.238	-1.426	.998	-2.584**	1.283	-2.220***	.478
-2 log likelihood	1571.298		244.289		455.781		267.715		533.102	
Sample size	1809		405		414		335		655	
ρ^2	.269		.179		.319		.123		.228	

Notes: * p < 0.1; ** p < 0.05; *** p < 0.01. B = coefficient; SE = standard error.

72

migrant households. Second, party membership for households in poverty neighbourhoods means less in terms of privileges but is rather an association with the established institution. For working urban households, a significant contribution to poverty generation comes from the existence of an unemployed family member. One unemployed family member raises the probability of becoming poor by more than 2.42 times. But when the head of household becomes unemployed, such an impact still exists but is reduced to 1.74 times. For the other two groups, the impact is between 1.52 for retired households to 1.82 for migrants. For migrants, the number of dependent children is very important, because this significantly increases living costs and reduces the ability of going to work (the mother may have to look after the children).

It seems that for urban working and retired households, the only critical impact comes from unemployment, because there is a significant difference between employed and unemployed households. The attributes of education (years of schooling) and party membership and dependent children are irrelevant. For them, as long as they remain in the state system, they are protected. However, for marginal groups, their years of schooling, association with the party, or the number of dependent children become relevant, as these might be the last push into or out of poverty. Migrants generally have a low educational attainment. But they work in the labour market. Even a low educational attainment can mean a big difference for their poverty experience.

A small yet steady effect on poverty rate is seen across all models. For every 1 per cent increase in the poverty rate of a neighbourhood, the chance of living in poverty increases by 4.4 per cent for all households. For working urban households, this figure is 3.4 per cent; for unemployed urban households, 5.2 per cent; for retired urban households, 3.0 per cent; and for migrant households, 4.6 per cent. There are some differences but they are not huge. There is a relatively constant poverty neighbourhood effect, that is the concentration of poverty in a neighbourhood does affect individuals' poverty incidence. The difference from an average of 4 per cent to 12 per cent could mean a 33 per cent difference in the probability of being poor, even though other aspects of household features are the same.

CONCLUSION

In contrast to studies on urban poverty that are based on national statistics of the general population, the findings reported in this chapter paint a picture of poverty incidence and patterns for specific social groups in low-income neighbourhoods. Despite the extremely low poverty rate and alleged national trend of declining poverty, our study provides evidence that the poverty issue should be contextualized in urban spaces. For the general population in the period of fast economic growth, rising income and employment opportunities, poverty might not be a problem. In the poverty neighbourhoods surveyed, however, poverty rates exceed the negligible level. Drawn from first-hand household survey data in low-income neighbourhoods in six major Chinese cities, our study reveals a poverty incidence of 22.4 per cent. This shows that despite a general decrease of absolute urban poverty, the spatial and social concentration of poverty has become an issue. Urban poverty rates might be reducing, but poverty in the city is concentrating. However, China is not experiencing poverty concentration in quite the same way as ghettos in the US or socially excluded neighbourhoods in Europe. Moreover, the dynamics and consequences of poverty concentration are very different. This study fills a gap in existing poverty studies in contemporary China by revealing in considerable detail, the morphology of poverty – its concentration and determinants (or strictly speaking, correlates) in different types of poor neighbourhoods and in the different social groups that live in those neighbourhoods.

Our study finds that urban poverty is highly concentrated in several neighbourhoods and social groups that endure multiple disadvantages. Some of the findings are consistent with conventional wisdom. For instance, urban poverty over-represents in the mid-age group, that is the 40s and 50s. Household head's schooling years is a useful predictor for poverty incidence too. More schooling years greatly reduces the risk of being poor. In terms of occupation, manual workers/social service workers and people with informal jobs are two very disadvantaged groups with the highest poverty concentrations. On the other hand, some of the findings are not consistent with conventional wisdom.

Among three types of poor neighbourhood in Chinese cities, old inner city neighbourhoods have the highest poverty concentration. Compared with urban residents, rural migrants are not necessarily the poorest group. This is an important finding: when a social group can manage its livelihood well through either market remuneration or institutional protection, it is less likely to fall into poverty. Migrant groups are not equivalent to the urban poor, despite low living standards. Migrant enclaves, that is urban villages, are not ghettos. They survive by engaging in market production. In the worst situation are those who are failed by both market and state institutions, that is laid-off workers who have failed to find re-employment. As the survey reveals, laid-off/unemployed workers have the highest poverty concentration. In this group, not only the poverty rate, but also poverty intensity and inequality are the highest of all groups.

Among groups with different housing tenure, poverty is highly concentrated in public rental housing, inherited housing and self-built housing, while private rental housing is not necessarily associated with a poorer population.

The study reveals a mismatch between actual hardship and deprivation perception. Groups used to having close ties with state institutions, such as occupants of workers' villages, the laid-off/unemployed group, the public rental housing group, and the subsidized/welfare housing group, tend to overstate their hardships: they have a strong sense of deprivation. Rural migrants, on the other hand, tend to understate their hardships, having a lower sense of deprivation. Being retrenched or eliminated from the SOEs, the former groups are no longer protected by state institutions. It is quite natural for them to be more pessimistic about their lives. On the other hand, rural migrants make positive comparisons with their former rural situation and with the anticipated future. They are, therefore, less likely to consider themselves as the urban poor.

This finding about the permanent poor and the migrant poor suggests the importance of understanding the difference between relative and absolute poverty. Relative poverty makes a comparison between oneself and others, but also between one's positions at different times. Individuals below an absolute poverty line or in a vulnerable position near to it, may have very different experiences and perceptions due to the income/well-being level to which they compare themselves. There is a strong tradition in migration studies, from Lewis (1954), Fei and Ranis (1964) to Todaro (1969) and beyond, that rural migrants make comparisons with their former (or intermittent) rural situation and with the anticipated future rather than, or in addition to, more established urban groups. In fact, the comparison with established urban residents is generally understood to be a positive comparison that gives hope and drives the migration decision. If migrants come to cities to emulate the urban classes it is not surprising if they do not identify themselves as poor as frequently as members of the urban class who have fallen into misfortune. By contrast, established urban residents who have lost their jobs as a result of mass unemployment have three comparators to make them feel miserable: their previous position of greater well-being; their lack of hope in the future (they have not generally made the migrants' decision to forgo present well-being for future gain); and the threat of migrants who generally work harder and under worse conditions and who compete for jobs, suppress wages and squeeze the benefit from selling their labour.

Through comparing MLSS coverage rates across different social groups, this study identifies a substantial gap in existing social safety nets and highlights certain blind spots of social assistance, for example rural migrants, elderly/retirees, households living in private rental housing and inherited/ self-built housing. As one of the most important means of state welfare provision, the distribution of MLSS subsidies is disproportionate to actual poverty concentration, especially for urban villagers, rural migrants, the private rental housing group and the self-built housing group. Under institutional discrimination, these groups are not recognized as official urban citizens and are consequently excluded from the formal institutions, remaining unprotected by any social safety net.

In examining the association between poverty generation and various predictors in different neighbourhoods and social groups, we generalize two major determinants of poverty. One is social welfare entitlement to MLSS subsidy, and to housing, education and health care benefits. This determinant is related to a number of variables, importantly, *hukou*, party membership, housing tenure, employer type, and SOE/CEO working experience. More social welfare entitlements mean a lower probability of being poor. The other determinant is market remuneration results, which roughly include three sub-categories: selling one's own labour/skills at a good price (in relative terms) by getting into regular and stable employment; selling one's own labour/skills at a depressed price by getting into informal and unstable employment; no success in selling one's own labour/ skills. This determinant is related to variables in our analysis that include *hukou*, age, years of schooling, occupation, weekly working hours, job change. Selling one's own labour/skills at a good price suggests a lower probability of being poor. On the other hand, selling one's own labour/ skills at a depressed price or being unsuccessful in finding work, is related to a higher probability of being poor, that is the working poor and the unemployed poor.

Poverty generation is determined by a combination of these two determinants. In general, these two determinants affect the probability of poverty equally, despite the fact that one determinant might have stronger effects in some neighbourhoods and groups than in others. Conventionally in China, being excluded from institutional protection/social welfare provision is believed to be one of the most important causes of urban poverty. Nevertheless, as China's urban economy is increasingly shaped by markets, we must recognize that market remuneration mechanisms are becoming a more and more important determinant of poverty, especially for people who have been eliminated or excluded from the state institutions, notably laid-off workers and rural migrants. Our study shows the rising importance of market remuneration mechanisms. For instance, for the laid-off/unemployed, changing jobs, that is attempts to sell one's own labour/skills in the market for a good price, is significantly (negatively) correlated with the probability of being poor. Also, our study reveals that laid-off/unemployed workers rather than rural migrants are the poorest group. This is mainly because under the redundancy policy, laid-off workers not only become jobless but are also stateless. In this sense, this group suffers dual difficulties of being deprived of social welfare entitlements formerly supplied by the SOEs and finding it difficult to sell their labour – or selling it for a depressed price. They have therefore become the very poorest in the city.

On the other hand, despite their disadvantaged status, rural migrants are more active in selling their labour, even for a lower price than their urban counterparts will accept. They are thus better able to survive urban poverty. They are willing to take low-profile jobs such as manual work and social service jobs, which temporarily but effectively help them survive hardships and avoid the trap of poverty. Nevertheless, most of them only manage to sell their labour for a very low price due to fierce competition from other migrants and from laid-off workers. This makes them much more vulnerable than their urban counterparts who find it easier to get into regular and higher-waged employment.

The determinants of poverty vary in different social groups and neighbourhoods. Nevertheless, a general finding is that the withdrawal of social welfare provision and exclusion from regular employment is an important factor in Chinese cities. In other words, an inferior position in urban institutions organized by the state (for example *hukou* status) and an inferior position in the market remuneration system, fundamentally result in the clustering of poverty by group and by neighbourhood that we have described in this chapter.

In addition, this chapter has revealed a small but not insignificant effect of poverty concentration on poverty generation in China. Living in poverty neighbourhoods increases the probability of being poor by a steady percentage (for every 1 per cent increase in poverty rate the chance is increased by 4.4 per cent). Having said this, Chinese cities are characterized by a relatively high level of social mix. Measured by an index of dissimilarity at the residents' committee level, the index ranges from 0.2 to 0.4 for most socioeconomic groups, indicating a relatively modest level of segregation (Li and Wu, 2008). Chinese cities therefore lack the very high poverty areas found in the US. In the US, high poverty areas are defined as those in which 40 per cent of the population is poor within a census tract (Jargowsky, 1997). Measured by the official poverty line, the poorest neighbourhoods identified in our six Chinese cities have an overall poverty rate of below 38.3 per cent. The average rate is at 22.4 per cent. As we argued at the start of the chapter, poverty in Chinese cities needs therefore to be examined at the points (spatially and socially) at which it clusters.

Our research reveals that the intersection of two dimensions of vulnerability – social vulnerability of laid-off and unemployed households and geographic vulnerability of old urban neighbourhoods – produces the worst deprivation in Chinese cities. For the social group in which the head of household has been laid off or is officially unemployed, a poverty rate of 44.2 per cent has been found. But living in old urban neighbourhoods pushes the poverty rate of this social group up to 50.6 per cent. Even when the basic demographic and socioeconomic attributes are controlled for, as an average, being a household head with laid-off/unemployed status increases the chance of living in poverty by 3.2 times, compared with rural migrants. Living in an old urban neighbourhood increases the chance by 1.6 times, compared with urban villages. The joint effect raises the chance by 4.7 times. Even in workers' villages, the joint effect is 3.8 times higher than the urban village reference group.

In urban China, the morphology of poverty is created by 'poverty of transition' processes. Namely, vulnerability is not simply attributed to the introduction of the market but rather the interaction between the market and state institution. This chapter has exposed a detailed picture of the institutional foundations of poverty concentration during China's urban transition. That is, the concentration of poverty is built upon the residential geography inherited from the socialist era. For example, since households in old urban neighbourhoods were more likely to be outside the state enterprise system in the socialist period, they did not benefit from housing privatization to the extent that core enterprise employees did. They carried their vulnerability into the market system, where they were further marginalized. The seeds of their vulnerability were sowed before market transition but reinforced by it. The state and market mechanisms of exclusion reinforce each other to produce a double-jeopardy vulnerability. Old urban neighbourhoods were systematically under-invested in during the state-run economy. Public housing tenants living in old urban neighbourhoods were generally outside the state enterprise system and were underprivileged in housing consumption (Logan et al., 1999). Those who live and work in old urban neighbourhoods are more likely to be laid off first during the labour market reform – a process of 'deterioration from the margin' of the state system (Wu, 2007).

Compared with unemployed households, retirees and rural migrants are two very different groups. Retirees share some similar characteristics with the urban working population because they maintain an institutional link with the workplace (that is they are not 'bought out of services'). They may experience some hardship, but measured with an extremely low official poverty line (literally $1 per day), as long as they continue to receive a state pension, they are relatively unlikely to find themselves in the poverty group. In a sense, they are protected by their state pension.

Rural migrants, on the other hand, do not have an institutional link with the state. They survive by taking low-paid and low-profile jobs in the city. Migrants, as a social group, are not necessarily a poverty group. They self-select into the city, following economic opportunities. As a result, they have a very high rate of employment. The hurdle of entering the city is high, owing to the lack of squatter opportunities. In workers' villages, private rental is limited. In urban villages, space is controlled by private landlords. As a result, these two types do not evolve into high-poverty neighbourhoods.

Poverty-stricken neighbourhoods in China therefore are co-products of exclusion under different systems. This is an important spatial context in which deprivation is shaped by reinforced market and institutional forces. Musterd and Murie (2006: 16) point out this spatial context by arguing, 'academic and research analyses or policy prognoses that treat categories of the population without any reference to where they live are likely to miss an important dimension of the experience of social exclusion'. Where to live is not just a matter of 'residential preference' but is shaped by the structure of opportunities. As we discuss in subsequent parts of the book, the legacy patterns of property rights inherited by the Chinese city in transition structures the geography of poverty. Within this pattern of housing market opportunities, poor households sort themselves. We have shown in considerable detail how spatial and social clustering of poverty interrelate and how households of different types face different opportunities according to the rights they are able to obtain or retain from market and state institutions.

3.   Poverty groups: livelihood and trajectories

The previous chapter describes poverty incidences among different social groups. This chapter discusses in detail their livelihood and poverty situation through our fieldwork observations. The first part of this chapter examines basic aspects of living under poverty, while the second part draws on personal life stories obtained through interviews. The purpose of this chapter is therefore to depict complex composition of poverty groups and their varied trajectories towards poverty.

As we have shown in the previous chapters, China's new urban poverty is composed of unemployed persons, laid-off workers, poor workers and retirees from failing or bankrupt enterprises, and poor rural migrants. This is different from the traditional urban poor in China – the 'Three Nos' (no relatives or dependants, no working capacity and no source of income) (Chen et al., 2006; Liu and Wu, 2006a). The majority of the new urban poor comprises newly laid-off workers and unemployed persons.

Since our survey samples were randomly selected to include different types of household in 25 low-income urban neighbourhoods, they allow us to contrast different social groups, vulnerable groups and less vulnerable groups; and also to compare poor households and non-poor households. This chapter presents a comprehensive portrait of the urban poor by looking at their demographic characteristics, social entitlements, housing conditions, neighbourhood interaction and social networks. Respondents are categorized into four social groups according to household heads' employment status: working group, unemployed/laid-off group, retired group, and rural migrants group. Each group is further divided into poor and non-poor households, poor households being those with incomes under the minimum income level as identified in Chapter 2.

Table 3.1 shows demographic characteristics of different groups. In general, poor households have a larger household size, except for the poor laid-off/unemployed group. Among all groups, poor retirees have the largest households, even larger than rural migrant households. This suggests that the impoverishment of the retired group is highly related to large household size. The poor also have a much higher percentage of unemployed persons in their families, not surprisingly. In the poor laid-off/

Table 3.1 Comparison of demographic characteristics indices

	Working		Laid-off/unemployed		Retired		Rural migrants	
	Non-poor	Poor	Non-poor	Poor	Non-poor	Poor	Non-poor	Poor
No. of cases	360	45	231	183	282	53	532	123
Household size	3.25	4.09	3.32	3.23	3.58	4.89	3.89	4.53
Unemployed people %	16.11	28.41	39.54	60.17	13.52	25.03	18.90	32.26
Dependent children %	18.32	20.30	17.49	18.84	7.52	10.84	21.84	23.82
Household head age	38.25	42.00	48.49	49.79	65.55	65.58	37.85	42.38
Household head years of education	11.47	10.49	9.98	8.47	8.27	7.72	8.57	7.20

unemployed group, the percentage of unemployed people is as high as 60.17 per cent, that is, on average about two-thirds of the family members are laid off or unemployed. A high percentage of dependent children in the family presents additional disadvantage to low-income households. This is particularly true for rural migrants. The heads of poor households are generally older than those of non-poor households. Obviously, for rural migrants and the working groups, an older household head is a particular disadvantage for a household. But for the laid-off/unemployed group, there is little difference with respect to household head's age. This is mainly because the middle-aged (40s–50s) is the major targeted group with respect to the redundancy policy. In terms of education, heads of non-poor households have more years of schooling compared with those of poor households in all groups, suggesting a causal relationship. Overall, both poor and non-poor working groups received more years of education than all other groups. Poor rural migrants are the poorest educated. Before we examine the livelihood of poverty groups, in the next section we provide a brief review of the literature on diverse poverty groups.

UNDERSTANDING DIVERSE POVERTY GROUPS

In Western market economies, prevailing structural interpretations regard the new urban poverty as an outcome of structural changes such as global economic restructuring and post-Fordist transformation (Neef, 1992; Gans, 1993; Morris, 1993; Wacquant, 1993; Wessel, 2000; Walks, 2001). The new urban poor mainly include poorly educated young people, long-term unemployed adults, workers in the informal sector, one-parent families, and immigrants (Mingione, 1993; Badcock, 1997). They are marginal in the labour market (Wilson, 1987; Sassen, 1991; van Kempen, 1994; Hamnett, 1996; Dorling and Woodward, 1996; Mohan, 2000). Since the labour market is regarded as the most important mode of integration in advanced market economies, the new urban poor, because of limited access to the labour market, are more vulnerable and become socially excluded. They therefore have limited welfare security (Silver, 1993; White, 1998; Musterd and Ostendorf, 1998) and weakened social support networks (Mingione, 1996; Musterd et al., 1999). Different poverty groups are subjected to different hardships. While poorly educated young people, long-term unemployed adults and low-income workers in the informal sector are excluded by economic restructuring, the lone elderly, single mothers and immigrants are mainly subjected to the contraction of the welfare state and the fragility of social networks.

There has been a sizeable body of literature on China's laid-off/

unemployed and rural migrants. Through examining retrenchment determinants and duration of unemployment for retrenched workers, Appleton et al. (2002) conclude that the urban redundancy programme is a potent source of poverty, insecurity and discontent. And retrenched workers are viewed as the new 'urban underclass' in China (M.Y. Wang, 2004; Solinger, 2006). In respect of re-employment, although there were increases in the number of jobs in the non-state sectors, the expansion was far from enough to compensate for the losses in the state-owned enterprises (SOEs). A study on the re-employment of laid-off workers conducted by Giles et al. (2006) confirms a strong positive association between education and the probability of re-employment and a negative relationship between age and re-employment, with these effects being particularly strong for women. They also found that social networks have significant positive effects on re-employment probabilities, while employment referral services provided by local residents' committees also play an important information role in re-employment, especially for women who are highly motivated to find a new job.

Nevertheless, as temporary shelters that manage and care for retrenched workers, the Re-employment Service Centres (RSCs) are far from a panacea in solving the re-employment problem. By and large, whether retrenched workers can succeed in getting back to work depends crucially on their personal attributes and the skills they acquired (Wong and Ngok, 2006). In fact, the majority of them are facing the risks of being poor due to various restrictions of their age, skill and education attainments. M. Wang (2004) illustrates that the reasons for retrenched workers becoming trapped in poverty lie not only in the obstacles of age, skill and education, but also the skill and spatial mismatch and the fierce competition among themselves and competition from rural migrants. Although certain measures have been taken by the state to protect and help retrenched workers, such as unemployment insurance, re-employment services, and Minimum Living Standard Support (MLSS), many of the existing social benefits available in Chinese cities are actually directed to the middle-income groups rather than the poor (Wang, 2005).

Migrant workers join retrenched workers to create a dual problem of legacy of labour market problems. Due to the lack of official statistics, not until very recently have the lives and housing conditions of poor rural migrants been understood (Shen 2002; Wu, 2002; Zhang et al., 2003; F. Wu, 2004; Wang, 2005; B.Q. Li, 2006; Liu and Wu, 2006a; Lu and Song, 2006). For instance, based on a survey conducted in Tianjin 2003, Lu and Song (2006) developed a wage regression model to study the determinants of the wage gap between rural and urban workers. Their findings show that in addition to economic and social-demographic factors such as ownership of business, education, experience and age, the restrictive *hukou* system has negatively influenced migrants' income.

Another study on rural migrants in Tianjin conducted by B.Q. Li (2006) suggests that employer provision and informal social networks partially, but ultimately inadequately, fill the gap in state provision of social services. Although urban social provision organized by the state had the potential to help rural–urban migrants to fend off various risks and participate in the urban society, the system was far from comprehensive. New government policies, which give rural migrants legal status so that they can stay in the cities, have only solved some of the problems. The vulnerabilities caused by social exclusion make it difficult for rural migrants to share the dividends of economic growth (Wang, 2005). Similarly, Shen (2002) argues that although low education levels and lack of skills are important causes of low income for the temporary population, it is clear that unequal government policy, especially the household registration system, is the main cause of the miseries of rural migrants. Starting with the next section, we begin to discuss three aspects of livelihood of the poor: social entitlement, housing and neighbourhood social interaction and networks.

SOCIAL ENTITLEMENTS OF THE POOR

In Table 3.2 we use six indicators to measure the social entitlements available to different groups of people. Entitlements are important in poverty studies since they help determine the capacity of households to survive and prosper. Along with the owned or acquired endowments of household labour, capital and land, social entitlements (transfer endowments) create safety nets and raise a household's ability to convert its other endowments into income and wealth. The first indicator we use is Chinese Communist Party (CCP) membership, since our analysis has shown its important effect in predicting poverty. In all groups, heads of non-poor households have a much higher percentage of CCP party membership than those of poor households. For the laid-off/unemployed, the contrast between poor and non-poor households is particularly striking. This suggests that being a CCP party member is a great advantage for the laid-off/unemployed in avoiding poverty.

The second indictor is the percentage of MLSS recipients. About two-thirds of the poor laid-off/unemployed group and half of the poor retired group have received this subsidy, while the ratio is much lower for the poor working group. The rate of MLSS receipts for rural migrants is extremely low due to various restrictions on MLSS eligibility. Rural migrants are not eligible for urban MLSS but a few of them receive it from their home

Table 3.2 Comparison of social entitlement indices

	Working		Laid-off/unemployed		Retired		Rural migrants	
	Non-poor	Poor	Non-poor	Poor	Non-poor	Poor	Non-poor	Poor
No. of cases	360	45	231	183	282	53	532	123
Party membership (%)	16.7	13.3	14.7	4.4	29.8	24.5	5.3	3.3
MLSS recipient (%)	0	37.8	0	68.9	0	49.1	0	7.3
Social welfare index	0.14	0.14	0.11	0.17	0.12	0.16	0.03	0.02
Amount of social welfare/benefits	150.61	160.16	138.10	244.78	236.24	214.89	32.28	44.85
Housing tenure (%)								
Rental	**39.4**	**44.5**	**29.4**	**34.4**	**17.0**	**32.1**	**74.8**	**58.6**
Private rental	29.7	28.9	16.0	12.0	1.8	11.3	72.2	54.5
Public rental	9.7	15.6	13.4	22.4	15.2	20.8	2.6	4.1
Homeownership	**60.6**	**55.5**	**70.6**	**65.6**	**83.0**	**67.9**	**25.2**	**41.4**
Self-built	6.9	15.6	11.7	9.3	10.6	9.4	17.3	33.5
Inherited	6.9	11.1	13.9	19.1	7.8	5.7	2.4	3.3
Privatized	26.9	20.0	31.6	21.3	50.4	37.7	2.8	1.6
Subsidized	12.5	8.9	10.8	14.8	9.2	13.2	1.9	2.4
Commodity	7.2	0	2.6	1.1	5.0	1.9	0.8	0.6
Second homeownership	10.6	8.9	10.4	0.5	5.7	1.9	23.5	8.1

town. The results show that even in the poorest neighbourhoods, the coverage rate of MLSS is not very promising. The MLSS is only a partial tool for alleviating urban poverty under the current institutions for allocating citizenship rights in China.

To assess the importance of a series of social entitlements, we introduced a simple index of welfare and benefits provided by employers and/ or local government, denoted as the social welfare index $= \Sigma X_i/7$, where $X = \{1,0\}$ depending on whether a household is or is not in receipt of seven kinds of benefit: housing subsidy; employer-paid unemployment insurance; employer-paid health care insurance; employer-paid pension insurance; subsidy for children's education; subsidy for disabled; MLSS subsidy. The value of the index is between 0 and 1. A higher value suggests a higher level of transfer entitlements, better safety-net protection and less vulnerability to poverty. These 1/0 values can be taken to signify a pattern of property rights over state transfers. In principle, they should shift a household's predisposition to poverty.

The differences between poor and non-poor households vary among different groups. In the working groups, there is no difference between poor and non-poor households. In both laid-off/unemployed and retired groups, poor households have higher scores on the social welfare index than non-poor households, while in the rural migrant group, the opposite holds. It is intuitive to expect that the poorer households would have more transfer benefits than wealthier households. This is true for urban households (working, laid-off/unemployed, and retired groups), although it is not so obvious for the working group. However, this is not applicable to rural migrants. Conversely, we can suppose that if the transfer entitlements are working as they should, those with more benefits should be less vulnerable to poverty. The result suggests that transfer entitlements are particularly important for rural migrants to escape the trap of poverty. The laid-off/unemployed group has the highest social welfare index score, while the retired group and the working group have slightly lower scores. For rural migrants, the social welfare index is extremely low, confirming that this group of people have to struggle to make it in the urban economy with few entitlements derived from their own labour.

The average amount of social welfare/benefits (seven kinds of benefit listed above) received by individual households is also calculated for each group. Poor laid-off/unemployed households enjoyed the highest amount of benefits. The retired group, poor or non-poor, receive a comparatively high amount of social benefits. Rural migrants receive the least social benefits. This result further confirms that institutional discrimination against rural migrants prevents them from obtaining equal rights to access state or employer-provided social welfare and benefits. For all groups, except for the retired group, poor households enjoy more benefits than non-poor households. This is consistent with the social safety-net policy which aims to ameliorate poverty. On the other hand, this result also suggests that insufficient social benefits lead to the impoverishment of retirees.

The fifth indicator is housing tenure. We view owner-occupant housing tenure as a form of social entitlement (acquired via exchange), since it is related to a range of rights, for example access to privatized, public rental housing, and public housing subsidies. Our survey confirms that more non-poor households than poor households have their own homes, and fewer of them rent, except for rural migrants. For both the laid-off/ unemployed group and the retired group (poor or non-poor), more than two-thirds of them have property rights over their home. Strictly speaking, these are leasehold rights, which are transferable in the secondary housing market. The percentage of homeownership among the latter is higher than the former, while both are higher than the working group. This reflects the results of State Owned Enterprise (SOE) reforms and housing reforms. In 1998 the employer-provided subsidized housing system was abandoned. People who did not catch the very last 'train' of welfare housing have had to purchase commodity housing (built commercially after housing reforms and sold on the market). This explains why the working group has a much lower percentage of homeownership. Non-home-owning households in the laid-off/unemployed group and the retired group are likely to be those whose work units in the centrally planned era were smaller and poorer, and therefore unable to afford to build homes for their own workers. As we have already noted, in the central planning era, work units functioned like micro territorial states, providing urban services and homes for their workers. Workers in small and poor work units tended to rent homes in the dilapidated pre-1949 housing areas in the central city, or to live on in their own houses – but with little ability to maintain them and with no effective ownership rights.

For all groups with urban *hukou*, the lack of homeownership correlates with poverty. Furthermore, non-poor households are more likely to own commodity housing, while poor households own more subsidized, inherited or self-built housing. Meanwhile, the non-poor working group owns the highest percentage of commodity housing; the poor laid-off/unemployed group owns the highest percentage of inherited housing and subsidized housing; while the highest percentage of privatized public housing is found in the non-poor retired group. Homeownership reported by rural migrants is comparatively low. Here we refer to homeownership in the city (including urban villages), rather than in the rural area, since most rural migrants own a home back in their villages. Interestingly, more poor rural migrants than non-poor rural migrants have homeownership in the city.

In fact, the majority of rural migrant 'homeowners' own self-built housing – housing not yet legally recognized by the local authority. It is understandable that poor rural migrants have to resort to this 'illegal temporary housing', since they cannot afford other types of housing.

As this discussion begins to reveal, from this survey data, we are seeing the emergence of social differentiation in Chinese cities. Some of this is being driven by the new institutions of housing markets but much is still determined by residual institutions from the pre-reform era. For instance, sheltered by the ambiguous property rights structures in urban villages (which places these neighbourhoods outside strict formal municipal control), to squeeze their housing costs, a few poor migrants choose to build crude houses as temporary homes in the urban fringe.

The structure of rental housing among the four groups also varies significantly. The working group (poor or non-poor) has a much higher percentage of private rental housing than the other two urban groups. Again, this is the result of SOE reform and housing reform. In all groups, more poor households than non-poor households live in public-rental housing. This suggests that public rental housing which has not been privatized is generally in poor condition and accommodates the poorest population in the city. Nevertheless, in the retired group, the percentage of private rental housing among poor households is much higher than that of non-poor households. This is mainly because with the majority being homeowners, renting is a great disadvantage for retirees, no matter whether it is private rental or public rental.

We also compare the percentage of second-home ownership among different groups. Since most rural migrants have their own homes back in their home town, which they consider as second homes, the percentage of second-home ownership for both poor and non-poor rural migrant households is quite high. As for urban households, the working group (poor and non-poor), has the highest percentage of second-home ownership. This result suggests that both poor and non-poor working urban residents are comparatively better off in terms of housing ownership. The second homes owned by poor working residents are privatized public houses or self-built houses. Among the other two groups, particularly the laid-off/unemployed group, the contrast between poor and non-poor households is wide.

HOUSING CONDITIONS

Housing is an important aspect in profiling the poor, especially rural migrants who commonly suffer from low-standard and overcrowded housing. Current urban housing reforms have focused on the needs of local residents and private housing for the better-off while overlooking the needs of migrant workers and low-income groups (Shen, 2002; Wu, 2002; F. Wu, 2004). Nevertheless, laid-off workers are not extremely poor in terms of housing, thanks to the welfare and housing systems established in the pre-reform period (Y.P. Wang, 2004). As the institutional reforms of China's state capitalism reached new depths, there was a great state sell-off of homes built and rented out by local authorities, state-owned enterprises and other work units. Millions of urban workers received the right to purchase the deeds to their homes following housing reform in 1988, especially after 1998. The prices paid by tenants were very low – the equivalent of a few thousand pounds in most cases – and the vast majority of urban workers took up the offer. The result was that most among this class of urban resident now do not face the expense of housing rent, an entitlement that raises their real incomes and in principle makes them less vulnerable than migrants to poverty.

Things are quite different for rural migrants. As an important element of the bundle of urban amenities associated with *hukou*, housing remains difficult to attain for migrants (Chan and Zhang, 1999; Wang and Murie, 2000). In general, company quarters/work place, rented housing and construction sites are the main types of accommodation for the temporary population in Chinese cities (Shen, 2002). Meanwhile, the emergence of urban villages (*chengzhongcun*) provides an alternative source of inexpensive housing for rural migrants (Zhang et al., 2003). Nevertheless, the housing conditions in urban villages are generally not good. Restricted access to urban housing, together with their temporary status, contributes to migrants' poor housing conditions (Wu, 2002). The general disadvantage experienced by migrants has much of its roots in the institutional restrictions associated with the *hukou* system, which outweigh the combined effects of socioeconomic factors (W.P. Wu, 2004).

Sato (2006) examined housing inequality and housing poverty in urban China in the late 1990s, using the 1999 CASS data and a simple measurement of housing poverty, that is, the proportion of rent actually paid in total household expenditure, with the poverty line being set at 30 per cent. The survey data shows that 21 per cent of migrant households experience housing poverty. Sato's research findings illustrate a large disparity in housing conditions between urban households and migrant households. A new type of housing poverty has been emerging among migrant households. Although more and more migrant households have been settling in urban areas, they are still alienated from housing reform policy (Sato, 2006). They do not benefit from the urban work-units' housing allowance scheme and housing privatization programmes; they cannot access subsidized low-price owned housing and housing loan schemes; they are also excluded from the local government's low-rent public housing (*lian zu fang*) programmes. In our study, housing differentiation resulting from institutional discrimination is shown through contrasting rural migrants and other urban groups.

We now use four indicators to measure the housing conditions of different groups. The first is average housing floor area per capita. The second, denoted by a housing quality index $= \Sigma X_i/6$, is a composite of six qualitative aspects of housing, each given a binary value $\{1,0\}$: private kitchen; private bathroom; electric shower; liquefied or piped gas; air conditioning; Internet. The third indicator, denoted by a Satisfaction Index$= \Sigma X_i/50$, compounds interviewees' satisfaction with their current housing situation on ten dimensions: housing area; housing quality; community services; schools and nurseries; markets and commercial services; transportation conditions; public security; hygiene; green space; overall satisfaction. A single-scale (0 = not applicable, 1 = very dissatisfied, 2 = dissatisfied, 3 = neutral, 4 = satisfied, 5 = very satisfied) is used to calculate the index. The fourth indicator used is the change in housing conditions in the last ten years (improved, no change, or deteriorated). Results are shown in Table 3.3.

In all urban groups, the average housing floor area of non-poor households is much higher than that of poor households. This is particularly true in the case of the working group, among whom the average housing area of the non-poor is twice that of the poor. By contrast, in the rural migrant group, non-poor households are only slightly better off, compared with poor households. This suggests that rural migrants generally suffer from crowded housing conditions. A higher income does not necessarily suggest more housing floor area, since migrants tend to squeeze their housing cost to allow for other household expenditures. There is a big gap between urban households and rural migrants in terms of housing quality index, arising from the various advantages of urban *hukou*. The non-poor working group has the best housing quality, followed by non-poor retirees. Poor rural migrants and the poor laid-off/unemployed have the lowest housing quality. The gap between poor and non-poor households is quite big within the working group and the laid-off/unemployed group, while the poor and non-poor gap is smaller within the other two groups. This suggests that housing commodification has resulted in housing differentiation in the working group and laid-off/unemployed group. Retired and rural migrant groups remain less affected. The former generally enjoy better housing quality as a legacy of the previous housing allocation system, while the latter frequently suffer from low-quality housing largely due to the deep urban–rural division inherent in the *hukou* system.

Despite the physical gaps between urban households and rural migrants,

Table 3.3 *Comparison of housing condition indices between different groups*

	Working		Laid-off/unemployed		Retired		Rural migrants	
	Non-poor	Poor	Non-poor	Poor	Non-poor	Poor	Non-poor	Poor
No. of cases	360	45	231	183	282	53	532	123
Housing area/capita (m^2)	19.99	10.24	18.99	12.18	19.26	13.24	19.79	18.61
Housing quality index	.63	.43	.55	.35	.57	.52	.39	.32
Satisfaction index	.58	.56	.56	.55	.56	.59	.54	.54
Change of housing conditions (%)								
Improved	35.0	22.2	24.7	22.9	22.0	7.6	35.6	27.6
No change	56.4	68.9	68.0	67.8	74.5	88.7	47.4	56.9
Deteriorated	8.6	8.9	7.4	9.3	3.5	3.8	17.1	15.5

in terms of housing floor area and housing quality, the satisfaction indices of the four groups are very close. The poor retired group and the non-poor working group have the highest satisfaction index, reflecting not only the actual housing conditions but also the subjective perceptions/comparative conditions. The greatest contrast between physical housing conditions and subjective perceptions is found in the rural migrants group. Similar to the finding in respect of self-perception of poverty, there is a mismatch between objectively measured housing conditions and the subjective sense of well-being. This indicates something profound about the dynamics of density. Rural migrants are apparently willing to accept high levels of space deprivation and compensate with other sources of satisfaction – earning an income higher than the rural alternative, saving, surviving, and building a future for their children and so on.

Finally, looking at the change in housing conditions, poor households generally have less chance to improve their housing conditions, and are more likely to have experienced deteriorating housing conditions in the last ten years. Compared with urban households, rural migrants have the highest percentage of people experiencing improved housing conditions and the highest percentage of people experiencing deteriorating housing conditions. This may be a significant finding in the context of Chinese cities, suggesting that housing differentiation is emerging within the migrant community, with the more capable ones moving up the housing ladder, while the less capable ones are becoming worse off. However, the high deterioration rate may also reflect migrants' shift from rural or small town living accommodation to highly congested city living. Densities and rents are higher in the city and housing poverty is a price to be paid for access to urban wages. In comparison, urban households' housing conditions are stable, especially for the retired group. Unsurprisingly, poor retirees have the least chance to improve their housing conditions.

NEIGHBOURHOOD SOCIAL INTERACTION AND NETWORKS

Four indicators are used to measure neighbourhood interaction and social networks (see Table 3.4). The first is the number of familiar neighbours. The second is an index denoted by a neighbourhood interaction index $=\Sigma X_i/20$, comprising five aspects of neighbourhood interaction: frequency of chatting with neighbours; frequency of visiting neighbours; frequency of experiencing mutual neighbourhood help; frequency of socializing, for example, eating with neighbours; and frequency of participating in community-organized activities. These are measured on a scale of 1 to

4 (1 = never, 2 = rarely, 3 = occasionally, 4 = often). Neighbourhood interaction indices range in value from 0 to 1. A higher score indicates a higher degree of social interaction. The third indicator is whether the respondent develops neighbourhood-based social networks, that is most of their acquaintances and friends are from the local neighbourhood. We also measure respondents' willingness to reside in the neighbourhood for the long term, and their attachment to the neighbourhood. The final indicator measures resources available to overcome hardships. Choices include government subsidies, social security schemes, *danwei* subsidies, help offered by friends and relatives, and the option of having no support or of not needing help.

Interestingly, poor rural migrants have the largest number of familiar neighbours. This is contrary to the perception that poor households usually have a narrower social circle. Nevertheless, this is not uncommon in China's urban villages, since rural migrants from the same place of origin tend to live in the same place after they have migrated to the city. For poor migrants whose social circle is mostly confined within the neighbourhood they live in, it is quite normal for them to become friendly with a large number of neighbours, most of whom are from the same place of origin. Considering the next indicator, there is no obvious difference in neighbourhood interaction index value between poor and non-poor households within each group.

The unemployed/laid-off group has the highest score, which means this group interacts with neighbours most frequently. The working group has the lowest score. The result reflects the different life patterns of these groups: working people are more often occupied by their work, thus they interact with their neighbours less frequently than other groups do. It is quite apparent that poor households are much more likely to develop neighbourhood-based social networks than non-poor households, except for the retired group. This suggests that poor households generally have a narrower social circle which is mainly based in the place they live. Not surprisingly, poor rural migrants hold the highest score of this indicator: for the majority of them, most of their acquaintances and friends are from the local neighbourhood. This is not quite applicable to retirees, probably because poor retirees are more likely to be chronically sick and are thus less actively involved in neighbourhood interaction.

When comparing the willingness for long-term residence and the attachment to a neighbourhood, poor households generally have higher scores than non-poor households. This suggests that the neighbourhood has a much more important meaning for poor households than for non-poor households. There are some exceptions though. For instance, a higher percentage of non-poor unemployed/laid-off respondents are willing to reside in the same neighbourhood on a long-term basis. A slightly higher percentage of non-poor working people have a sense of attachment to their neighbourhood than poor working people do. Despite these deviations, the message is quite clearly conveyed: poor people rely on their neighbourhood-based social networks more heavily than non-poor people do. This difference is most obviously shown in the contrast between poor and non-poor rural migrants.

Finally we look at the resources available to different groups to overcome economic hardships. The survey data shows that for all groups, support from relatives and friends is the major resource that sustains a household through economic hardships. Rural migrants are most likely to rely on relatives and friends for support, reflecting their lack of access to alternative resources, for example social security entitlements, government and *danwei* subsidies. Government subsidy is one of the most important resources for overcoming economic hardships for poor urban households, but rural migrants have very little access to this resource. Generally, poor households rely much more heavily on government subsidies than non-poor households to overcome hardships. In contrast, non-poor households receive more supports from their employers to overcome economic hardship. This is mainly because *danwei* subsidies are closely related to the rank, scale and economic performance of the enterprise, which also has a direct connection with respondents' poor and non-poor status. Those who are employed or who used to be employed by a 'good' employer are less likely to be poor, and have more access to *danwei* subsidies. Meanwhile, social security schemes have become an important source for urban residents to overcome hardships. Many more poor unemployed/laid-off and poor retirees resort to social security schemes than non-poor households do, because social security insurance has increasingly become part of the support package provided to poor urban households in recent years. However, only a very small proportion of rural migrants, even fewer with poor migrants, manage to participate in social security schemes. Still a large proportion of poor households, especially poor rural migrants, have no resources to overcome hardships at all – neither a paid social security safety net nor friends/relatives who can help.

In addition to our six-city survey, we conducted more than 50 interviews with people from different poverty groups, of which the majority were laid-off workers and rural migrants. The number of interviews with the working poor and poor pensioners was smaller, following the proportion they form of the urban poor. When put alongside our household survey data from the six cities, these interviews provide rich information on the different trajectories of pauperization faced by each poverty group. In the rest of this chapter, we use this interview data to discuss in greater depth

Table 3.4 Comparison of neighbourhood interactions and social network indices

	Working		Laid-off/unemployed		Retired		Rural migrants	
	Non-poor	Poor	Non-poor	Poor	Non-poor	Poor	Non-poor	Poor
No. of cases	360	45	231	183	282	53	532	123
Number of familiar neighbours	55.84	57.60	78.41	59.60	63.00	53.69	67.12	127.57
Neighbourhood interaction index	.57	.57	.60	.60	.59	.58	.58	.59
Neighbourhood-based social networks (%)	43.1	64.5	58.3	63.2	70.0	62.0	58.1	73.2
Willingness to reside for long term (%)	39.2	48.9	49.4	45.4	56.7	60.4	41.0	47.2
Attachment to neighbourhood (%)	25.3	24.4	32.5	39.3	44.7	49.1	18.4	35.8
Resources available to overcome hardships (%)								
Government subsidy	1.1	13.3	2.2	15.8	1.8	13.2	1.3	1.6
Danwei subsidy	14.2	11.1	6.5	3.3	18.4	9.4	2.1	1.6
Social security schemes	5.3	6.7	4.3	27.3	3.5	13.2	0.4	0.8
Relatives and friends	41.7	33.3	49.4	36.6	35.5	30.2	56.7	53.7
None/don't need	37.8	35.6	37.7	16.9	40.8	34.0	39.5	42.3

the four poverty groups, that is, laid-off workers, rural migrants, poor pensioners, and the working poor.

POOR LAID-OFF/UNEMPLOYED WORKERS

From State Workers to Laid-off Persons

China was institutionally divided into two systems of urban and rural sectors through the introduction of a *hukou* system in the 1950s to guarantee the priority development of city-based industrialization. 'Urbanite' (*shimin*) and 'peasant' (*nongmin*) became the respective identity labels of those who had urban residence registration and those who had rural residence registration. In the centrally planned system before 1978, urbanites were allocated to work units (*danwei*) in urban areas, and peasants were organized into communes (*renmin gongshe*) in rural areas. According to the centralized allocation policy of labour, all young workers in urban areas were directly allocated to enterprises after graduation from high school. A 51-year-old laid-off worker recollected his employment experience for us:

> Before being laid-off, I was a worker at a state-owned chemical plant. . . . In the past, the government took the responsibility for arranging jobs. After graduation [from high school], I was directly assigned to this plant, working while apprenticing. I didn't change my job until I was laid off last year. (Interview, August 2005)

The economic reform started in the early 1980s. While the state permitted the development of private enterprises such as the self-employed and joint ownership units, the public ownership sector was still in a dominant position in the economic system. Under such circumstances, while some employees in the state and collective sectors had left their employment units to become self-employed or to work in private enterprises, the majority of workers chose to stay in the public ownership sector to maintain access to comprehensive welfare. The state was still responsible for providing jobs to urban workers, because the socialist planned system was still functioning at that stage. Years of service were compensated with cash. After his years of services were compensated by a one-off payment (*maiduan gongling*) in 2003, one 42-year-old man became unemployed. Before that, he was a salesman for a state-owned commercial company:

> After I graduated from senior high school in 1979, I waited for a job (*daiye*) at home. Three years later, it was arranged for me to work in my father's unit through substituting him in his post (*dingzhi*) . . . When I got married in 1985,

the municipal housing bureau allocated this house to us, and the rent is very low. I received regular pay, and I could also enjoy the health care welfare. Our living conditions were not bad. But since being laid-off, our life has gone from bad to worse. (Interview, March 2007)

Although gradual reform in urban China since the late 1970s has led to a new economic style and the emergence of new social groups such as employees in private enterprises and peasant workers, in the 1980s the economic system remained essentially unchanged (Li, 2004). Public ownership was still the dominant position. By 1992, employees in public ownership units still numbered 145.1 million, constituting 92.8 per cent of total urban employees (State Statistics Bureau, 2000). During the whole period of the planned economy, while workers in SOEs and COEs were subjected to low living standards, they obtained steady employment and income, and also enjoyed comprehensive welfare.

Since the early 1990s, the old style of socialist economic planning has given way to a Chinese-style socialist market economy (Y.P. Wang, 2004). The centralized allocation system of labour has been gradually dismantled, and the full employment policy has been abandoned. Such reforms severely affected publicly owned enterprises. COEs and the medium-to-small SOEs were the first to be pushed towards the market and faced with competition from private enterprises, forcing most of them to transform their owner-ship and management mechanisms. In this context, many workers in such enterprises were laid off or dismissed, and were pushed into the new labour market. A laid-off worker who worked in one collective enterprise for 16 years now makes a living doing a temporary job:

I was allocated to this plant in 1980. . . . In 1996, our plant stopped producing. We, all of the workers, went back home and had nothing to do. In fact, the effi-ciency of our plant had become poor since 1992. Since then, our salaries have been delayed. After bankruptcy [of this plant], we still cannot get our salaries. (Interview, June 2007)

Since 1995, the reform of large SOEs has also been carried out to achieve economic efficiency and to compete with other new private enterprises. Following a capital-intensive approach for upgrading technology and pro-duction equipment, 'downsizing in the interest of efficiency' has become the major feature of reform. The number of employees in publicly owned enterprises has greatly decreased. Many workers in such enterprises were made redundant before they reached their retirement age. A 51-year-old man became an early retiree in 2003:

I have worked in this factory for over 30 years. The efficiency of this factory was not bad before, but it became worse several years ago. The state-owned enterprises are more or less the same. . . . Our plant was not a small enterprise. It used to employ over 2000 workers. Nevertheless, it failed to survive the SOE reform. In December last year, our plant was merged with a private enterprise. The majority of workers were laid off. (Interview, May 2007)

In moving the economy from planning to market, millions of industrial workers have been influenced by the market-oriented reform. To avoid potential social turbulence from large-scale unemployment, the government has adopted a series of measures to help laid-off workers to become re-employed, such as establishing 're-employment service centres' (RSCs) in 1999. The bulk of laid-off workers were assigned to these centres. In principle, laid-off workers in a RSC can enjoy a basic living allowance, and receive relevant re-employment training. Three years later, if they still cannot get a job, they have to leave the RSC. A policy was implemented in 2002 to transform their status into two types: if a worker has worked in a work unit for less than 25 years, the years of service are bought out. Then the worker disengages from the work unit and enters the market. Workers who have worked in work units for more than 25 years will receive early retirement, but continue to receive a small wage according to the unit's degree of profitability. Work units are also responsible for buying endowment insurance for them. However, not all of these policies have been achieved (Solinger, 2002). A 40-year-old woman who was laid off with the offer of a one-off payment (*maiduan gongling*) in 2002 now makes a living by doing temporary work:

I entered the [reemployment] centre after being laid off in 1999. In the centre, we were asked to take part in a training course for re-employment. The course instructed us to create job opportunities by ourselves, for example running a small business. We are all low-quality and have no money, so how can we become a business owner? (Interview, July 2007)

A 47-year-old man, who was previously a worker in a collective enterprise, received early retirement in 2002, and now makes a living through peddling:

Several years ago, our plant was merged. My wife and I were both laid off and only got about 100 Yuan [US$12] for living expenses. Afterwards, we entered the centre. We can get over 200 Yuan for basic living expenses, it is not bad . . . but, in 2002, my wife was *maiduan gongling*. She got about 4000 Yuan for compensation. The standard is that for one year of working you can get one month's average salary. . . . So she only got this compensation. Our unit is not very efficient, so the average salary is lower. . . . I worked in this plant for about 23 years. The unit gave me special treatment because my household is poor. I was considered as an early retiree so that the unit helps me to buy endowment insurance, but I cannot get a salary from the unit. . . . The compensation is not enough to afford our living expenses. (Interview, July 2007)

Excluded by the Labour Market

The limited monetary compensation given to laid-off workers is not enough to maintain the basic living expenses of their households, forcing them to seek jobs in the new labour market. These laid-off workers do not have enough capital to become self-employed due to their long-term low income in publicly owned enterprises. At the same time, being older and having only low levels of education and skills due to the old employment training system, most of them also lack competitive advantage in the market place. They are typically excluded from the new niches of the formal employment markets and become unemployed, which results in the loss of regular income. A laid-off worker told us with great disappointment:

> I only finished junior high school. At that time, few people entered senior high school. We all only had education to the level of junior high school. Now it is different. Most people have graduated from senior high school or university. . . . After graduation, I was allocated to the factory. I didn't change my job until I was laid off. In the unit, I was only an ordinary worker. Now I am laid off, with a low level of education and no skills, it is difficult for me to get a new job. (Interview, December 2006)

The 48-year-old unemployed man who has been staying at home for two years since *maiduan gongling* is not optimistic about re-employment:

> I want to find a job, but it is very difficult to get one. Many enterprises want young people. . . . Even if some small enterprises would like to employ me, the work would be too hard. I am too old to manage it. For us, the low-quality workers, if you are over 40 years old, it is very difficult to find an appropriate job. . . . I have been looking for a job in the labour market for a long time, but no unit wants me. (Interview, December 2006)

Laid-off workers and unemployed persons have thus been gradually pushed into the new labour market. However, considering individual factors plus the severe employment situation, the majority of them cannot be absorbed by the market. Many of them lost a regular income after becoming unemployed or have had to resort to temporary jobs, leading their households into vulnerable living conditions.

Limited Welfare Security

While the work-unit-based welfare system is gradually being dismantled, the social welfare system has not yet been developed. The new urban poor depend entirely on limited welfare security. To deal with increasing lay-offs, unemployment and new urban poverty, many cities have set up a three-tier safety network based upon three programmes from the late 1990s, including the Labour Security Programme (LSP), the Unemployment Insurance Programme (UIP) and the MLSS for urban residents which we have already described (Liu and Wu, 2006a). However, the LSP and the UIP only provide living allowances to those laid-off workers who had contracts in the formal sector, and have nothing to do with the unemployed and poor workers. Even so, the living allowance of an average 270 Yuan per month (US$32.5) does not enable laid-off workers to lead a decent life, as we have noted already. Moreover, many laid-off workers either do not receive their allowances on time due to enterprises' poor efficiency, or cannot obtain allowances owed by enterprises that have closed.

Since the late 1990s, the MLSS has been set up to provide absolute poverty households with basic living expenses. Unemployed persons, laid-off workers and their families are now the main recipients of this programme. However, the standards in all cities are kept at subsistence level, as already mentioned. As the final 'safety net' for maintaining basic living standards for urban residents, the standard of the programme is set low and its coverage is narrow. A 40-year-old unemployed woman told of her experience of applying for MLSS subsidy:

> I am a divorcee; I now live alone. Two years ago, I was made unemployed. So far, I have been unable to find a formal job. I have no other way except to apply for *dibao*. It was difficult to get it. The ex-director of the residential committee told me: 'There are too many applicants. You are still young, you should go to work'. Yes, I want a job, but I cannot find one. . . . The current director is very nice, she cares about us. So I got the *dibao* this year. . . . We, these recipients of *dibao*, only get 220 Yuan for living expenses and we still need to do some volunteer work for the residential committee. I would rather find a job, I don't want *dibao*. (Interview, July 2007)

A 45-year-old single man was laid off in 1993. He lives with his mother. In 2002 he was retired early. They live only on his mother's pension:

> I am ill and cannot do hard work. Now I have nothing to do, and I just stay at home. The only income in our family is my mother's pension, about 500 Yuan a month. . . . So I want to apply for *dibao*. But the residential committee did not approve the application. Because the standard of *dibao* is that the monthly per capita household income is less than 220 Yuan, we do not qualify. . . . But mother's pension is actually not enough for our living expenses. (Interview, July 2005)

The stories of laid-off workers depict a particular pauperization trajectory. For them, the redundancy policy fundamentally changed their fate from being a privileged class enjoying lifetime employment, highly subsidized housing and children's education and so on, to a proletariat because the state abandoned the *danwei*-based welfare regime. These laid-off workers are not only excluded by the institutions of the modern labour market, but are also trapped in the predicament of limited welfare security and a sense of relative poverty compared to their previous experience.

RURAL MIGRANTS

From Farmers to Peasant Workers

In the pre-reform era, due to the restrictions of the *hukou* system farmers were strictly constrained in rural areas to work in farming. The commune, as the basic institution in rural areas, was responsible for organizing rural labourers to participate in collective farming. Rural land was collectively owned. Farmers could get points through collective farming. According to their points, they could get grain rations. However, 'the united production and consumption' under the egalitarian ideology during the pre-reform period resulted in low incentives among producers and low efficiency in production. Reform was necessary.

In the decade after reform, gradual and experimental changes started in rural areas. Household responsibility was introduced in 1980 to dismantle the collective agricultural production of communes (Y.P. Wang, 2004). Farmers were disengaged from the collective. According to household size, they received the rights to use of a certain amount of farmland leased from the local government under a land contract (*tudi chengbao*). However, the improvement in agricultural productivity and the large-scale growth of population in rural areas exacerbated the problem of surplus labour, which had been hidden in the form of underemployment in the former communes (Fan, 2004). By the late 1980s, along with market reform of the grain circulation system, some peasants began to flow into cities to seek employment. An Anhui man left his village in 1989 to be a temporary worker in the city. He came to Nanjing to collect waste seven years ago, and currently rents a room in an urban village with his wife and two children:

> We, three brothers, helped our parents to farm before. The amount of farmland in my village is quite small. My oldest brother can take care of the farming, so my other brother and I have to make a living in the cities. (Interview, June 2007)

The migration of rural labourers into urban areas was not only the result of 'push' factors from the rural areas, but also of 'pull' factors from the cities. In the early days of rural–urban migration, living conditions were not necessarily always poor. A 36-year-old Shandong man who works as a cleaner in Nanjing comments:

> Before [about the late 1980s], just a few peasants came out [to work]. At that time, there were also few laid-off workers [in cities]. Urbanites were unwilling to do those dirty and difficult jobs. We peasants can endure hardship. I got this job, with good pay. Apart from my daily expenses, I still saved some money. (Interview, July 2007)

Excluded from the Regular Labour Market

In the 1990s, the urbanization of the population accelerated. More and more peasants flowed into urban areas. The institutional structure to support this adjustment in the spatial labour market was slow to change, however. First, rural migrants have been institutionally excluded from regular urban employment and are thus restricted to certain sectors. A 36-year-old Shandong woman came to Nanjing to do temporary work with her husband four years ago. They rent a 6 square metre room to live in with two children:

> My husband is a cleaner of this residence. His salary is 300 Yuan a month. The low income is not enough to cover our living expenses. So I set up a booth along the street to sell vegetables, earning 5 to 6 Yuan a day. One month ago, my booth was confiscated by the police. Local people (urbanites) also set up booths, and they have been allowed. But we peasants are forbidden to do so. . . . I have nothing to do now. (Interview, July 2005)

A 50-year-old Anhui man told of a similar experience:

> Several years ago, I came to Nanjing and used a tricycle to deliver goods for a restaurant. One day, while I was delivering goods in the Xinjiekou area [city centre of Nanjing], the police sequestrated my tricycle, and I was fined 100 Yuan. I don't know why. . . . local people can work in this way, but, we [peasants] cannot. . . . There is no other way, I can only work as a porter in a wholesale market, and get paid 450 Yuan a month. (Interview, June 2005)

The rural migrants do not obtain fair institutional treatment in the urban labour market. They are also excluded from certain formal and steady occupations, and can only undertake hard, dangerous and dirty labour-intensive jobs (Liu and Wu, 2006a). Consequently, many rural migrants have low and unstable incomes, and live in poor conditions (State Statistic Bureau, 2006).

Excluded from the Urban Society

Rural migrants face subsistence hardship in the cities as they are denied access to social entitlements. Without urban *hukou*, rural migrants cannot obtain the institutional rights to enjoy urban services. They are still subjected to paying the extra costs of living in cities, including unsubsidized housing, children's education and health care. Unsubsidized living costs have become the primary factors dominating rural migrants' living conditions in cities (Chen and Yang, 2005). One couple from Henan province are both cleaners in the same neighbourhood; they have been renting a room to live in the city for about eight years, with one 15-year-old daughter:

> We got the job via an acquaintance. . . . It is too hard, but we have no choice. Currently it is difficult to find another job. . . . We can earn about 800 Yuan a month between us. But our living expenses are higher than that. We need to pay 150 Yuan for renting the room, only 10 square metres. . . . Our daughter studies in a junior high school in this sub-district. Because we do not have local *hukou*, we need to pay an additional contribution fee for her education here, 500 Yuan annually. . . . She will go to senior high school next year. By that time, we won't be able to afford her education fee, because it will be 6000 Yuan annually. We will have to send her back to our hometown. (Interview, July 2005)

The education fee is a heavy burden for rural migrants. Therefore, most rural migrant households prefer to leave their children in their home town to study. An Anhui man reported,

> My wife and I both collect waste here: our son was left in the countryside. We have no choice, we can't afford his education fee here. (Interview, July 2005)

In addition, medical fees are another extra cost for poor rural migrants. To one Jiangsu couple who are hawkers, child health care is their biggest expense:

> My son is only 5 years old. He often falls ill. Because he is a child, you have to take him to see a doctor. We are different, we are adult. If we are ill, I just buy some medicine. . . . Every time, we need to pay several hundred Yuan for our son's health care. . . . We are different from the urbanites. They have a health care subsidy. (Interview, July 2005)

Lack of Welfare Security

Unlike urbanites, poor rural migrants enjoy no welfare security and face vulnerability, becoming a marginal group in urban society. The traditional welfare system mainly served urban residents, and the ongoing reform of the social welfare system still bypasses rural migrants. A short-term unemployed woman from Shandong province, who previously had a temporary job, expressed her dissatisfaction:

> We are peasants, so the [urban] government does not take care of us at all. They only care for urbanites; nobody thinks of our life and death. If an urbanite is laid off, he [or she] can get living subsidies. Also, the urban poor can apply for the *dibao*; we [peasants] have nothing. . . . We have got used to these things. In the countryside, the government doesn't bother about us much. So in the cities, we do not expect government help any more. (Interview, June 2005)

Rural migrants are often isolated by urban society. They face social exclusion by discriminatory attitudes. Urbanites do not regard migrants as part of the urban population and are unwilling to live close to them. The behaviour and habits of peasants are usually looked down upon. Three Anhui sisters came to Nanjing to be sewing workers three years ago. They rent an 8 square metre room together in an urban village.

> Our household is poor in a rural area, so we cannot go to school. . . . In this [urban] society, illiteracy is a problem. If you cannot read, you have to do some temporary work in cities. . . . We, the peasants, are poor. We do not wear good clothes, and our skin looks darker, so urbanites do not want to have anything to do with us. They look down on us. . . . We prefer to rent a room here because the majority of people here are from the countryside. We seldom have any contact with urbanites except for making a deal with them. (Interview, July 2005)

Many migrants feel that it is difficult to communicate with urbanites, and their social networks in cities are usually composed of those from their original villages and peasant worker colleagues. For rural migrants, the only security is contracted-out agricultural land in their own villages. The scale of land loss is significant in coastal areas where large-scale constructions have been initiated. Once they lose both their leased lands in rural areas and their jobs in urban areas, they are very likely to fall into poverty.

POOR PENSIONERS

Chronic Illness and the Lack of Social Security Insurance

One major impoverishment factor for pensioners is chronic illness. Incurring excessive health care costs, chronic illness pushes those unfortunate pensioners' families into the poverty trap. Under the background of market transition, the lack of social security and insufficient welfare provision makes chronic illness a particularly adverse risk factor for these families.

One of our interviews was with an old couple, both 79 years old and living in Pingshijie, one of the typical low-income neighbourhoods in Nanjing. The husband, Mr. Zhang told us:

> I was educated to junior high school level, and my wife was illiterate. When I was young, my family ran a small ironware shop, which was closed down after a few years. After that, I have been switching jobs constantly between clerk, construction worker, and temporary workers . . . I was single until my late 50s. When I met my wife, she was a widow with three children. She has been working in different factories since 1958, such as a coking plant, steel works, and a lacquer plant. Her eldest girl was sent to Urumqi and suffered from chronic illness, her son died few years ago, and the youngest girl was laid off. She spent a lot of money to support her children when she was still working. But after retirement, none of her children are able to support us. The main sources of income for the family are our pension and the MLSS subsidy, which add up to 560 Yuan per month. However, my wife has been suffering from illness for a long time, and has had several operations on her legs. Neither of us have health care insurance. Medication costs therefore have been a heavy burden for the family . . . On average she needs to spend 50–60 Yuan on medication every month, and much more when she is worse. Every now and then, we receive a small amount of money from our neighbours and the local residents' committee. They helped us a great deal to survive these hardships. They are really good people. We have tried to repay them, but we don't have the money. (Interview, March 2007)

Another pensioner in Wubaicun, a low-income workers' village in Nanjing, has a similar experience. Mrs Chen, a 65-year-old widow told us:

> My husband died 7 years ago, and left us nothing. Right now I live with my son's family. My son was only educated to junior secondary school level, and has no stable job. His wife has no job and is a full-time homemaker taking care of my 3 year-old granddaughter. I only went to primary school, so I could never get into a good enterprise. I also had a car accident 18 years ago. Soon after that, I had to retire before reaching the retirement age. Since then I have been suffering from chronic illness. Right now my monthly income is about 500 Yuan including my pension and MLSS subsidy. But I have to spend at least 100 Yuan per month on medication and have to support my son's family as well. All of my income and my son's income can barely cover the basic subsistence of the whole family. Therefore we have to restrict our household expenditure to a minimum. We have an electric fan, but we never use it unless it's extremely hot or only when some guests come. We have no refrigerator, no telephone. All of our furniture and clothes are donated by neighbours. We don't go to hospital even if we are ill, unless it's very serious, because none of us are covered by health care insurance. So we have to pay for everything. I was very ill last year, and had to borrow several thousand Yuan to go to hospital. Now I still owe my sister and my neighbours 3000 Yuan. I don't know when I can pay off the debt. (Interview, March 2007)

Underlying Pauperization Factors under Market Transition

The general background of market transition cruelly interacts with and exacerbates poverty risk factors such as chronic illness among pensioners. The enormous number of laid-off workers and the highly underdeveloped welfare system after the abandonment of the *danwei*-based welfare regime are the underlying cause of impoverishment of pensioners. Apart from some extreme examples, most poor pensioners' households usually have one or more laid-off family members. In the waves of SOE and COE reform, pensioners become the main breadwinners for the whole family. The disadvantage of laid-off workers contributes to the vulnerability of the whole family. For some poor pensioners, the pension from their employer is far from adequate, especially when the whole family is depending on it. These pensioners are most likely to work in loss-making enterprise or small factories which suffered the most under market transition and become marginal in the market economy. It is not uncommon for grown-up children to live with their retired parents and depend on their pensions. With most family members being laid-off, the income from retired parents is the only income source for the whole family. This is most commonly found in SOEs where the sons or daughters were allowed to replace the retired parents' positions. After the SOE reform, they were laid off and had to depend on their retired parents again. In these cases, a large family size, especially a large number of dependants, creates a huge disadvantage for pensioners, making them very vulnerable to poverty.

Mr Lin used to work for a steel plant. He became an early retiree at the age of 51. He told us his story:

> I came to work in this factory right after I graduated from secondary high school in 1970. Until 1997, our factory was running quite well. But the competition from factories in other places and the shrinking state investment was a great threat to our enterprise. In 2000, a great number of workers were made redundant. I was one of them. I was asked to retire even though I still had 9 years to go. My pension is only 600 Yuan per month. It was 500 at the beginning. We are all getting the same amount, although I used to earn a higher salary than some of the other co-workers. They [the employer] intentionally kept our pension to a minimum . . . My wife died two years ago. I live with my son's family. My daughter's family lives next door. Both of them worked in the same factory as mine. After graduating from high school, my daughter was allowed to replace her mum's position, since both of us were working in the same factory. But in 2002, both my son and daughter were laid off. My son and his wife's monthly income is only 500 Yuan, and they have a 9-year-old girl who goes to primary school. My daughter's situation is not much better. Their monthly income is 800 Yuan. But their son is going to university next year, which will cost them a lot of money. So I have to support them every now and then. Although my pension is so small, I have to help them if I can. I can't

watch them suffering and do nothing. So I have to squeeze every penny and save it for my children and grandchildren. I don't normally go to hospital even if I am ill. (Interview, April 2007)

Another interviewee, Mr Xie, 62 years old, retired from a chemical factory two years ago. He told us a slightly different story:

> After I graduated from senior high school, I was sent to the countryside at the age of 19. I met my wife and got married there. In 1980 we came back to the city with our two sons. I was assigned to a chemical factory and worked there until 2 years ago. However, my wife remained as rural *hukou*, and she didn't manage to find a proper job in the city. She stays at home and finds some temporary jobs occasionally. Right now the major source of income for the family is my pension, which is about 700 Yuan per month . . . We didn't have the money to send our sons to university. Our eldest son was educated to senior high school level, and my second son dropped out of junior high school. Neither of them managed to find a stable job. Several years ago, my eldest son went to Guangdong province to find a job. But he returned within half a year and complained about the harsh working conditions there. He married a girl from the countryside two years ago. Both of them can only find temporary jobs. The girl is clever, but she also has a rural *hukou*, which makes it particularly difficult for her to find a job. Their monthly income is less than 500 Yuan. It is barely enough for their basic subsistence. If they have a child, things could be even worse. So I have to send them some money once in a while. My second son is even worse off. He is low-skilled and lazy, and never works on the same job for more than a month. He can't even find a wife. He lives with us and depends on us right now, and never gives us money. My wife worries about him all the time. But there is not much we can do. We are still struggling for a basic existence. (Interview, April 2007)

In Mr Xie's case, a combination of multiple disadvantages, such as his wife's and his daughter-in-law's rural *hukou*, his sons' unemployment and his retirement pushed the family into the grip of poverty.

Since the late 1990s, the number of retirees in China has rapidly increased. This is due to two reasons. One is that China has become an ageing society. The other reason lies in the large number of early retirees as a result of SOE and COE reform. Under the redundancy policy, not only were a vast volume of workers retrenched, but also a number of workers were retired before reaching their retirement age. The amount of pension that retirees receive is highly geared to the efficiency of the enterprises that they used to work for. The difference in pension received by retirees from different enterprises can be huge. Retirees who used to work for lose-making enterprises are usually offered the minimum level of pension, regardless of their previous wages. This minimum amount of pension is usually barely sufficient to cover pensioners' basic subsistence. The coverage of social security insurance also varies. For most loss-making SOEs and COEs, pensioners are not covered by health care insurance. Chronic illness is therefore not in itself a determinant of poverty, but it is when it interacts with the rule that relates health care subsidy with the historic performance of the previous place of employment.

THE WORKING POOR

Adverse Personal and Household Characteristics

Large household size has a critical effect on the impoverishment of the working poor. For those who earn little salary and have to support a big family, poverty is never far away. One of our interviewees, 25-year-old Mr Su, told us his story:

> I'm the eldest child in our family. I dropped out of school at the age of 18. I was accepted by a good university, but my parents couldn't afford the tuition fee and I have a younger brother who was going to junior secondary school during that time. So I had to quit and worked as a clerk in a small private enterprise. Of course, I was very sad, but for the sake of the whole family, I had to make a sacrifice. My parents made sacrifices for us too . . . They retired 2 years ago, and their pension was very small, adding up to only 500 Yuan per month. My salary is not great either – 700 per month. My brother went to university in Beijing last year. His tuition fee and monthly living expenses are a huge burden for the family. To save some money from the return tickets from Beijing to Nanjing, he hasn't come home for a year. We miss him very much, but can't do much about it. My grandpa is now living with us. Fortunately, he is still in good health. Otherwise, we couldn't afford his medication costs. I have to spend every penny I earn on the family. I don't even have a girlfriend yet – nobody wants to date a bloke like me. (Interview, April 2007)

It is also not uncommon that the working poor suffer multiple disadvantages as described vividly in this quote. When multiple misfortunes hit a family, the family becomes deeply trapped in poverty with very little scope for getting back on the ladder of adequate subsistence, never mind prosperity; 49-year-old Ms Zhang told us her unfortunate story:

> My husband was diagnosed with lung cancer a year ago. Fortunately we discovered the disease at an early stage, but it will take a long time and cost a lot of money for him to recover. He is now on medication and goes to hospital every month. On average, we need to spend 1200 Yuan per month. My husband was laid off 6 years ago, and is not covered by health care insurance. So we have to bear the costs all by ourselves. I work as a saleswoman in a department store – long working hours and low pay. My salary plus my husband's subsidy is 1500 Yuan per month. We need to spend most of the

money on my husband's medication. We have a girl who has just graduated from university. She can support herself now. It is really a relief. My parents are still living with us.

They help us a lot: taking care of my sick husband, doing household chores. They even supported us sending our daughter to the university. Without them, my husband and I might not have been able to get through all these hardships. But their pensions are very limited too. The two of them only receive 800 Yuan per month. We are still depend on them to a great extent. But they're getting old – both of them are 72 years old now. My mum has had asthma for a long time. But she doesn't go to hospital unless it's really serious [the interviewee was weeping]. My family is leading a miserable life. Some neighbours take pity on us, they help us occasionally. (Interview, December 2006)

Market Discrimination and Institutional Discrimination

A considerable number of working poor are converted from laid-off workers. As the research finding of other scholars suggests, re-employed laid-off workers usually earn less than those who have never been retrenched from their work (Appleton et al., 2006). This suggests that being laid off has become a permanent disadvantage for them; even getting re-employed does not necessarily lessen their vulnerability to poverty. This is particularly true for female laid-off workers. Being discriminated against in the labour market, re-employed laid-off workers find it difficult to find well-paid and stable jobs. One of them, 49-year-old Mr Liu, who currently works in a small private enterprise, told us,

I used to work in a large-scale state-owned enterprise as a welder since graduating from a technology school. My income wasn't very high, but I earned enough money to feed my family. Things have changed so rapidly in the early 2000s. I was retrenched from the factory and was only offered a monthly subsidy of 300 Yuan. My wife was laid off as well the next year, and was offered a monthly subsidy of 250 Yuan. Fortunately, I managed to find another job, since I have welding skills. However, it's nothing like my previous job. My first job was stable and well-paid – 1000 Yuan per month. Now I work longer hours and get less pay, which is only 750 Yuan per month. Anyway, it's better than nothing – my wife has only been able to find temporary jobs since being laid off. She brings home 300–400 Yuan per month at the most. We have a son who just went to university last year. We need to pay his tuition fee of 6000 Yuan per year, and 450 Yuan per month for his living expenses, which is already a really low amount compared to his fellow students. But this amount of money is a heavy burden for my family. My wife and I have to minimize our daily expenditures, just to save some money for our son. He is the only hope the family has. (Interview, June 2006)

The poor working migrants who work often live among people who have migrated from different places of origin, either from rural or urban areas. This is because they both live in a lower quality environment. Even if migrants are able to earn similar or even slightly higher salaries compared to their local counterparts, their expenditure is in fact much higher than that of the latter for an equivalent lifestyle due to institution-based discrimination. Those migrants who do not earn a great amount of money and have school-age children, are particularly vulnerable to poverty. Mr Yang, 32 years old, is one such example:

> I am originally from a small town in Sichuan province. I came to Guangzhou 8 years ago, after graduating from a small college. I changed my job a few times since I came to this city. My first job was quite good. I worked as an accountant in a small private company and earned 1200 Yuan per month. But the company closed down two years after I arrived. Since then I have not been able to find an accountant's job. There are too many people coming to Guangzhou to look for a job. And most of them have better qualifications and are more experienced. Also most employers would prefer local people. Now I work as a clerk in a small printing factory. My monthly salary is only 800 Yuan. My wife is from the same town as me. We got married just before I left home. She came to join me one year later, but didn't manage to find a stable job. She stays home most of the time, to take care of the family. We have a 7-year-old boy who is going to primary school this year. I think I'm better off compared with those rural migrants. But I have the same problem as them too when it comes to children's education, although I have an urban *hukou* from my home town. Apart from the 500 Yuan fees, I have to pay an extra 300 Yuan per semester for my son to go to a local primary school. It is only an average primary school. If my son wants to go to a better school, I have to pay more. I can't imagine how much I will need to pay when he goes to high school and university. I will have to work and save harder. But I'm not optimistic about the future. With my son just starting primary school, my family is already not far from poverty. And we are not eligible for local MLSS subsidies because we don't possess local *hukou*. We have to resort to relatives and friends from whom we ask for help to get through hardships every now and then. I feel like a stranger in the city although I've been working here for many years. (Interview, March 2007)

CONCLUSION

The new urban poor do not belong to a unified group. Labour market reform has led to massive redundancies and generated a group of poor permanent residents, who are marginalized by their low human capital endowment. Meanwhile, the influx of surplus rural labourers into the urban area is also creating an informal class, of which a considerable proportion becomes the urban poor, largely due to institutional discrimination. Besides these two poverty groups, poor pensioners and poor working people are on the increase compared to the pre-reform era. The emergence of these two poverty groups is also closely related to the special institutions that have governed market transition in the Chinese urban economy.

Urban poverty groups experience different pauperization processes, and are subjected to distinctive processes and experiences of social exclusion. Our study has investigated four major impoverishment factors: 1) individual characteristics, such as chronic illness and large household size; 2) market exclusion, especially exclusion from formal labour markets; 3) institutional exclusion, in particular the constraints of the *hukou* system; 4) related institutional effects such as the influence of *hukou* and former workplace on personal access to social security. A combination of these different factors results in various trajectories of pauperization for the four poverty groups.

Laid-off workers and unemployed persons experience a status change from being beneficiaries of the planned economy to being victims of the market economy. In the planned economy, urban workers benefited from a work-unit-based welfare system. The state-organized work units were like mini-states, providing access to jobs, housing and necessary public goods and services. The transition of the economic system pushed them into the market, where they lost their state-organized protection. Constrained by their age, their low skills and lack of capital, most of them have ended up excluded from the labour market. The new urban poor become a vulnerable group characterized by market exclusion and limited welfare dependency.

The marketization process has also given a chance to younger rural migrants to work and live in the city. They, however, are excluded from social services by the discriminative *hukou* system. Without an urban *hukou*, they are excluded from formal urban employment. Most are compelled to enter the informal labour market, and have begun to compete with laid-off workers. Rural migrants have to pay the full costs of urban services. As a result, they face lower real incomes compared to urbanites with comparable skills and other qualities. They tend to suffer from isolation and cannot integrate into urban society because of formal institutional barriers and discrimination that leads to social exclusion. Their social capital is constrained by the lack of networks in the city, and they continue to be exploited by the market. And with an infinite supply of low-cost migrant labour, they end up selling their labour at a very high price in terms of deprivation accepted. But they have no other choice. Their low human capital endowment is one of the decisive factors for their poverty status, and their vulnerability largely results from institutionally based exclusion. Farmers became institutionally discriminated against, being seen as inferior during the era of urban-based industrialization in the pre-reform period, and this has continued in the contemporary city. This is reinforced by the continuation of the *hukou* system. It is the pressures from large-scale unemployment and the lack of urban public goods and services that have forced urban governments to retain the *hukou* system. The unfortunate result is the superimposition of deep-seated rural–urban social divisions upon a newly emerging set of class divisions.

We have also discussed the plight of poor pensioners and the working poor. Although the incidence and intensity of these two poverty groups are not comparable to the two major poverty groups, they are part of the emerging new urban poverty and deserve further investigation. As conventional wisdom would suggest, the impoverishment of pensioners and working people is largely the result of personal characteristics or household characteristics, such as long-term illness, and large household size. The disadvantages of chronic illness or of a large number of dependent family members, or the combination of the two, result in the miseries of tens of thousands of poor families. But as with the other categories of poor, these factors are amplified by institutional factors, particularly in the case of these groups, of the laws governing redundancy and welfare subsidy. Our interviews with poor pensioners and the working poor reveal that in addition to adverse personal and household characteristics, market transition is the underlying reason for pauperization.

This is precisely the difference between the traditional urban poor (the Three-Nos) and the new urban poor. Market reforms and the legacies of the planned economy have directly resulted in the formation of two big poverty groups, the laid-off/unemployed and rural migrants. Laid-off family members, an inadequate pension, and lack of social security insurance are important pauperization factors for poor pensioners. For the working poor, the underlying pauperization factors include laid-off family members, market discrimination against re-employed laid-off workers in terms of low wage and lack of security, and institutional discrimination against 'outsiders', in terms of social benefits and education.

Market transition and institutionally based exclusions have produced different characteristics in the four poverty groups. China's new urban poor disproportionately bear the social cost of rapid economic development and urbanization under market transition. While the long-term low pay system and low living standards in the planned economy gave them the ability to endure their present living predicament, and while the prosperous Chinese market economy has provided them with many potential chances to better themselves, the emergence of new urban poverty has begun to cause certain types of social unrest. Protests and resistance are on the rise. This will intensify in the coming economic downturn. Social inequality under China's rapid economic development has also intensified. Central and local government experiments with re-employment policies and policies attempting to address some of the disadvantages of migrants indicate that the new urban poverty is being paid serious attention. In this context, our detailed look in this chapter at the profile and experience of the different groups of poor inhabitants of the poorest neighbourhoods in Chinese cities provides a rich site of evidence with which to measure and test welfare reform ideas.

4. Impoverished neighbourhoods

Although the mechanisms of urban poverty generation in China have received a great deal of attention in the past few years, there has been very little focus on the spatial distribution of poverty. There is therefore a need to understand 'spatiality' of poverty. Here, we use the term 'spatiality' specifically to indicate the importance of space in poverty generation. Our scope is more than the spatial distribution or the urban poor per se. We try to understand how poverty is generated in specific individual neighbourhoods, for example, contingent upon the position of a neighbourhood in the spatial framework of development. In this chapter, we examine poor neighbourhoods and relate them to state development strategies and public policies. In short, we argue that poverty concentration is formed through spatial differentiation driven by a set of institutional factors.

SPATIALITY OF THE NEW URBAN POVERTY

Although urban poverty is a relatively new phenomenon, its spatiality should be traced back to the uneven development of urban space going back to the pre-1949 era. In the period of state socialism, systematic under-investment in the old city enabled the state to accumulate capital needed to build new industrial areas. These industrial areas were located at the periphery of the city, forming an industrial belt, and now that commodity housing has led to rapid sprawl, the inner suburbs. Underinvestment in the built environment created a chronic housing shortage problem in the 1950s–1970s. There was very slow change in the urban landscape of the old areas and these became backward, marginalized places in the state-led industrialization process. Residents who were better educated or skilled, and their offspring who graduated from tertiary education, were absorbed into the state work-unit system dominated by state-owned enterprises. The remaining residents thus mainly consisted of low-skilled workers who worked in street-run collective factories and were domiciled in housing provided by the municipal housing bureau and in the residual privately owned housing that somehow managed to escape the mass conversion of property rights into state ownership.

In contrast, in the inner suburbs, the development of industrial areas along with the construction of 'workers' villages' led to the concentration of workers in state manufacturing industries. The social areas in Chinese cities are thus characterized by a tight relationship between workplace and residences which, during the state-planned era, were differentiated into occupational areas. Such differentiation, because of the relatively egalitarian urban policy and the homogeneous living standards of urban residents across occupational sectors, was less salient in terms of social spatial inequality (although there have now been a number of sophisticated studies showing a unique dimension of inequality along the state redistributive function, such as differentiation according to the rank and size of state workplaces; see Logan et al., 1999). Whereas there was relative homogeneity across the city itself, the city and the rural areas were divided by formidable institutional barriers, including household registration, which classified citizens according to their parents' household registration status. Although the division has begun to experience some change, first by the flooding of rural migrants into the city and later by an ad hoc response through commodification of the *hukou*, it still has profound implications for the spatiality of the new urban poverty. Rural migrants are still considered lower-status and are persistently discriminated against, as we have evidenced in previous chapters. There is no doubt that there is a two-class society in the making in China (Chan, 1996).

The market-oriented reform has led to an unprecedented level of sociospatial mobility in urban China. In particular, the establishment of a real estate market effectively started in the 1990s has given individual households the right to choose residential locations, although it is still subject to various constraints. The reshuffling of residents first began with the relocation of state employees among multiple residences developed by the workplace. Since the introduction of comprehensive urban development from the mid-1980s, through which state work units were encouraged to cooperate in developing larger residential areas instead of their own living quarters, the integrated structure of workplace-residence has been gradually dismantled. In the 1990s, many workplaces stopped building their own staff quarters but, instead, purchased commodity housing from real estate development companies. This further paved the way for a more differentiated social space according to the market principle of affordability, and further strengthened the inequality that started to emerge in the planned economy. For example, in the case of multiple work-unit compounds, housing allocation criteria tended to favour those who were currently employed and had a higher status within the work unit. The side effect of the demise of egalitarian housing allocation was the concentration of low-status and retired workers in the worst workplace compounds, which were often built in the earlier stage of staff housing development (many being built in the 1970s and early 1980s) and located nearer to industrial estates than were later work-unit housing estates. Moreover, in old urban areas, residents who were affiliated to more 'profitable' or powerful workplaces were more likely to leave the place through subsidized commodity housing purchase. As a result of reinforced market and institutional mechanisms, social stratification is thus leading to the emergence of 'area-based' poverty and marginalization.

We see a process of 'residualization' similar to that documented in Britain. In Britain, better-off residents have begun to move out of council housing since the adoption of the 'right to buy', which has resulted in the concentration of minorities and low-income and low-skilled tenants in council housing in a process of 'residualization' (Burrows, 1999; Forrest and Murie, 1990; Hamnett, 1991, 2001). Under housing commodification, rich and high-income residents have left municipal housing in the dilapidated old urban areas and the work-unit housing in degraded workers' villages in Chinese cities, and this has led to the concentration of the residual unemployed, laid-off workers, low-income workers and retirees. As for rural migrants, because of their rural residence registration they have no right to enjoy low-rent municipal housing and are excluded from the public service domain in urban areas. Housing marketization gives them a chance to live in the urban areas, but the majority of them, especially poor rural migrants, can only afford low-rent housing in certain urban villages and have become clustered in these villages due to their inability to compete in other parts of the housing market. There is also some evidence (from our interviews) that a rental market for migrants is slow to develop in former work-unit compounds because of the discriminatory attitude of owner-occupiers in those compounds. Many of these neighbourhoods typically retain a strong residual collective ethos and organization, notwithstanding the distributed property rights. This means that collective interests can act as effective gatekeepers in the selection of tenants – more so than in the typical unorganized neighbourhoods of Western cities where neighbourhood change (and 'tipping') typically happens spontaneously. So the clustering of migrants happens by market process, as a function of bidding power in the housing market, and by social exclusion, as a function of discriminatory attitudes.

The rich and the middle classes have moved into gracious neighbourhoods such as villa, town-house and apartment building complexes produced by the marketization, not just of housing production but of the production of entire neighbourhoods. The less well off and the socially excluded groups have a much more constrained choice of residential relocation. They remain in old, urban, dilapidated neighbourhoods or in degraded workers' villages in the inner suburbs, or clustered in rural migrant enclaves in the urban periphery.

SPATIAL DISTRIBUTION OF THE URBAN POOR

The unique process of social area formation under socialism has led to an uneven distribution of the new urban poor. In this section we examine the detailed spatial distribution of poverty in the city of Nanjing to illustrate this uneven pattern. We also briefly refer to the city of Guangzhou to see how similar patterns can be found in different cities. Because of data constraints, we cannot extend this level of analysis to the other cities we have surveyed. But we present the quantity of low-income households (measured as the number of MLSS recipients) in the districts of those cities (see Table 4.1).

In general, the MLSS ratio in each city reflects its industrial and economic development level. Not surprisingly, Wuhan has the highest MLSS ratio among the six cities, as a city suffering from radical industrial restructuring. Harbin and Kunming are located at the north-east and southwest corner of China respectively, both in a comparatively undeveloped hinterland, and therefore also have a relatively high MLSS ratio. Xi'an, as the most developed city in the less developed north-west region, has a MLSS ratio that is slightly lower than Wuhan, Harbin and Kunming. Guangzhou and Nanjing are two comparatively developed cities located in the fast-developing Pearl River Delta and the Yangzi River Delta respectively; and have the lowest MLSS ratio of the six cities. Within each city, the distribution of MLSS recipients is also uneven, with some districts having much higher MLSS ratios than others. This is further evidence of the emergence of spatially concentrated poverty in Chinese cities, and of the need to study poverty from a neighbourhood perspective. The distribution of MLSS recipients helped us select the poorest neighbourhoods in each of our six case study cities.

In the remainder of this section we focus on the city of Nanjing to give a more detailed picture of poverty distribution. The city of Nanjing shows that historical legacy partly determined the distribution of the urban poor. Before 1949, Nanjing was divided into several functional areas, according to 'the Capital Construction Plan' under the nationalist government. This included political, industrial, commercial, cultural and educational, and residential areas. The construction of the Xinjiekou commercial centre and the gracious Yihelu residences is representative of how the northern part of Nanjing city became the priority area for urban development at that time. Meanwhile, most governmental sectors and universities were concentrated in the northern part, where Gulou and Xuanwu districts are now. The construction of upmarket residential areas since the late 1990s in the northern part of the city follows that area's traditional status of being the educational and administrative area with a concentration of

Urban poverty in China

Table 4.1   The distribution of MLSS recipients in six large Chinese cities (2006)

Cities	Recipients of MLSS	Total population	Ratio (%)
Nanjing	**70659**	**5246378**	**1.35**
Xuanwu	4664	489022	0.95
Baixia	8176	466149	1.75
Qinhuai	7391	247704	2.98
Jianye	5794	204397	2.83
Gulou	5690	696225	0.82
Xiaguan	8800	299326	2.94
Pukou	7619	504418	1.51
Qixia	11242	414318	2.71
Yuhuatai	5207	207202	2.51
Jiangning	3160	845459	0.37
Liuhe	2916	872158	0.33
Guangzhou	**40840**	**6231192**	**0.66**
Liwan	9527	705134	1.35
Yuexiu	7197	1150782	0.63
Haizhu	11636	890280	1.31
Tianhe	2464	644890	0.38
Baiyun	3366	760954	0.44
Huangpu	1181	193427	0.61
Panyu	1634	935687	0.17
Huadu	1707	636442	0.27
Nansha	1194	147181	0.81
Luogang	934	166415	0.56
Wuhan	**253735**	**8188431**	**3.10**
Jiang'an	40266	651706	6.18
Jianghan	36349	464416	7.83
Qiaokou	30625	533161	5.74
Hanyang	25331	524932	4.83
Wucang	35081	1069075	3.28
Qingshan	13736	455615	3.01
Hongshan	9637	946091	1.02
Dongxihu	1126	260660	0.43
Hannan	2475	106506	2.32
Caidian	9368	444413	2.11
Jiangxia	14753	643839	2.29
Huangpo	18469	1112346	1.66
Xinzhou	16519	975671	1.69
Xi'an	**127556**	**6358800**	**2.01**
Xincheng	24459	639200	3.83
Beilin	21602	849000	2.54
Lianhu	28402	739700	3.84

Table 4.1   (continued)

Cities	Recipients of MLSS	Total population	Ratio (%)
Baqiao	11012	542300	2.03
Weiyang	9912	562900	1.76
Yanta	10063	1103300	0.91
Yanliang	3213	249100	1.29
Lintong	10636	666000	1.60
Chang'an	8257	1007300	0.82
Kunming	**51068**	**2319600**	**2.20**
Wuhua	10637	663800	1.60
Panlong	6521	410800	1.59
Guandu	7165	487800	1.47
Xishan	9494	448100	2.12
Dongchuan	17251	309100	5.58
Harbin	**112723**	**4727220**	**2.38**
Daoli	20923	690282	3.03
Nangang	18059	1049895	1.72
Daowai	29013	686270	4.23
Xiangfang	18396	737267	2.50
Pingfang	5413	158349	3.42
Songbei	1314	196992	0.67
Hulan	7493	623236	1.20
Acheng	12112	584929	2.07

Source: Information gathered from the Ministry of Civil Affairs.

intellectuals and political elites. In contrast, the southern part of the city, known as *chengnan*, literally 'southern city', which broadly covers the area between Xinjiekou and Yuhuatai, has remained as a traditional old urban region in which handicraft workers, small stores and other ordinary urbanites have concentrated. Chengnan was also the area in which rural migrants and refugees concentrated during and after the war years. In 1949, over 200,000 people lived in 309 shanty areas scattered over *chengnan*, primarily along the railway or near the city wall (Chen et al., 2006). The north–south segregation (the rich north and the poor south) of the city was the prominent characteristic of urban development in that era.

Between the 1950s and 1980s, socialist state-led urban development became the dominant factor in creating the urban spatial structure of Nanjing and in shaping the distribution of urban population. The municipality of Nanjing city prioritized investment in the construction of industrial areas in the inner suburbs. Like other socialist cities, the city of Nanjing was characterized by a lower level of urbanization compared with the level of industrialization. As a result, and considering the restriction of natural conditions by the Yangtze River in the west of the city and Zijing Mountain in the east, the city's development extended further towards the north of the city outside Zhongyangmeng (the 'central gate' of the city wall) and to the south-west inner suburbs. Meanwhile, many houses built in the Qing Dynasty have remained in the old urban areas of *chengnan*. Many of the historical shanty areas and dilapidated old urban areas in *chengnan* were redeveloped as worker areas in the 1980s but have been left out of the modern redevelopment boom. Most residents there are tenants of municipal housing, and the area has an over-representation of the aged, the retired, the jobless, low-income households and employees in low-ranking collective units. On the other hand, as one of the most important industrial cities, Nanjing developed large-scale state-owned enterprises in traditional industrial sectors during the period of the centrally planned economy. New industrial areas were built, extending from Zhongyangmeng to Maigaoqiao in the northern part of the city and from Yuhuatai to Banqiao in the south-western inner suburb of the city, containing the machinery and electronic industries respectively. Most neighbourhoods in these industrial areas were dominated by a few large state work units, and became areas in which the workers in these plants lived.

In the 1980s, the municipality of Nanjing city implemented a policy of urban development under the slogan 'regeneration of the old city integrating with development of the new areas'. The object was to deal with a severe housing shortage. Consequently, most of the shanty areas and some old urban neighbourhoods were redeveloped into mixed residences together with commercial areas. The development of new areas was presented as the large-scale construction of workers' communities in the 1980s as a way of providing housing for workers (including returned *xiafang* persons) in these SOEs. This kind of development dominated the then urban fringe, such as Nanhu to the south-west of the city, Wubaicun in the north-west and Wusuocun in the north. This sealed the concentration of industrial workers.

Since the 1990s, because the financial ability of the state to renew the old city has been limited, redevelopment of old urban areas has been left to the market. However, market-oriented real estate development is less effective in regenerating the worst dilapidated residential areas. In those areas, which often have lower accessibility and a high concentration of poorer residents (such as the east part and west part of Zhonghuameng – the south gate of the city wall – in the *chengnan* old urban area), redevelopment has become extremely difficult. Better-off residents have gradually moved out of these areas, and residents there are mainly composed of the aged, the jobless, the laid-off and unemployed persons and their families.

Since the 1990s Nanjing city has experienced industrial restructuring, from labour-intensive industries to capital-intensive and technology-intensive industries; and from traditional manufacturing sectors to modern manufacturing sectors and services. Consequently, state-owned enterprises in the traditional manufacturing sector have faced closure and rationalization, which has led to widespread lay-offs and unemployment. Laid-off workers and unemployed persons accounted for 14.2 per cent and 3.6 per cent respectively of the labour force in Nanjing in 2001 (State Statistics Bureau, 2002). The closure of the work unit had a disastrous effect on many workers' villages and workers' communities, such as Nanhu, Wubaicun and Wusuocun.

Through computing the location quotients (LQ) for the new urban poor, the residential concentration of poverty at the scale of street-office area (sub-district) can be measured quantitatively and compared to the concentration of urban poverty throughout the urban areas. We use the number of MLSS recipients in the street-office areas in 2002. The number of the new urban poor is computed by subtracting the traditional poor (that is the 'Three-Nos') from the total number of MLSS recipients. The location quotients range from 0.2 to 2.71 in 42 street-office areas of the city zone. These street-office areas can be divided into five categories based on the LQ classification (using equal interval classes). The two categories with the highest values represent street-office areas with greater concentrations.

There are several obvious pockets of poverty concentration: Mufushan and Baotaqiao in the Xiaguan district; Jiankanglu in the Baixiaqu district; and Nanhu in the Jianye district. Mufushan and Baotaqiao belong to the traditional industrial areas near the port along the Yangtze River in the north of the city; Jiankanglu represents the old urban dilapidated areas in *chengnan*; and Nanhu is a typical workers' village in the south-west of the city. Figure 4.1 also indicates, as a whole, that the southern part of the city, the south-west and the north outside Zhongyangmeng have seen higher poverty concentrations, because they either belong to the old areas or have developed into industrial uses and workers' villages. In contrast, the central and east districts such as Gulou and Xuanwu function as the political, cultural, educational and commercial centres, and have lower poverty concentration.

As Nanjing is the provincial capital and a modern large city, a great number of rural migrants have been attracted to its urban area since the 1980s. According to the data of the Fifth Population Census, there is a migrant population of 0.75 million in Nanjing city, amounting to 17.0 per cent of the total population (NCO, 2002). While a few rural migrants rent housing in inner city areas with central locations such as Gulou, Jianye and Baixia, the majority cluster around employment opportunities in

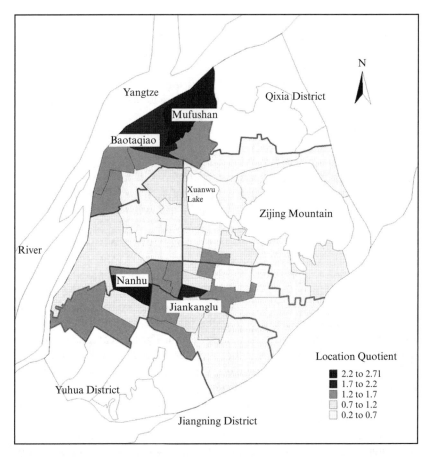

Source: Liu and Wu (2006b).

Figure 4.1   Location quotients for the urban poor (measured in MLSS recipients) in Nanjing

the urban fringe and inner suburbs. The intense construction of industrial areas in the north of the city outside the central gate and large-scale
wholesale markets such as the southern group of wholesale markets for
structural materials have been major attractors. The urban villages in
these expanding fringes of the cities have provided private rental housing
for the migrants, producing migrant enclaves such as Suojie (Henancun)
and Xiyingcun.

Figure 4.2 maps the location quotients for the migrant population in
the Fifth Population Census for street-office areas. The LQ ranges from

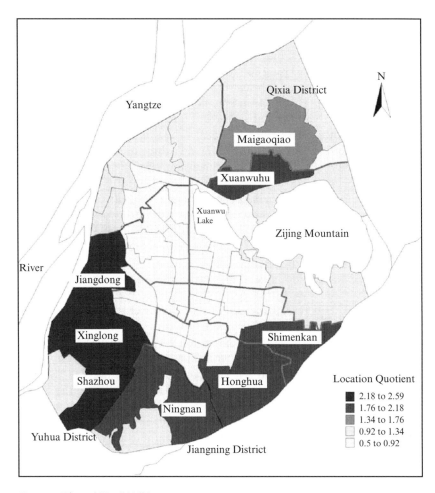

Source: Liu and Wu (2006b).

Figure 4.2   Location quotients for migrant population

0.5 to 2.59 in 55 street-office areas of the city zone and the inner suburbs. These can be divided into five categories, based on an equal interval classification. From Figure 4.2, we can see that the higher concentrations of migrant population include Maigaoqiao in the Qixia district, Jiangdong in the Gulou district, Shimenkan in the Baixia district, Honghua in Qinhuai district, Xinglong in Jiangye district, and Shazhou and Ningnan in the Yuhua district. All of these areas are located in the urban fringe or the inner suburbs.

The distribution of urban poor in Guangzhou has been studied by Yuan and Xu (2008). Using the Fifth Population Census data and MLSS data in 2005, they developed an index of deprivation, including income, employment, education and housing conditions. Five main factors of comprehensive poverty were selected through factor analysis (eigenvalue higher than 1.5). They are, respectively: economic poverty, occupation disadvantage, housing facilities, employment status and family burden. The cumulative explained variance reached 66.4 per cent. The average score of the main factors is 0. A score greater than 0 for any dimension in a sub-district means that there is poverty in this dimension. The higher the score, the deeper the poverty.

In terms of the development process, the administrative boundaries of the built-up area of Guangzhou city are divided into two: inner city and peri-urban area. The former consists of the original Yuexiu, Dongshan and Liwan districts, totalling 33 sub-districts; the latter includes Haizhu, Tianhe, the original Fangcun, and Baiyun districts, totalling 64 sub-districts. We then overlaid these main factors and identified 24 inner city sub-districts and 12 peri-urban sub-districts with at least three factor loading scores greater than 0. This reveals the cumulative characteristics of comprehensive poverty. The comprehensively poor sub-districts form 37 per cent of the total sub-districts. The triple-dimension poor sub-districts form 22.7 per cent of the total; sub-districts with four dimensions of poverty form 13.4 per cent of the total; and one sub-district has quintuplicate poverty. We calculated the total score of each sub-district according to the factor loadings. The average total score is 0.97. Sub-districts are divided into five grades. Fifty-five sub-districts belong to the first and second grade with the score below 0, and 42 sub-districts fall into the third to the fifth grades with their scores above 0, indicating the presence of multiple deprivation.

From Figures 4.3 and 4.4, we can see that the inner city and part of the peri-urban area in Guangzhou city are characterized by cumulative multiple poverty, displaying an overall 'concentric and partial radial' pattern of spatial distribution. The concentric pattern corresponds to the urban development circles of different historical periods. The partial radial pattern is created by the industrial zones of the planned economy and the urban villages surrounding them. The multiple poverty areas show corresponding occupational characteristics. That is, the poor in the inner city are primarily those who work at the lower end of the service industry, while the poor in peri-urban areas are primarily industrial workers.

In sum, state-led urban development and housing provision has helped the concentration of the new urban poverty. These patterns of concentration are discernible at the street-office scale. This might still be too coarse a scale to reflect all of the systematic socio-spatial patterns of poverty,

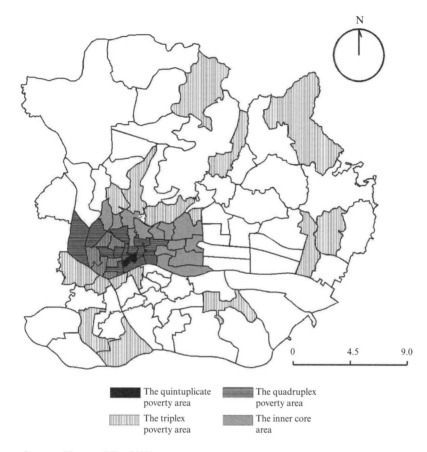

N

0   4.5   9.0

■ The quintuplicate
poverty area

▨ The quadruplex
poverty area

▥ The triplex
poverty area

▦ The inner core
area

Source: Yuan and Xu (2008).

*Figure 4.3   Spatial distribution of multiple deprivation at the sub-district
level*

however. To deepen the understanding of poverty concentration at the neighbourhood level, we select three neighbourhoods in Nanjing to examine the dynamics of poverty transition in greater detail.

TYPOLOGY OF POOR NEIGHBOURHOODS

Table 4.2 shows the three major types of poor neighbourhood in Chinese cities. This is a conceptual framework which will be discussed with cases later in this chapter.

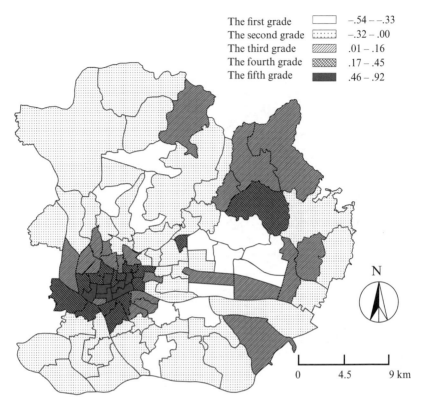

The first grade   ☐   −.54 − −.33
The second grade ▦   −.32 − .00
The third grade   ▨   .01 − .16
The fourth grade   ▩   .17 − .45
The fifth grade   ■   .46 − .92

N

0   4.5   9 km

Source: Yuan and Xu (2008).

*Figure 4.4   Composite scores of multiple deprivation at the sub-district
level*

Dilapidated Inner Neighbourhoods

The first type of poor neighbourhood is the dilapidated older or inner
neighbourhood in the central areas. These areas largely conform to the
distribution of shanty towns and shack dwellings in the pre-revolution era
and have been left out of the real estate development. These areas were not
thoroughly redeveloped in the socialist transformation in the 1950s, not
only because urban redevelopment was limited to a few 'model' workers'
villages due to the deliberate constraint on consumption-oriented investment, but also as a result of the state-led industrialization strategy which
favoured large-scale, capital-intensive and heavy industries. In other
words, although it is undeniable that the living standard of inner-city

Table 4.2   Three types of urban poor neighbourhood

Forms	The legacy of socialist development	New impacts of market transition
Inner-city dilapidated residences	Underinvestment in the built environment Peripheral to the organized industrialization and state workplaces	Selective redevelopment and exclusion of the poorest areas Marginalization of informal labourers due to competition from rural migrants and laid-off workers
Concentrated industrial areas (workers' villages)	Minimized cost of construction and low-standard Concentrated manufacturing areas Occupational-based services and welfare	Lack of commercial value of redevelopment and high cost to redevelop multi-rise buildings Large-scale economic restructuring from manufacturing to service industries Selective mobility of residents within workplace compounds and commodity housing market
Rural migrant enclaves in urban fringes	Rural–urban division by household registration Extraction of rural surplus into state-led industrialization	Continuation of exclusion from the formal labour market Restrictive labour policy resulted from local protectionism Inaccessible urban housing markets and fragmentation of land-use systems where the urban fringe sees the management vacuum.

Source: F. Wu (2004: 416).

dwellers has improved, they have remained in a peripheral position in the state occupation-based welfare system. Many of them still work in private small shops and collectively owned street factories; their workplaces often make little profit and are unable to provide additional benefits in housing and health services. These small businesses are vulnerable to economic changes. In the early stage of economic reform, relaxation of stringent economic control and the introduction of markets benefited these small businesses, because the reform was initiated in the spheres where planning was not dominant. The scope for embryonic private businesses has been

squeezed by the increasing competition in commerce and the shift from a
shortage economy to an over-accumulated regime in the 1990s. The lack
of effective demand haunted the economy in the late 1990s. The informal
workers such as street hawkers, small shop owners, and low-skilled shoe
menders, locksmiths and knife sharpeners are marginalized because of
increasing competition from the laid-off workers and rural migrants.
Most residents there are tenants of municipal housing. The area has an
over-representation of old-age, retired, laid-off and low-income households. The market-oriented real estate development is less effective in
regenerating the most dilapidated residential areas. In the accessible areas,
redevelopment has displaced the original residents and thus led to a changing community profile, but in the areas that are less connected to the road
with a high concentration of poorer residents, redevelopment has become
extremely difficult.

Degraded Workers' Villages

Workers' villages, usually located in industrial districts and with a concentration of the employees of state-owned enterprises (SOEs), have
experienced the most dramatic change in employment profile. With industrial restructuring and the bankruptcy of SOEs, the jobs in state-owned
manufacturing industries have been fast disappearing. While not all
workers' villages are poverty-stricken areas, these communities were worst
hit by the redundancies under SOE reform. The large-scale construction
of workers' villages has contributed to the concentration of state industrial employees. Because of the lack of maintenance, together with the
initial low quality, these workers' communities are now deteriorating into
dilapidated residential areas. Furthermore, since the early 1980s, in order
to improve housing conditions for the workers of SOEs and to provide
housing for the returned *xiafang* population (*xiafang*, literally means
'sending-down' – urban residents were sent down to the countryside in
the anti-urban campaign in the mid and late 1960s) mainly employed in
SOEs, the state and the SOEs collaborated in the large-scale construction
of workers' villages in the inner suburbs. This further concentrated state
industrial employees in particular neighbourhoods.

Rural Migrants' Enclaves

The third type is 'urban villages', that is *chengzhongcun*. After land reform,
Chinese cities saw rapid urban expansion and sprawl. In suburban areas,
there has been large-scale construction of industrial areas and commodity
housing. Under state-led urban development, the state takes responsibility

for requisitioning farm and village land and relocating local residents. In order to support the development of industry, large quantities of farmland have been converted to urban use. However, many of the villages themselves (as distinct from the farmland) have been left to the local villagers to avoid the high relocation compensation costs. As a result, many urban–rural fringe villages have been encroached upon by urban land development and have become 'urban villages'. Due to the co-existence of two land use systems (the urban land lease system and collective land ownership in rural areas), the urban village is therefore characterized by chaotic land use and a dense mixture of housing tenures (Zhang et al., 2003). It is easier for local villagers to lease rooms because of the lack of regulation, and it is cheaper for migrants to find private rental housing in these villages. The concentration of rural migrants in urban villages is to some extent the result of institutional restrictions.

There is a general disadvantage facing all migrants with respect to access to urban housing as they are largely excluded from the mainstream housing distribution system. Although some rural migrants can indirectly rent municipal housing through private sub-leases, it is impossible for the majority of migrants to acquire the right of use or ownership of work-unit or municipal housing in urban areas. While a few migrants possess higher socioeconomic status, most of them are limited to heavy, dirty, dangerous and low-paid jobs, leading to lower socioeconomic status. As a result, although housing marketization gives migrants the right to purchase commodity housing, most migrants, especially poor rural migrants, do not have the economic means to gain access to such housing. Consequently, renting has become the best choice for migrants who live in urban areas.

The emergence of the urban village provides the possibility of accommodation for the majority of rural migrants for several reasons. First, urban villages are mainly located in the urban fringe, in which economic functions are concentrated in the form of industrial areas and the great wholesale markets. Increasing employment opportunities attract migrants to concentrate in these areas and rent housing in urban villages. Second, the availability of rental housing, especially at a lower rent than inside the city and with a larger living space, is another factor attracting migrants to live in urban villages. The concentration of rural migrants in *chengzhong-cun* has produced migrant enclaves (Ma and Xiang, 1998; Wu, 2002). Private rental housing has brought a steady income to local farmers in urban villages, and local governments sometimes benefit from charging a fee to migrants (a kind of tax), which further encourages illegal construction and exacerbates residential crowding. However, with the lack of efficient management and planning, some enclaves of poor migrants appear as dilapidated and crowded bungalows, illegal shacks in narrow alleys, unpaved and often filthy streets amidst the typical urban landscape of the suburbs.

A PILOT STUDY OF THREE IMPOVERISHED NEIGHBOURHOODS

We select three representative neighbourhoods in the city of Nanjing to conduct a pilot study of concentrated poverty areas (Liu and Wu, 2006b). These are Pingshijie, Wubaicun and Xiyingcun, which respectively represent old, urban, dilapidated homes, degraded workers' villages and rural migrants' enclaves. Their locations are shown in Figure 4.5. The survey was conducted in these three poor neighbourhoods in 2004.

Pingshijie: A Deteriorating Old Urban Residence

Pingshijie is situated in the southern old urban area of Nanjing in which ordinary residents traditionally lived, and is near the south-west of Xinjiekou, the modern commercial centre of Nanjing city. The neighbourhood was originally built in the Ming Dynasty of the fifteenth century, and matured in the late Qing Dynasty of the late nineteenth century. All of the one to two-storey buildings in this neighbourhood were wooden, and every large residential building has five to six cascading entry doors, forming the architectural style of the strip courtyard. In the feudal era, this neighbourhood was the area in which the common people were concentrated, and typical cafes and restaurants were laid out along the Pingshijie road. In World War Two, Nanjing city was invaded and heavily damaged, and subsequently the former prosperity of Pingshijie disappeared. Fortunately, those buildings of the late Qing Dynasty remained. In the last years under the nationalist government, as traditional commercial streets and the residence of the common people, this neighbourhood became in turn a community with a concentration of middle- to low-income retailers and craftsmen.

After the coming to power of the Chinese Communist Party (CCP), all of these retailers and craftsmen were recruited into collective units to become industrial workers according to the cooperative system of the public and the private (*gongsi heying*). Meanwhile, against the background of the concentrated construction of industrial areas in the inner suburbs of Nanjing, Pingshijie as well as the whole old urban area were left out of redevelopment due to the lack of investment. Due to long-term war and lack of housing construction, the housing shortage was an acute problem in Nanjing as in other Chinese cities. Since the housing in Pingshijie was

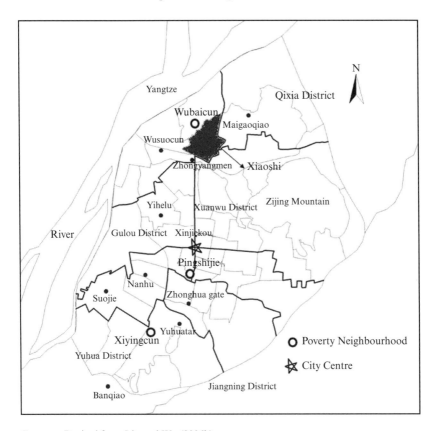

Source: Revised from Liu and Wu (2006b).

Figure 4.5 Locations of poverty neighbourhoods and some districts in Nanjing

assigned to be managed by the municipal housing bureau under public transition of property, in addition to a few inherited private houses (about 1 per cent of all housing retained a restricted right to sell), some workers in small and collectively owned enterprises which could not provide living quarters for their employees were ordered into this neighbourhood to share its housing. As a result, several households had to live in partitioned housing that had previously served single families. As a whole, with a high population density, Pingshijie became a neighbourhood with a concentration of the elderly, the jobless and employees in small, low-ranked units.

Since the 1980s, despite the state-driven redevelopment of the old city in Nanjing, this area has still been neglected because of the high population density in this central location. Under housing marketization in the 1990s, the neighbourhood was overlooked by the municipality and real estate developers because of the high cost of compensation associated with such a dense population. In fact, Pingshijie has now become a typical old, dilapidated, urban residence surrounded by modern buildings with a population of about 4000 living in an area of 8 hectares. Buildings in this area still retain the architectural styles of the late Qing Dynasty; however, many of these old wooden houses have deteriorated and have become dangerous through lack of maintenance. Moreover, due to the high natural growth in population and the consequent enlargement of household size (average 3.4 persons per household, in contrast with the Nanjing city average of 2.9 persons), the population density here has increased by 100 per cent from the 1950s to 1980s. Now almost every large residential building is shared by more than 20 households, and many extended families are often packed into one flat of less than 25 square metres. The gross housing area in Pingshijie, which is greater than the actual dwelling area, is only six square metres per capita, while the average for Nanjing is 20 square metres per capita. Consequently, some residents have chosen to construct shanties around their houses to enlarge their housing space.

Overcrowding and bad living conditions have become the primary problem in Pingshijie. Intolerable housing conditions have driven relatively better-off families (about 21 per cent of the total number of families, more than 1000 people) to relocate to other areas through purchasing commodity housing. The houses vacated by these families were not shared by the other local residents, but have been sub-leased to rural migrants. The migrants, about 8 per cent of the total population in this neighbourhood, have gradually occupied the houses through private rental, attracted by its central location. The residual group of local residents now mainly comprises older people, laid-off workers, and the unemployed and low-income families who cannot afford to move. According to the official statistical data from the residents' committee, older people over 60 comprise one-fifth of the total population, and registered laid-off workers and the unemployed who were originally employed in collective enterprises (the majority of them having become bankrupt in the market transition) form about 10 per cent of the total population. Therefore, Pingshijie has become a poor neighbourhood. According to official statistics, the income level here was very low. In 2004, about 70 per cent of households had an income level below 1000 Yuan (about US$120) per month (about 303 Yuan per capita), and the highest monthly household income level was only between 1500 and 2000 Yuan. The statistics indicate that the percentage of people in absolute poverty in the total urban population, that is the percentage of MLSS recipients (the minimum living standard in Nanjing was 220 Yuan per person per month, or about US$26.5), was 4.5 per cent, which is far higher than the Nanjing city average of 1.6 per cent.

Wubaicun: A Degraded Workers' Village

Wubaicun, with a population of about 5000 and an area of 7.5 hectares, is located in the northern industrial area of Nanjing, with the central gate of Nanjing city just to the south. To its immediate east and north are industrial factories, and some larger enterprises have developed residential communities with good living conditions to the immediate west and south of this workers' village. Before 1979, it was a vegetable plantation and a self-contained rural village in the northern inner suburbs of Nanjing city. In 1979, the state initiated the construction of a workers' village in this area to provide housing for the returned *xiafang* population, who were employed in collective or small state-owned enterprises because of their low skills and low qualifications.

Meanwhile, the original villagers were transformed into urban residents and employed in the surrounding enterprises. Consequently, the physical and sociological characteristics of the neighbourhood have been changed by the development of the state-built housing estate. The concentration of 5000 people into public (work-unit) housing meant a concentration of industrial workers. This comprised 58 apartment blocks, with between two and six levels. Most of the apartments have one or two bedrooms and a few of them three. The floor space of an apartment is on average 35 square metres, with a maximum of 60 square metres and a minimum of 20. At the beginning, the state promised that these apartments were only temporary accommodation for returned workers, for about five to eight years. As a result, the construction quality is very poor, and there are no balconies or toilets in the buildings. However, the promise did not materialize. So far the majority of the initial residents still live in these degraded apartments. Most of this social housing has deteriorated to the point of the buildings being dangerous. This is a compounding result of poor construction quality and lack of maintenance.

Twenty years have gone by and the descendants of the initial residents have grown up. Consequently, the average dwelling area of 25 square metres initially distributed to each household is no longer enough for the extended family. To enlarge their housing space, residents have constructed shanties near to their housing. These appear as disorderly bungalows and illegal shacks, without green land or public places except for one main street (Wubaicun road), along which there are some shops. Since the 1990s, Wubaicun has become encompassed within the urban district due to urban sprawl. As a result, this village became a concentrated community of traditional industrial workers. However, the majority of these district-owned or sub-district-owned collective units went bankrupt one after the other under the industrial restructuring and reforms of the late 1990s. This has meant that there is a very high percentage of laid-off workers in this community – higher than in areas in which there has been a more diversified occupation structure.

It is difficult for these laid-off workers to be re-employed in modern enterprises or service sectors, because most of them have a low education level and tend to be above the age of 45. The residence has now become a typical degraded workers' village, with a concentration of laid-off workers and unemployed population. According to the official statistics, the percentage of the registered laid-off workers and unemployed people among the total residents is about 40 per cent. At the same time, older people over 60 also occupy a higher percentage, about 17 per cent of total population. Because most of these older people are also older low labour market quality *xifang* returnees, their descendants' education has been neglected and their quality is also lower. Consequently, while most old people have a retirement pension, their households often live in poverty because their descendants either cannot find good jobs or are jobless. According to our interviews, adults depending on their older parents (*lao yang xiao*, literally the elderly fostering the younger generation) is a general phenomenon in Wubaicun. This kind of household poverty is one of the prominent problems of this degraded workers' village. According to the statistics, the percentage of people in absolute poverty (the recipients of MLSS) in the total urban population is as high as 5 per cent. About 65 per cent of households had an income level below 1000 Yuan per month in 2004 (about 303 Yuan per capita), and households with an income level below 1500 Yuan reached 93 per cent of all households.

Xiyingcun: A Marginal Rural Migrants' Enclave

Xiyingcun is situated in the southern inner suburbs of Nanjing city, and has an area of 5.5 hectares. Originally, this neighbourhood was a self-contained rural village similar to Wubaicun. Due to urban growth and the construction of nearby industrial areas, Xiyingcun has, since the late 1980s, gradually been swallowed up by the urban built-up area and, in particular, by surrounding industrial uses. Dating back to 1982, the Nanjing Lumber Company, a state-owned enterprise, requisitioned part of the village's farmland (the near west area of Xiyingcun) to construct a lumber yard. Subsequently, a variety of small timber retail companies settled nearby. By the late 1980s, the timber market group Saihongqiao Jiancai Shichang (supplying construction materials) had developed in the west and north of

Xiyingcun. In the early 1990s, living quarters for state-owned enterprises were constructed in the near east and south of Xiyingcun. Commercial buildings such as Yingqiao Wholesale Market and Runtai Market have gradually encroached on the residual farmland. Consequently, Xiyingcun has been surrounded and has become an isolated urban village. In 1994 it was transformed from a suburban village into a residents' committee area administered by Saihongqiao sub-district. While its rural farmland was requisitioned to meet the demands of industrial development and urban extension, the built-up village land is still owned by the village collective (in the name of all of the local villagers). This reduced the compensation liability facing Nanjing municipal authority, which developed the industrial land.

Accordingly, changes have taken place in the socioeconomic profile of the population in Xiyingcun. Since the late 1980s, the local villagers in Xiyingcun have gradually been recruited into collective enterprises such as the Nanjing Sartorial Factory and Boiler Factory, and have become industrial workers as compensation for losing farmland (in some cases such as these, the compensation package includes an alternative job). Moreover, with the transformation from village to residents' committee area in 1994, all of the local villagers became urban residents by being awarded urban *hukou*. In recent years, because these collective enterprises have closed down one after the other, these villagers have become unemployed. Fortunately, they still possess the right of use of their housing land in the built-up village and have used this to develop high density migrant worker housing. Since the mid-1990s, with the construction of many large wholesale markets near Xiyingcun such as Saihongqiao Timber Market, Kuashiji Decoration City and Yinqiao Market, Xiyingcun and nearby residential areas have become popular as migrant quarters.

The village's location on the urban fringe means relatively low rent and relatively convenient traffic routes, and these factors have added to its attraction for rural migrants. As a result, and with migrants' families joining them in the urban village, the migrant population of Xiyingcun has greatly increased in the last few years. While the number of local villagers in Xiyingcun is 843 people, the number of rural migrants shows a seasonal fluctuation from 4000 to 6000 individuals. Rural migrants therefore constitute over 70 per cent of the total population in Xiyingcun. They tend to have low-paid manual work, such as construction, repair and delivery, and a larger number of dependants. With a fixed supply of housing land in the village, this has meant bad living conditions. About 82 per cent of migrant households had in 2004 an income level below 1000 Yuan per month (about 295 Yuan per capita), and almost all migrant households had an income level below 1500 Yuan.

Overcrowding, jumbled buildings and poor infrastructure are prominent problems in Xiyingcun. Local villagers have made many large-scale illegal constructions, mainly two to four-storey buildings, to acquire higher income from rent. The local households in Xiyingcun have on average 20 rooms per household (because many are rented out). The local residents live in the biggest room, about 15 square metres. Other rooms, averaging 6 to 8 square metres, are rented to migrants. In Xiyingcun, there is almost no green land or public space except for one main street along with many retail stores and disorderly stalls. With a lack of toilets in the rented rooms, two public lavatories are not enough for so many migrants. There is no public space for the construction of public lavatories. Litter and waste disposal is a big problem, with all forms of environmental sanitation being very poor in Xiyingcun.

Summary

We have used the city of Nanjing to illustrate the distribution of the urban poor at different spatial scales, including in three neighbourhoods. Pingshijie, as an old dilapidated, urban area, has been left out of urban redevelopment due to its high population density and relatively high regeneration costs, and has become a clustering area for the urban poor and rural migrants. Wubaicun, as a workers' village constructed in the late 1970s, has deteriorated into a different kind of poor neighbourhood, acting as a filter that concentrates laid-off workers, unemployed persons and early retirees. And Xiyingcun, as an encroached urban village since the early 1990s, has attracted many rural migrants to rent housing there due to its location near large-scale wholesale markets, and has become a poor rural migrants' enclave. In sum, low socioeconomic status and poor living conditions constitute the common profile of these three poor neighbourhoods.

Poverty concentration has been widely acknowledged in Western literature, and many studies suggest that the spatial concentration of poverty is a major cause of social problems such as joblessness, poverty and crime (Jencks, 1992; Massey et al., 1994; Wilson, 1987, 1996; MacDonald, 1997; Galster and Zobel, 1998). Some argue that in these poor neighbourhoods there is a 'culture of poverty' (Lewis, 1969). Residents in these neighbourhoods develop a negative attitude towards society (Greenstone, 1991). However, our study of poor neighbourhoods shows that these poor Chinese neighbourhoods are less isolated from mainstream society. Many residents participate in the current mainstream economy. The boundary between poor and non-poor neighbourhoods is less rigid. Many poor neighbourhoods such as urban villages only have a short history. Poor and better-off neighbourhoods co-exist and have a geographic proximity, unlike clear segregation between decayed inner cities and wealthy suburbs in many western countries (Huang, 2005). The government also tries to demolish poor neighbourhoods. So many poor neighbourhoods vanished after redevelopment programmes. The attitude of residents in poor neighbourhoods seems to be more positive than that of ghettos in the West. We have discussed the trajectories of poverty formation in terms of life chances of the poor in Chapter 3. At the very least, we suggest poverty concentration in China is closely associated with state-led urban development policies and the specific system of housing provision.

POOR NEIGHBOURHOODS: A SURVEY OF 25 NEIGHBOURHOODS

After studying three neighbourhoods in 2004, a major household survey was subsequently conducted, as detailed in Chapter 2. The purpose of this section of the book is to provide detailed case material of these different types of villages in a way that allows for comparison and nuanced understanding.

Degenerated Workers' Villages

Degenerated workers' villages are enclaves for industrial workers who used to work in large-scale state-owned enterprises (SOEs). These living quarters or compounds were deemed as mini-societies, providing housing and social services. Now many are laid off and unemployed. Some lost the support from their workplaces and become the urban poor. Some benefited from public housing privatization and became homeowners. Some of them managed to capitalize on their possession and make a fortune, while the others at least possess housing security compared with non-homeowners. Figure 4.6 shows seven workers' villages surveyed in this study. We describe them in detail in the following.

Yiyin neighbourhood in Xi'an is the work-unit compound of the state-owned Shaanxi No.1 Printing and Dyeing Mill. This neighbourhood accommodates more than 2000 households, about 8000 people, of which 1800 are laid-off workers and the rest are their family members or retirees. There are more than 500 households in the neighbourhood receiving MLSS subsidy. The MLSS coverage rate is as high as 25 per cent, suggesting a relatively high poverty rate in the neighbourhood. It also suggests that former SOE employees have better access to state welfare provision. Shaanxi No.1 Printing and Dyeing Mill was established in the 1950s. It

Yuhua No. 2 New Village, Nanjing

Yama, Harbin

Yiyin, Xi'an

Huaxingli, Wuhan

Lingang new village, Kunming

Jueyuan, Harbin

Guangdan, Guangzhou

Figure 4.6   Degenerated workers' villages surveyed in six cities

was among the top three profit-making industries of Shaanxi province before 1984. Facing fierce competition from Zhejiang province and Jiangsu province, it became a loss-making industry from 1994, and finally closed down in July 1997. However, the SOE has not officially announced its bankruptcy. All manufacturing equipment was sold, and all workshops were rented out. In 1999, housing reform allowed employees to purchase their homes at cost price.

Since 2004, more new houses have been constructed and sold to senior and better-off employees at a discount price of 1100 to 2000 Yuan per square metre, which is much cheaper than the market price. The construction of new housing has been funded by the enterprise, although it suspended production. Junior employees and those who could not afford to buy houses were offered public rental housing with shared kitchens and toilets. Laid-off employees were offered a benefit package including a lay-off subsidy of 230 Yuan per month, and a comprehensive social security insurance package worth 295 Yuan per month, including pension, health care and unemployment insurance. The central government, the provincial government and the enterprise each contribute one third of the cost of the benefit package. Most laid-off workers do not manage to get a job due to their lack of skills and their age. The next generation of these laid-off workers and earlier retirees who did not succeed in getting into colleges and universities, have also become chronically unemployed.

Yuhua No. 2 New Village neighbourhood is located to the south of the city ring road of Nanjing. It now accommodates about 1900 permanent urban residents and more than 500 migrants. Permanent residents are mainly former workers from several nearby SOEs, such as the Nanjing Sewing Machine Manufactory, Bicycle Manufactory, and Farming Machine Manufactory. Most of these workers have been laid off since 1990. This neighbourhood also accommodates a number of residents relocated from other old inner urban neighbourhoods. This is a highly mixed work-unit compound. The majority of laid-off workers from nearby SOEs and relocated residents are chronically unemployed. Many people are experiencing economic hardships; however, only 72 people are MLSS recipients. The MLSS coverage rate is 3 per cent. Most residents are not covered by any social security insurance scheme. For laid-off workers, the only security is housing; most of them have purchased public housing from their employers at a comparatively low price during the housing reform in the late 1990s. For relocated residents, they also enjoy a relatively low rent or even private ownerships of their resettlement housing.

Over time, some better-off indigenous residents have moved out of the neighbourhood. Some remaining residents have also managed to expand their houses by invading public space. Owners of these vacant houses and expanded houses capitalize on their possession by renting out rooms to migrant workers. In contrast to other work-unit compounds which are managed by a single large-scale SOE and thus are under greater control, this neighbourhood has a more developed housing rental market and accommodates more migrants. Since houses have for a long time lacked proper maintenance and have been greatly expanded, the built environment in this neighbourhood is comparatively poor. It is a declining residential complex which was initially associated with industrial development in the earlier stage and is now reshaped by market reform and the development of tertiary industry, as well as the flourishing informal sector.

Huaxingli neighbourhood is the work-unit compound of Wuhan No. 4 Cotton Textile Manufactory, accommodating more than 660 households, about 2157 people. During the SOE reform, more than 200 workers living in the neighbourhood were laid off. The No. 4 Cotton Textile Manufactory was the best among seven cotton textile factories in Wuhan. From the late 1990s, the textile industry has been in a downturn. This enterprise inevitably started to lose profit. In December 2004, it was privatized and restructured into Wuhan Yudahua Shareholding Co. Ltd. The newly established company failed to absorb laid-off workers from the former SOE, and did not take the responsibility of providing lay-off subsidy. Most laid-off workers managed to find temporary jobs or informal jobs, and the MLSS coverage rate is comparatively low.

In terms of housing, all employer-allocated housing was privatized after 1996. This was sold at the relatively low price of 500 Yuan per square metre. Many of these houses are now in very poor condition and are without private kitchens and toilets. This means employees of the former SOE did not really benefit from the privatization of public housing, since they neither have a comfortable home, nor are they able to capitalize on their housing assets. Many residents have expanded their houses into public space. This is a relatively poor urban neighbourhood in terms of socioeconomic profile and built environment. Since there are not many vacant houses available and they are under strict control, very few migrants choose to reside in this neighbourhood.

Yama neighbourhood is the work-unit compound of Harbin Flax Spinning Mill. This neighbourhood accommodates 3600 households, about 9600 people. Most residents are workers of the Flax Spinning Mill and family members of these workers. Migrants only account for 5 per cent of the total population. This neighbourhood was developed in 1951 along with the establishment of Harbin Flax Spinning Mill. This large-scale SOE was recognized as one of the most significant 512 SOEs in the whole country. However, since the 1990s, the enterprise stopped making a profit, and ended up with a huge debt of 1.1 billion Yuan. In 2004, the spinning mill was privatized and restructured into Harbin Changlong Flax Spinning Co. Ltd. After the SOE reform, a great proportion of workers were laid off, especially those in their middle age, with low or simple skills. Laid-off workers were offered a monthly subsidy of 260 Yuan, which is barely sufficient for basic living necessities.

The MLSS coverage rate in the whole neighbourhood is as high as 5 per cent and the neighbourhood also has a high percentage of retirees. In many families where the younger generation is laid off or unemployed, the retirement pension is the only income source for the whole family. Since SOE reform, neither workers nor laid-off workers are offered a social security insurance package by their employer. Housing reform in the late 1990s has privatized 80 per cent of former public housing. Those who could not afford to purchase housing still reside in public rental housing owned by the enterprise, which is relatively low quality. To encourage and to support re-employment of laid-off workers, the neighbourhood committee provides free training courses and employment information. There is also a three-year tax-exemption policy in Harbin for those laid-off workers who start their own small businesses. Nevertheless, the re-employment rate is still relatively low, and many laid-off families struggle for basic necessities.

Jueyuan neighbourhood is the work-unit compound of Harbin Insulating Materials Plant. There are 2365 households, about 5860 people living in the neighbourhood, of which more than 1000 people are laid-off workers, and 155 households are recipients of MLSS subsidy. The MLSS coverage rate in the whole neighbourhood is as high as 6.6 per cent. Harbin Insulating Materials Plant was established in 1956, and was the largest comprehensive insulating material plant in China. Before the 1990s it was a profit-making enterprise, but soon after began to make a loss. More than 1000 out of 2800 workers were laid off. In 1998, the enterprise was reformed and became part of the Harbin Electronic Equipments Group. However, those laid-off workers were neither absorbed into the new enterprise, nor were they offered lay-off subsidies. Those who are approaching retirement age were required to pay a lump sum cost of pension insurance out of their own pocket before they could qualify for their retirement pension.

In terms of housing, most public housing has been privatized since the late 1990s. For MLSS subsidy recipients, they are also offered a subsidy for health care insurance and children's education besides the MLSS subsidy itself. For instance, children in households receiving the MLSS subsidy are offered a subsidy of 2000 Yuan if they get into university. However, those who are not eligible for the MLSS do not enjoy any social benefits. Due to the limited quota for MLSS recipients, many poor households did not get into the scheme, and were put on the waiting list. Since most laid-off workers are about 45–50 years old and with low or simple skills, they are not able to or not willing to be re-employed. It is also quite common that the household head's retirement pension is the only income source of the whole family. Many households are struggling for their basic living necessities. This neighbourhood has become the poorest in the sub-district.

Lingang new village is the work-unit compound of Yalong Metallurgy Co. Ltd based in Kunming. It accommodates more than 1100 households, about 3000 people. Yalong Metallurgy Co. Ltd was a state-owned steelworks. Since 1996, the SOE reform has retrenched a number of redundant workers. In 2006, the steelworks was privatized, and became part of the Yalong Metallurgy Group. A large proportion of workers was laid off or became early retirees. Laid-off workers were paid a lump sum compensation corresponding to their length of service. After that, they no longer receive any subsidy from their former employer. Most laid-off workers and early retirees did not manage to find a new job due to their age and skills. Many of them are now facing economic hardships. There are about 110 households in the neighbourhood receiving MLSS subsidies.

The MLSS coverage rate is 10 per cent, much higher than the average level in Kunming and other impoverished neighbourhoods. There are two types of housing in the neighbourhood: a) purpose-built apartments with private kitchen and toilet; b) employee dormitories without private kitchen and toilet. Purpose-built apartments have been sold to employees at a discount price according to length of service. The average housing price was 400 Yuan per square metre, which is much cheaper than the market price. Dormitories are rented to employees who have a comparatively short length of service for a comparatively low rent, for example, 2 Yuan per square metre. Most residents in Lingang new village are not covered by social security insurance. There are very few migrant workers in the neighbourhood due to the strict control and the undeveloped rental market.

Guangdan neighbourhood is situated at the north-west periphery of Guangzhou. It is the work-unit compound of Guangzhou Nitrogenous Fertilizer Plant, now accommodating 9600 people, of which 7200 are registered urban population. There are about 100 people on MLSS subsidy. The MLSS coverage rate is relatively low, considering that the majority of residents in this neighbourhood are disadvantaged groups, for example, the laid-off/unemployed and elderly. There are more than 3500 elderly people in the neighbourhood, more than 3000 laid-off workers, and more than 600 early retirees. The Nitrogenous Fertilizer Plant was established in 1957 as a nationally recognized large SOE. Since the late 1980s and the early 1990s, this SOE was facing fierce competition from Hunan province and Fujian province. The increasing water and electricity rate and the rising labour costs in Guangzhou further pushed the Nitrogenous Fertilizer Plant into difficulties. In 1998, employees were only paid 70 per cent of their former salaries.

In 2001, the SOE was deeply in debt, and closed down soon after. After the bankruptcy of the plant, fewer than 1000 former employees were re-employed by other work units. The 3000 laid-off workers were offered a lump sum payment equivalent to their monthly salary multiplied by years of service. In this case, the maximum payment was only about 50,000 Yuan, which could not last for long. In the first 6 to 24 months after being laid off, employees were offered a subsidy of 340 Yuan per month plus health care insurance worth 45 Yuan per month. Afterwards, these laid-off workers had to develop their own survival strategies. However, most laid-off workers did not manage to find stable, formal sector jobs. In terms of housing, most work-unit housing was sold to employees at a cost price of 500 Yuan per square metre in the late 1990s, which has now increased in value to 4000 Yuan per square metre. However, only employees who had a certain length of service were allowed to purchase those purpose-built apartments. Those disqualified employees could only rent work-unit dormitories with shared kitchens and toilets. Some of these dormitories were also rented to migrant workers.

Old Inner Urban Neighbourhoods

Old inner urban neighbourhoods usually have a highly mixed population, including laid-off workers from small-scale SOEs and collectively owned enterprises (COEs), people running small businesses and those engaging in the informal sector, as well as rural migrants. Some of these old neighbourhoods are situated in historical districts and are characterized by an over-crowded and dilapidated built environment due to the long-term lack of proper maintenance and investment. Other old neighbourhoods have long been shanty towns in the inner city. All these neighbourhoods have been neglected and marginalized in both the pre-reform rapid industrialization period and the post-reform high commercialization period. Figure 4.7 shows the dilapidated landscape of the seven neighbourhoods of this type surveyed in our research. Residents of old inner urban neighbourhoods are very disadvantaged. Most have long been marginalized and have few possessions, such as housing, which could be capitalized in the market.

Dongdayuan neighbourhood is situated very close to the ancient city of Xi'an in the central area. It accommodates 4000 households, of which 50 per cent are migrants. The registered urban population in the neighbourhood is more than 6000. Among them, more than 300 are MLSS recipients. The MLSS rate is 5 per cent. There are also about 200 people unemployed, laid-off or disabled. The neighbourhood also has a high percentage of elderly residents: about 500 people are over 60 years old. This is a typical dilapidated inner urban neighbourhood. It has long been a neighbourhood accommodating low-income residents and migrants, being a shanty town before 1949. Since the 1970s, residents have improved their houses in an incremental way, with two-storey wood and brick structure houses replacing the shanties. The housing quality and infrastructure are still comparatively poor, and better-off households have gradually moved out and rural migrants moved in. Both the built environment and the socioeconomic profile of the neighbourhood have therefore steadily deteriorated over the years. This is a Chinese example of spontaneous neighbourhood tipping.

The overcrowded living conditions have led many residents to expand their living space into the public space, which makes narrow streets and alleys even narrower. The construction density is extremely high, while infrastructure and public facilities are extremely undeveloped since the densification has happened as a result of many independent and unco-ordinated small investments by households. On average, more than 100 households have to share one public toilet. Despite its central location, this neighbourhood has lacked proper maintenance for decades and has resisted redevelopment because of the high redevelopment cost caused by high population density. However, as land values in the city increase at a rate much greater than the annual inflation of compensation costs, redevelopment is almost inevitable and this village, in its prime location, is expected to face the bulldozer before long.

Gaogangli neighbourhood is situated just to the south of the ancient city wall of Nanjing and to the north of Qinhuai River, a major waterway of the city. It is one of oldest urban neighbourhoods in the city with several hundred years' history. Gaogangli neighbourhood now accommodates more than 1300 households, about 3200 people, not including several hundred migrant workers who are not registered with the residents com-mittee. There are 140 households on MLSS support, giving a relatively high MLSS coverage rate of about 10 per cent. Most houses in Gaogangli are low-rise one to two-storey houses owned and managed by the munici-pal housing authority. Located in a central area, it is now surrounded by a forest of high-rise buildings. The houses are rented to residents for a nominal rent, and many residents have been living in these overcrowded houses with shared kitchens and toilets for most of their lives. Over time, better-off residents have moved out and have rented their vacant houses to rural migrants. Despite the unsatisfactory conditions, many migrant workers have been attracted to this neighbourhood because of its central location and relatively inexpensive rent. The neighbourhood has a highly

Gaogangli, Nanjing

Dongfanghong, Harbin

Dongdayuan, Xian

Tujia, Wuhan

146

Laojie, Kunming

Zede, Guangzhou

Yangrendong, Guangzhou

Figure 4.7 Old urban neighbourhoods surveyed

147

mixed population, including laid-off workers and early retirees from a small-scale collective-owned enterprise, craftsmen, small business owners, and rural migrants working in the informal sector.

In general, the majority of residents do not have stable jobs. The neighbourhood has long had a comparatively low socioeconomic profile. The out-immigration of better-off residents and the incoming rural migrants who accept the pitifully low housing standards for the modest savings on rent compared to urban villages at comparable locations, have established this neighbourhood as one of the most deprived areas in the city. Few residents in the neighbourhood are covered by any social security insurance scheme. Some residents struggle for their basic living necessities, and they are hoping that the municipal authority's proposed redevelopment plan will improve their housing conditions and offer some compensation to support their family.

Tujia is located very close to the commercial and business centre of Wuhan. It is part of the old city core of Hankou district. There are 4514 registered urban residents and more than 1000 migrant workers in the neighbourhood. A large proportion of local residents are laid-off, unemployed and early retirees. There are 200 households that are MLSS recipients, giving an MLSS coverage rate of 4.4 per cent. About 80 per cent of residents still live in public rental housing owned and managed by the local housing authority. Similar to many other old inner urban neighbourhoods, Tujia neighbourhood was marginalized in the earlier industrialization period and remains in a marginal position in the late market-oriented reform era. Former workers and early retirees from the small collectively-owned enterprises that used to be located here were neither offered the opportunity to purchase privatized public housing, nor were they offered the social security insurance package enjoyed by some laid-off workers from large-scale SOEs. A few early retirees in this neighbourhood were offered a monthly subsidy of 150 Yuan from their employers.

The legacy of the industrialization period barely left these laid-off workers and early retirees anything to rely on after being retrenched. Most of them have not managed to find re-employment, especially the middle-aged women. Many of the younger generation of these families have become unemployed as well. Most of our interviewees expressed discontent with their lives. In this neighbourhood, migrant workers who have managed to find a stable job seem to lead a better life than the indigenous urban *hukou* holders. This is in stark contrast to the situation in urban villages.

Dongfanghong is a dilapidated residential block located at the north of the inner city of Harbin. It accommodates more than 4640 households, about 10 000 people, of which 3640 are registered urban households and

1000 are migrant households or temporary households relocated from other places in the city. About one third of the population are elderly, and a large proportion of the working-age population are unemployed or laid off. There are 340 households receiving MLSS subsidy, giving a coverage rate of about 7 per cent. This is another neighbourhood that was originally a shanty town located at the city fringe before 1949. Urban expansion meant that this former peripheral shanty town became part of the inner city. About 75 per cent of houses in the neighbourhood are privately-owned, most of these being privatized work-unit housing. The rest are owned and managed by the local urban housing authority. There is also some semi-illegal self-build housing constructed by local residents for rent. The poor conditions mean relatively low rent and this has attracted many migrant workers and urban households seeking temporary housing. As with the other old city urban neighbourhoods described above, this area is experiencing progressive downgrading in terms of the built environment and socioeconomic profile. A small section of the neighbourhood was redeveloped in 1998 through a commercial housing development project, while the rest of the neighbourhood remains overcrowded and dilapidated. It is one of the poorest inner urban neighbourhoods of Harbin.

Laojie is a historical district located in the central area of Kunming. Historically it was part of the commercial and political centre of Kunming, but this old neighbourhood has now become a dilapidated residential block accommodating more than 800 households, about 1000 people. It has a mixed population of indigenous people and migrants. The migrants (30 per cent of the population) mainly work in the nearby flower and pet wholesale market. Most of the indigenous residents are elderly and laid-off/unemployed. There are about 30 MLSS recipients. Most houses in this district are more than a hundred years old. About 80 per cent of houses are owned and managed by the local housing authority. The rest are inherited private housing that survived state expropriation in the socialist era because of their poor condition. Many houses along the main streets have been modified into shops and restaurants, generating considerable rental income for the houseowners and job opportunities for migrants. The old residential districts in surrounding areas have been gradually demolished and redeveloped since 1994. The better-off residents have started to move out. Meanwhile, some migrants are attracted to the neighbourhood by the abundant job opportunities in the old city centre. It represents a typical degenerating old inner urban neighbourhood. In fact, this neighbourhood is very likely to be redeveloped in the near future.

Yangrendong neighbourhood is located in a historical district of central Guangzhou. This neighbourhood accommodates 1968 households, about 5800 people. There are only 26 households receiving MLSS subsidies: 152

households with laid-off household heads; and more than 400 households with retired household heads. There are also some migrant workers who are not officially registered with the residents committee. Yangrendong is one of the oldest neighbourhoods in Guangzhou. At one stage, it was the commercial centre of the city and home to the city's wealthy businessmen. In the 1950s, all shops and wealthy homes were confiscated and allocated to ordinary residents. Most of the new residents of the gracious homes were workers from nearby SOEs and COEs. Then after the market-oriented reforms of the 1980s and 1990s, commercial districts and wholesale markets reappeared in parts of the neighbourhood and surrounding areas.

Now, about 25 per cent of the ground floor area has been converted to commercial use. These are mainly leased to retailers and wholesalers by the local government landlord. There is very little private investment, however, since residents are not motivated to invest in and maintain their rented houses. There is also a lack of investment from the local government, however, and the physical state of the neighbourhood continues to deteriorate. Many houses are dilapidated and without private kitchens and toilets. Nevertheless, due to its central location, the housing rental price is relatively high, above 900 Yuan per month for a one-bedroom apartment. Property owners are therefore comparatively well off, since they can capitalize on their possessions in the market. This neighbourhood is an example, therefore, of an area of the city in which the property rights structures inherited from the socialist and pre-1949 era are conferring differential advantage to people who started off in the reform period as equally poor. This is clearly the case in urban villages where many villagers have become a conspicuous rentier class. It is not so obvious in old neighbourhoods because it is more difficult to identify the properties still in private ownership – and the proportion of these tends to be much lower than in urban villages.

Zede neighbourhood is located to the north-west of the expressway surrounding central Guangzhou. It accommodates 8349 people, of whom 7677 are permanent urban residents; the rest are migrants. There are only 10 households receiving MLSS subsidy. Strictly speaking, this is not an inner urban neighbourhood. It is part of the affordable housing and resettlement housing projects developed for residents relocated from the inner city of Guangzhou. Since its population is mainly from former dilapidated inner urban neighbourhoods, we selected this neighbourhood based on its population composition. About one third of houses in the Zede neighbourhood are classified as affordable housing, which was sold to mid- to low-income residents at a discounted price. The other two-thirds of houses are resettlement houses for residents affected by inner city redevelopment, which is also owner-occupied housing.

Residents from different parts of the inner city started to move into Zede in 1996. Many of them still retain their *hukou* in the inner city, and have not registered with the local residents' committee. This neighbourhood has a highly mixed population. Since the neighbourhood was developed especially for low- and mid-income households, many residents have a comparatively low socioeconomic profile. A number of them are chronically unemployed, but few receive MLSS subsidy. Compared with old inner urban neighbourhoods, housing quality in this neighbourhood is much better. Subsidized by public investment from the city government, housing prices are also comparatively affordable in this neighbourhood. Nevertheless, local amenities and facilities, such as schools and hospitals, are highly underdeveloped; many residents prefer to send their children to schools in the centre and commute to hospitals in the centre.

Urban Villages

Urban villages are unique among the various patterns of low-cost development found in cities across the world. They are formed by land requisition and give rise to a mixture of landless farmers and an influx of rural migrants. Unlike the old inner neighbourhoods described already, in most urban villages, the majority of residents are rural migrants rather than indigenous villagers. The latter become relatively privileged landlords. Our study included urban villages to be able to understand this fascinating intra-neighbourhood dynamic as well as to be able to compare this kind of low-income neighbourhood with others. More than that, because of our survey design, we are able to gain insights into the poorest of these low-income neighbourhoods. Figure 4.8 shows the 11 urban villages surveyed in our study. There are no official statistics or reports examining these people's lives – hence the importance of this kind of survey. Within neighbourhoods, systematic sampling ensured a sample of indigenous villagers as well as the majority migrants. Building houses on their housing plots and renting them out is the easiest and most commonly adopted living strategy for these landless farmers.

In some villages, the collective economy endures through small township and village enterprises (TVEs) or through a village committee-organized residential or industrial rental business (renting houses, land and workshops). The collective ownership of land in these neighbourhoods therefore provides some security and benefits to villagers. Nevertheless, these are generally only temporary strategies for the collective and for villagers, and are relatively insecure because the city government can easily take away property rights by redeveloping the urban village. Although indigenous villagers are generally better-off, the distribution of fortune among

Nanhe, Xi'an

Tanghusi, Wuhan

Renyi, Xi'an

Tuanjie, Wuhan

Tengzi, Nanjing

Hada, Harbin

Suojie, Nanjing

Hongmiao, Kunming

Figure 4.8   Urban villages surveyed in six Chinese cities

153

Sanyuanli, Guangzhou

Beiting, Guangzhou

Gangtou, Kunming

Figure 4.8 (continued)

them can be rather uneven. Some villagers struggle because they do not have the resources, for example capital and loans, to start a rental business. Others lost their rights to a share of village land in the early stages of economic reforms and now have no landed assets to rent. Since urban villages close to the city centre and villages in the suburbs have often had very different experiences during the reform period, we selected 11 urban villages from a mix of inner and outer locations.

Renyi village is located very close to the southern ancient city gate of Xi'an. It specialized in vegetable cultivation from the 1950s to the early 1980s. Following several stages of land requisition starting in the late 1980s, most farmland has now been converted to urban land, while about 200 *mu* of housing plots remain (15 *mu* = 1 hectare). The compensation for land requisition has varied over the years. In 1988, the village was offered a gross compensation of 80,000 Yuan per *mu*, while in 1993, it was 160,000 Yuan. In 1993, villagers over 16 years old received 27,000 Yuan per person, while under 16-year-olds received 5000 Yuan. Now located very close to the city centre, the value of land that once belonged to Renyi village has increased dramatically. The local state and land lessees have benefited from land value increase of the former farmland but the collective and the displaced peasants have no rights to a share in this. As part of the compensation deal, peasants were offered the right to urban *hukou*, which they had to pay for at a price of 2000 Yuan per person.

Although villagers have officially become urban residents, they have not had access to any social security entitlements to date. A scheme was devised to bring the local state, the collective and the peasants together to purchase social security insurance for the displaced peasants. Under this arrangement, each party would offer one third of the total payment. However, the scheme has been pending for several years because the state has been reluctant to offer its one third and the collective has claimed a lack of resources. Many villagers say they would like to pay their share. After land requisition, just 20 jobs were made available in a variety of small SOEs. Most of these have now become bankrupt and the 20 villagers have been laid off. About 80 per cent of the villagers of working age have not managed to find a job. The main reasons cited by them and by officials are low skills, low educational attainment and a lack of discipline. There were and are no TVEs in the village and there is therefore no collective enterprise to support villagers. The major income source for most villagers has become the rent from their houses.

Nanhe village is located to the west of the outer ring road of Xi'an. There are more than 380 households, about 1220 people in the village. The village also accommodates more than 2000 migrants from Sichuan province, Zhejiang province, and nearby townships and villages. During the industrialization period of the 1950s and 1960s, several large-scale state-owned textile factories were built in the surrounding areas. Some villagers stopped farming and made a living by running family spinning businesses. After two stages of land requisition from 1998 to 2000, and from 2003 to 2006, the farmland in Nanhe village has shrunk from 1000 *mu* to 400 *mu*. Now, 70 per cent of villagers have lost their farmland. The compensation standard was set at 30 000 Yuan per *mu* to the collective ownership, that is to the village. On average, every villager received a cash compensation of 5000–10 000 Yuan. After losing their farmland, most villagers did not manage to find a job. Some still run spinning businesses; others have a succession of temporary jobs, and some have migrated to other places to work. For most villagers, their major income source is house rental.

There was a collectively owned small textile TVE in the village but it was closed down not long after it started, due to competition from surrounding large-scale textile factories. In the early days of liberalization, there was little to guide collective entrepreneurs in succeeding in a competitive environment. The small family spinning businesses have had a difficult time since 2003. In 1997, the village collective developed a residential project on their farmland. However, since the title deeds of these houses are still not available, these houses were sold at a relatively low price of 800–1000 Yuan per square metre. From this project villagers receive a dividend of 200 Yuan per year. The rest of the income is used to improve infrastructure in the village. Other income sources are from renting land. In total, villagers receive 700–1000 Yuan per year from the collective, plus rental income from housing they have developed on their village housing plot. This amounts to around 200–400 Yuan per room monthly. In general, most villagers live well above the poverty line. However, the situation varies from family to family. Those who cannot afford to build houses for rent, still struggle for basis living necessities, while those who manage to build houses for rent in the best locations, have made great fortunes. What worries villagers the most is the lack of social security and health care. Villagers are not covered by any social security or health care scheme. Should the remaining (housing) land in the village be requisitioned, villagers' livelihoods will be seriously threatened.

Tuanjie village is located very close to a commercial and business centre of Wuchang district in Wuhan. It accommodates more than 4900 households, about 19,600 people. Among these households, only about 1200 households are indigenous villagers, the other 4800 households being migrant workers. There are no MLSS recipients in the village. Tuanjie village experienced three stages of land requisition, which took place in 1975, 1982 and 2006. During the first two phases, only one person in each household was offered a job and urban *hukou* as compensation. In the third phase, villagers were offered cash compensation. However, they had not been paid by the time we visited the village in 2007.

In 2005, the villagers' committee established a shareholding company and offered shares of stock to each remaining villager according to their age. Those who were offered employment opportunities in the earlier periods of urban development were not eligible for shares. Ironically, their move from rural to urban *hukou* and from farmer to urban worker meant that they are no longer considered privileged members of the community. For senior members of the village, the value of their shares of stock has risen from 300,000 to 700,000 Yuan. After the establishment of the shareholding company, villagers were expected to take responsibility for their own social security insurance. Most villagers have built multi-storey houses (up to eight floors) on their housing plots and rent to migrant workers. Tuanjie village has developed into an extremely high density settlement, comparable to urban villages in Guangzhou and Shenzhen. One village household could have up to 40 tenants. The monthly rent for one room in the village ranges from 100 Yuan to 350 Yuan. Therefore the income from housing rental is significant, and is sufficient to give villagers access to commodity housing elsewhere in the city. In this village, landless peasants are therefore relatively well off. Urban poverty only exists among the migrant households.

Tanghusi village is situated in a newly developed urban area in Hankou district, Wuhan. It accommodates 2110 indigenous households, about 3560 villagers. Located in a new district offering an abundance of job opportunities in the logistics and building industries, this village has attracted more than 10 000 migrant workers renting houses from local villagers. As in Tuanjie village, the collective has been turned into a shareholding company running a small-scale TVE and workshop rental business. All villagers above 16 years old are eligible for shares of stock, which offer each villager an average annual dividend of 2000 Yuan. In addition, the village collective has purchased a comprehensive social security insurance package for each villager. Some villagers are employed by the TVE too. Most villagers also have their own rental businesses, which generate a substantial income. They are therefore relatively better off. Only three households in the village are MLSS recipients, who received urban *hukou* at an early stage of redevelopment but became redundant. Besides the standard subsidy from local government, these MLSS recipients also receive an extra subsidy of 456 Yuan every three months from the village collective. Urban poverty mainly exists among migrant workers who are renting houses in the village.

Tengzi village is on the periphery of Nanjing, where Zhongyangmen coach station, railway station and a major logistic centre of Nanjing are located. It accommodates more than 880 households, about 2000 people. Tengzi has a highly mixed population combining SOE workers, indigenous villagers and migrant workers. About 600 people are workers from the nearby Nanjing Automobile Manufacturing Group, and about 1400 are indigenous villagers. Besides these, there are about 20,000 rural migrants crowded into this small village. In the early 1990s, the city government requisitioned a great proportion of farmland from the village and established the Nanjing Automobile Manufacturing Group. To accommodate workers in the automobile factory, the employers purchased housing plots from the village and constructed houses for their employees. As compensation to the village, more than 200 indigenous villagers were employed by the Nanjing Automobile Manufacturing Group and were offered urban *hukou*. About 100 villagers were also offered jobs in surrounding small-scale SOEs and COEs. Most of them have now been laid off after the SOE and COE reform of the late 1990s. The remaining villagers were offered a lump sum cash compensation of 10 000 to 20 000 Yuan.

At present, most villagers have built multi-storey houses for rent and have become petty landlords. The highly accessible location has attracted thousands of rural migrants into the village. On average, each indigenous household has built housing equivalent to 500 square metres for rent. The biggest renter in the village built over 1000 square metres of housing and rents to 72 tenants. The average rental income for each indigenous household exceeds 7000 Yuan per month; about three times higher than the average income of Nanjing households. The highest rental income for an indigenous villager is 20 000 Yuan per month. However, the quality of these massive 'village' houses is extremely low. More than 30 tenants typically have to share a bathroom. The infrastructure of the rapidly developed village is extremely poor. The village collective has established a shareholding company that runs a car wash centre and a small transportation company. Only a few villagers – those with high influence and access to capital – have shares of stock, and are offered a considerable dividend. The other villagers are only offered an annual dividend of 500 Yuan, which is far less than their rental income. This two-tier ownership model reflects the fact that the land is collectively owned, but the capital for the businesses is provided by a few. It is a kind of collective-private-partnership and an example of the complex property rights arrangements that have emerged in urban villages. Social security insurance is purchased by villagers themselves on a voluntary basis. Housing rental is the major income source for most villagers. Reaping the profit from their rental businesses, most villagers are not willing to find other jobs. The migrants who provide this income to the villagers bid against each other for a limited number of homes, and as a result, force the price up and value for money down, living in very small, crowded and unhealthy spaces. They will bid a price for almost any spaces that the petty developer-rentier villagers can produce. The poorer quality the living space, the lower they have to bid and the more they have to spend on other expenditures such as remittances to their family and children's education.

Suojie village is located at the west of Nanjing city, in the new development area known as *hexi* (the western area of the river Qinghua). There are 3574 indigenous villagers and more than 8000 migrant workers in the village. In 1985, part of the village farmland was taken away by the city government in the name of infrastructure construction. In 1995, all villagers were offered urban *hukou* and officially became urban residents. Since most of the farmland requisitioned by the city government was not fully developed until 2000, villagers continued their vegetable cultivation on the vacant land. They remained as peasants but with urban titles; an unusual phenomenon. In 2000, the Nanjing Hexi New Town project was rapidly built and the villagers of Suojie village were finally transformed into real urban residents. After land requisition, only 175 villagers were offered jobs by the city government. The rest were offered a lump sum cash compensation of 5000 Yuan per person on average. The cash compensation was soon used up and villagers had to rely on their own wits for survival. Again, the easiest way was to build housing and rent it to migrant workers. The influx of rural migrants created great opportunities for rental and related commercial business. Driven by the chance of high profits, villagers built multi-storey houses, despite the rules and regulations against dense development. The village has been turned into an extremely high density residential block with very poor infrastructure and facilities. Without a drainage system, street lamps and very few public toilets, the village has become an unruly and filthy place. The local crime rate is high and it is known as a lawless place and a centre for prostitution.

Nevertheless, migrants are still willing to live in such conditions and housing rental has become the only income source for about 80 per cent of villagers. The highest rental income per villager exceeds 10000 Yuan per month. But not all villagers have been able to capitalize on their property rights on their housing plots. About 20 households in the village are MLSS recipients and few villagers or migrant workers are covered by social security insurance schemes. The local primary school was run by the village collective and has now become a migrant school mainly serving the children of migrant workers. Most indigenous villagers prefer to send their children to a public school nearby, which is more expensive but of better quality. There are plenty of convenience stores in the neighbourhood, mostly run by migrants from the village, but some indigenous villagers prefer to shop in bigger supermarkets in surrounding areas. It is quite obvious that a two-tier society is emerging in the village, where indigenous villagers are developing a set of preferences and patterns of behaviour that set them apart as landlords and better-off neighbours within this mixed community.

Hada village accommodates 15 000 people, of whom only 4000 are original villagers and 11 000 are migrants. In the 1950s, there were fewer than 100 residents in this suburban village of Harbin. In the 1990s, the population expanded to 3000. After two rounds of land requisitions in 1987 and in 1994, the farmland of the village shrank from 700 *mu* to less than 200 *mu*. About four-fifths of the villagers lost their farmland in that period and with it their major source of income. The total cash compensation offered to villagers was 30 000 Yuan per person and there were no alternative jobs offered. There is no TVE or any other form of collective economy in the village, which means villagers have to find their own way to survive in the urban economy. After land requisition, villagers were allowed to convert to urban *hukou* after going through various procedures, including paying an administration charge.

Now, only 800 villagers have become official urban residents with an urban *hukou*. A wholesale fruit market was constructed on some of the land that used to belong to the Hada village. This wholesale market has attracted many migrant workers, who have then sought inexpensive rental housing in the village. Similar to other urban villages, many villagers make a living by constructing houses and renting it to migrant workers. Some of the villagers have migrated to other cities to look for job opportunities, and have become migrant workers themselves. A small population of villagers, whose farmland was not invaded by the urban sprawl, still make a living by planting vegetables. This village thus presents a very mixed landscape combining urban and rural features. In most parts of the village, unplanned low-quality two-storey houses litter the narrow alleys. At the fringe of the village, there are agricultural fields planted with vegetables. This is not untypical in some fringe urban villages. The infrastructure in the village is comparatively poor, even for an urban village, with muddy and narrow streets, no drainage system or firebreaks. Compared with urban villages in the coastal cities that have highly developed rental businesses and high-rise informal houses, this urban village still retains the characteristics of a rural settlement.

Hongmiao village is located in the inner city of Kunming. It accommodates more than 500 indigenous villagers and more than 5500 migrants. Since 1986, its farmland has been requisitioned by the city government in several stages. By the early 1990s, all farmland had been taken away. Villagers were offered two compensation options: a lump sum cash compensation of 8000 Yuan per person or a job opportunity in a nearby SOE. Those who chose to be workers have now mostly been laid off after SOEs reforms. In 1992, a shareholding company was established to manage the rental businesses of the village. Indigenous villagers are offered two types of stock share. The first is calculated based on the length of service in the village before land requisition. As shareholders, villagers can get a maximum annual dividend of 2015 Yuan from this source. The second type is based on optional investment. Every villager is allowed to purchase shares of stock of no more than 30 000 Yuan. The first type of stock share is offered to every villager for free, while the second type is purchased on a voluntary basis.

In addition to the dividend from these collective entities, most villagers have built their own houses for rent. Each household has at least one house of four to six storeys. Due to the village's central location, most houses have been rented out at the relatively high price of 15 Yuan per square metre per month.

Having two income sources – from house rental and from dividends – most indigenous villagers are relatively well off. They are also covered by a subsidized health care insurance scheme in which villagers pay four-fifths of the total cost, while the other fifth is covered jointly by the government and the collective. Other kinds of social security insurance, such as pension insurance, are purchased by individual villagers themselves. Migrant workers in the village mainly work in the building industry and the informal sector, or run small family businesses. Their income varies substantially. Some are quite well off, while others are still struggling for their basic living necessities.

Gangtou village is located in the periphery of Kunming city. It accommodates more than 1000 indigenous households, about 3375 villagers. The number of migrant tenants varies at different periods of the year. Most of the time, there are about 3000 migrants renting houses from the villagers. These migrants mostly work as street vendors, running small family businesses, or working in the building industry of Kunming. At periods of high employment opportunities, for example when there have been large-scale construction projects nearby, the numbers of migrants can reach 8000. Between 1992 and 2001, the village farmland was requisitioned by the city government in a piecemeal manner and from 2002, urban construction has invaded this suburban village. Like many other suburban urban villages, Gangtou started off specializing in vegetable cultivation and has now been fully transformed into a dense urban neighbourhood, with all villagers receiving urban *hukou*. In 1992 and 1993, some villagers affected by land requisition were offered jobs as gardeners and guards but in later stages of requisition such job offers had dried up.

By the time we visited the village, about 70 per cent of villagers were chronically unemployed. A few were employed by the Kunming Cigarette and Tobacco Manufactory, which was developed on some of the land that used to belong to the village. Land requisition compensation was based on the area of farmland and varied in different periods. On average, every household received a total compensation sum of between 100 000 and 300 000 Yuan.

Most villagers have now built multi-storey houses for rent. However, due to the relatively peripheral location, only about 30 per cent of these houses are permanently rented. Compared with other places, the rent is comparatively low too. The village collective has also built several warehouses and rented them to the Kunming Cigarette and Tobacco Manufactory. The income was used to pay the start-up costs for a comprehensive social security insurance package for each villager, on the understanding that villagers would then pay subsequent premiums themselves. Many villagers have now left the insurance scheme, which seems to have been ill-designed. In general, the villagers of Gangtou village are better off, compared with their situation before land requisition. However, their future is uncertain, especially considering the prospect of their cash compensation being used up and with no social security insurance cover.

Sanyuanli village is one of the oldest urban villages in Guangzhou. It is situated at the northern fringe of central Guangzhou. This is a relatively large village accommodating 8985 registered local residents, and more than 20 000 migrant workers. Since the 1980s, Sanyuanli village has been gradually urbanized, with villagers starting to leave their farmland and becoming petty landlords. After more than 20 years, it has now become one of the biggest urban villages in the city. Five to six-storey houses were built to excess on any available land in the village. In total, there are 9581 houses/rooms available for rent in the village. The total housing floor area in the village is about 1 600 700 square metres, of which more than 600 000 square metres are for rent, while the total land area of the village is only 3 558 000 square metres. Land and housing rental has become the major income source for the village collective and individual villagers. Now, fewer than 600 villagers are employed. The others rely purely on rental income. The village collective has been converted into a shareholding company that runs land and housing rental businesses. All indigenous villagers were offered shares of stock according to their length of service before land requisition. By the end of 2006, the capital assets of the village shareholding company were 780 million Yuan, and the total income was 160 million Yuan. On average, the annual income of indigenous villagers was about 48 000 Yuan in 2006, which included a dividend of 39 000 Yuan from the village collective, and individual housing rent of about 9000 Yuan. Their income is much higher than the average for Guangzhou. With a subsidy from the village collective, about 30 per cent of indigenous villagers have participated in pension insurance and health care insurance schemes. For those villagers who are not covered by social security schemes, they are offered a monthly health care subsidy by the village of up to 130 Yuan. Elderly villagers who are not covered by a pension insurance scheme are also offered a monthly pension of 900 Yuan from the village collective. However, these benefits are only for indigenous villagers. The majority of residents in the village are migrant workers. Most of them work in the informal sector or only have temporary jobs and are not protected by any form of social security. Many of them struggle to survive in the urban economy.

Beiting village is situated on a small island called Xiaoguwei Island in the southern suburbs of Guangzhou. It accommodates 1231 indigenous households, about 4070 people, and 1656 migrant workers who are registered with the residents' committee. There are also several hundred migrants who are not officially registered, who are more mobile and stay temporarily. Officially they should all register but in practice those who move frequently may not register before they settle down. In 2003, Guangzhou University Town invaded Xiaoguwei Island. Beiting and three other villages were spared but all other villages on the island were removed, and villagers were relocated to other places. Meanwhile, all the farmland of the remaining four villages was taken away by the Guangzhou University Town development. Beiting thus became an urban village, and villagers were urbanized with an urban *hukou*. Every villager over 16 years old was offered a lump sum cash compensation of 20 000 Yuan. Only a few villagers were offered job opportunities in the Guangzhou University Town project.

By the time we visited the village, about 90 per cent of villagers were chronically unemployed after losing their farmland. But all villagers had been offered a comprehensive social security insurance package by the city government. About 10 households receive the MLSS subsidy. As with all other urban villages, housing rental became the major income source for the landless peasants. However, unlike Sanyuanli village where the location is much better and the rental business is highly developed, Beiting village only attracts a small number of migrant tenants and the number of migrants fluctuates in different periods, depending on the job opportunities available in surrounding areas. Most houses built by villagers are low-rise two to three-storey constructions and the monthly rental is only 80 Yuan per room, which is much lower than the price in many other urban villages in Guangzhou. There is no collective enterprise in the village and villagers are clearly worse off compared with those in Sanyuanli village.

Summary

Overall, the 25 surveyed neighbourhoods represent three types of poor neighbourhood, and show the general profile of poor urban neighbourhoods in China. Even within the same type of neighbourhood, however, each area has different dynamics of impoverishment, suffers from a different level of poverty, and hence creates its own particular social and physical landscape. The villages' fortunes are related to a number of intrinsic and extrinsic factors. These include population composition, especially the percentage of marginal groups including laid-off/unemployed and migrant workers; the location of the neighbourhood within the city; the location and level of economic development of the city; the composition of housing tenure, especially the proportion of public housing and privately owned housing; employment and socioeconomic status of residents; the productivity and economic efficiency of the remaining or former enterprises in the case of workers' village; the time period at which redevelopment occurred; and the efficiency of organization within the village.

The combination of these different factors contributes to the formation of different kinds of poor urban neighbourhood, with different kinds of and degrees of poverty problems. For the degenerated workers' village, the dynamics, degree and landscape of poverty are mainly shaped by the scale, ranking, economic performance, and welfare policy of the (former) state-owned enterprise. For old inner urban neighbourhoods, population composition and housing tenure composition have shaped the neighbourhoods' misfortunes, being determined by the development history, location, economic development of the city, degree of marginalization during the socialist era and the filtering dynamics during the market era. For urban villages, location within the city is particularly important since these areas are the major source of low-income housing for migrant labour. Other important factors determining the dynamics, degree and landscape of urban village poverty also include policies governing the transitional property rights of landless farmers, and the capital and skills of migrants and landless farmers. In all, the 25 neighbourhoods we have surveyed tell a consistent story, but one that is differentiated in subtle ways. The causes of poverty in each are all to do with the transition between administrative and market systems of resource allocation, but this transition plays out in very different ways in different parts of the city and among different groups.

THE 'LITTLE MARKET': TRANSITION FROM INDUSTRIAL DISTRICT TO IMPOVERISHED NEIGHBOURHOOD

To explore the formation of poor neighbourhoods further, we examine the transformation of one of Nanjing's suburban industrial districts into a poor neighbourhood which has come to be known as the 'Little Market'. The notion of a poverty of transition is developed to show how such a transformation occurs in the aftermath of state-led industrialization. The case illustrates the argument we have already posited: that neighbourhood impoverishment results from a set of interacting institutional changes associated with (a) transition from the socialist era; and (b) market deepening.

The Little Market is located outside Zhongyangmen (the 'central gate' of the city wall) and on the trunk road leading to the major industrial areas of Nanjing (see Figure 4.5). It belongs to Xiaguan District, the major industrial district of Nanjing. The community is governed by a Street Office, which can be regarded as an administrative area, the functions of which are evolving under transitional dynamics (Whyte and Parish, 1984; Zhang, 2003). Strictly speaking, the street office is not a government in itself but rather the agency of the district government. Since the consolidation of local governments in China, the street office has literally become the lowest level of government, responsible for implementing various policies designated by the district and city governments. Under the so-called new mode of societal provision of welfare, welfare provision has been transferred from work units to the street office. This has meant that Street Offices have grown in size, status and budget. They are embryonic modern local governments that have very rapidly evolved from less formal structures within the socialist administrative hierarchy. In that system, they were residual authorities, taking responsibility for infrastructure and population falling between work-unit territory and welfare and employment jurisdiction.

As a sub-district located adjacent to the built-up area before the 1950s, the Little Market has a mixture of different land uses. In total, there were 50 254 residents in 2003. The sub-district has different types of residential area: work-unit compounds, self-built housing and housing managed by the municipal government. Its low status is evident from the low levels of educational attainment and a relatively high proportion of minimum living standard (MLSS) recipients. In the 2000 population census, 34.8 per cent of its population over 6 years old had only received middle school education. Only 3.9 per cent of residents in the Little Market have university degrees, while the respective figures for two other central districts, Gulou and Xuanwu, are as high as 17.4 per cent and 14.7 per cent. Its low status is attributable to its status as an industrial district of Nanjing.

Because MLSS is implemented city-wide using a uniform criterion, the rate of MLSS can be used to show the overall poverty situation (for the city-wide poverty distribution see Table 4.1). In 2003, there were 541 MLSS households and 1247 MLSS recipients in the Little Market, giving a rate of 2.48 per cent, much higher than the respective figures in Xuanwu (1.07 per cent) and Gulou (1.18 per cent). The poorest neighbourhood in the Little Market is Wubaicun, a residents' committee area (equivalent to the neighbourhood). According to the population census in 2000, there were 2311 households in Wubaicun, with a total population of 6259. In 2003, the total number of households increased to 2433. Among them, there were 1516 registered households (with 3850 residents), 863 non-registered long-term households (with a population of 2710) and 154 households temporarily without registration (with a total population of 308). The Wubaicun neighbourhood has 91 MLSS households, with 297 individuals in receipt. As the MLSS is only applicable to registered households, the ratio of MLSS households to registered households can be calculated. The figure is 6.0 per cent, which is almost twice that of the Little Market as a whole. The ratio of MLSS recipients to registered population is 7.7 per cent, slightly higher than the figure measured by households.

One interesting feature of this and all the other poor Chinese neighbourhoods we have studied, is that the rate of poverty is rather low, compared to that of high-poverty areas in the United States. This is partially due to the stringent criteria for MLSS entitlement, which effectively renders it a safety net to prevent absolute poverty, destitution and starvation (see earlier discussion in Chapter 1). However, the figure was obtained after the implementation of the principle of *yingbao jinbao* ('granting a MLSS entitlement to all those who should be supported', which has led to the dramatic expansion of MLSS). It is also partly due to the absence of rural migrants in MLSS statistics. Wubaicun, for example, is a laid-off workers' village which is also an area with a concentrated migrant population. Migrants account for 44 per cent of the total population, and almost half of the population in Wubaicun is not registered. However, according to our fieldwork, there is no reason to believe that the poverty ratio among the migrant population should be significantly higher than that of permanent residents, although the living and working conditions for the migrants are much tougher (see the discussion later). Counting the poverty rate of migrants and local residents together, it is still unlikely the figure would exceed the 40 per cent threshold for the 'high poverty area' in the US. We understand that MLSS is a measurement of absolute poverty, and therefore measured in relative terms, the poverty rate in this neighbourhood could be higher.

In sum, the poorest neighbourhood in the Little Market cannot be characterized as a concentrated 'underclass' area. This is because many residents are still working, and they are not dependent upon state welfare provision. In fact, in the whole city of Nanjing, there is no such thing as a 'ghetto' that is comparable with the 'high-poverty area' in the US. This is also reflected in security, which is generally good. The Little Market has no 'no-go areas'. The community represents a microcosm of industrial suburbs in the former socialist era.

The Survey

Data collection for this study of the Little Market was carried out through a questionnaire survey in July 2003 by means of face-to-face interviews, which were preceded by fieldwork in 2002. We also conducted intense fieldwork in 2004 in the Little Market. The sampling method was based on stratified sampling for three groups: permanent urban households (without MLSS status), MLSS households and rural migrants. Within each group, the sample was proportional to the total target population in the small area. For permanent households, 5 residents' committee areas (neighbourhoods) out of 13 were randomly selected. From each neighbourhood, we randomly selected one major urban road and one minor road. The number of addresses was then counted and the sample interval calculated based on the sample quota and the total number of addresses. Sampling was then based on equal intervals. For residential compounds or multiple households at the same address, the first household on the left after the entrance was selected. For a failed sample, the next address was chosen, while other sampling addresses were kept the same. MLSS households were randomly selected from the name list, covering 13 residents' committee areas. The unit of sample was the household, because MLSS operates on a household basis. The size of the sample was distributed in proportion to the total number of MLSS households in each neighbourhood.

At the time of sampling in 2003, in total, the Little Market had 1247 MLSS recipients and 541 MLSS households; the size of the sample was aimed at 10 per cent of MLSS recipients. This is equivalent to the coverage of 24 per cent of MLSS households. As for migrants, they were randomly selected from the name list maintained by the local street office. It is generally known that migrant enumeration is difficult and such a list is often incomplete and only includes more established migrants. However, partly because this is a well-organized industrial area, the management of migrants is relatively good, with neighbourhood cadres maintaining close contact with the migrants inside the neighbourhood. Unlike neighbourhoods that have grown around urban villages, the Little Market has relatively few farmers' houses rented out to migrants (because the Little Market was a periphery rural village). There is also an economic reason why it was possible to identify migrants: the neighbourhood office often provides temporary housing to migrants in order to earn rent for the local office. We were therefore able to use this list as a sampling frame.

The sampling was undertaken in the same way as the sampling of MLSS households.

In total, 303 valid questionnaires were conducted, providing data that can be generalized to the Little Market Street Office.

Deindustrialization and the Deteriorating Margin

The Little Market is a peripheral community in the inner suburbs of Nanjing. The community serves an industrial area, the major industrial area in the north of Nanjing. Because of state-led industrialization in the 1950s, the area has a concentration of manufacturing workers. About 81 per cent of permanent non-poor households work or have worked (if not currently working) in SOEs and collectively owned enterprises (COEs). Only 8 per cent work in the private sector and another 8 per cent are self-employed as 'individual workers' (*getihu*). The concentration of SOE employees is higher than in other places in Nanjing. In the city of Nanjing, there are 562400 employees in the state-owned sector, 78200 in the collectively owned sector, 417000 in the private sector and 173300 individual workers, giving percentages for SOEs and COEs, the private sector and the self-employed respectively of 52.0 per cent, 33.8 per cent and 14.1 per cent in 2002 (Nanjing Statistical Bureau, 2003). Figure 4.9 shows the landscape of the industrial district of the Little Market. Workers' apartment buildings are in poor conditions. Over time, low quality housing has been passed to poor households in the workplaces.

The local economy of the Little Market is still affected by this historical legacy and the new private sector is underdeveloped. The dominant source of employment for local residents is the state-owned sector. Because of the concentration of industrial workers, deindustrialization has had a particularly detrimental effect on this community. The poverty groups mainly comprise laid-off workers and the unemployed population.

The concentration of poverty in the Little Market is caused by deterioration at the margin. That is, industrial workers and those who were at the margins of the local economy were the first to suffer from a deterioration in the job market and then to begin to slip into the poverty trap. To establish the relationship between the poverty group and the state sector, the survey asks whether the head of the household (defined as the main income provider) has ever worked in the state sector (for example, government institutions and SOEs). Of permanent non-poor households, about 31 per cent have never worked in the state sector. However, 54.1 per cent of MLSS recipients have never entered the state system. This difference suggests that almost half of MLSS recipients were already at the margin in the era of state-led industrialization. In other words, marginal groups (such as those who worked in small enterprises, COEs, the self-employed and the informal sector) are vulnerable during the transition because their employment is more likely to be subject to bankruptcy than in the core SOEs. The decline in state-sector employment has triggered a series of economic changes in the low-income community and has made those living at the margin more vulnerable. Economic hardship in the era of state socialism is transformed into urban poverty in the market-oriented economy. The deteriorating margin also occurs at lower educational levels. The survey recorded the highest educational attainment of households.

MLSS households share educational attainment similar to that of migrants. Only 9.4 per cent of MLSS households have a family member with a university education, while overall 24 per cent of permanent non-poor households have at least one member who has a university education. The profile of MLSS households is slightly better than that of migrants in that there are 41.4 per cent of MLSS household heads with a high school education while the figure is as low as 25.7 per cent for migrant household heads. This generally reflects the division between urban and rural areas. Unless MLSS households have a skilled worker in the family, they are no more competitive than migrants. About half of MLSS household heads have below middle school education and compete directly with migrant household heads. Another issue for MLSS recipients is whether job training can upgrade their skills so that they can specialize in a different segment of the job market. So far the effort to convert laid-off workers into self-employed or 'private entrepreneurs' has not been successful. Several interviewees mentioned that the re-employment programme did not fit their needs as they had no 'business experience', a poor educational level, limited financial resources and a limited social network.

While it is named the 'Little Market', the community has few commercial activities for permanent non-poor households. Only 8.2 per cent of residents worked in the commercial and trade sector. Most employment for permanent residents comes from manufacturing industries, accounting for 76.5 per cent. The percentage of 'higher' tertiary sectors such as finance, insurance and real estate, or cultural and educational sectors, is extremely low, accounting for only 3.1 per cent of permanent non-poor residents. For MLSS recipients, the percentage working in manufacturing industries is 47.9, much lower than the figure for permanent non-poor residents. In contrast, the percentage in social service (including domestic helpers) is 35.4, higher than the 7.1 per cent of the permanent non-poor households. However, many migrants use the Little Market as a cheap location from which to commute to urban markets nearby. Two large urban markets operate on the premises of previous warehouses. About 95

(a)

(b)

Figure 4.9   Landscape of worker's housing in the Little Market: (a) shared corridors, (b) apartment buildings

per cent of migrants work for the trade and catering sector and the social service sector.

To sum up, the lower occupational profile of poor households suggests that they are vulnerable during economic restructuring. When manufacturing jobs disappeared, residents had to shift to low-level services such as trade and catering and the informal sector. However, these sectors have been filled up by migrants, who are more tolerant of hard working and living environments. Poor urban residents are constrained by low educational attainment and have no competitive advantages over the migrants.

The Changing Labour Market: The Influx of Rural Migrants as the Working Poor

Has the influx of rural migrants contributed to poverty generation in this low-income community? To address this question, households were first asked to evaluate their living standards and then the ratio of food expenditure to total expenditure and income was used to verify the result. Among permanent non-poor households, about 23 per cent evaluated themselves as poor. This on the one hand indicates the limited coverage of MLSS, while on the other hand it shows the feeling of relative deprivation.

For migrants, a relatively larger proportion, 23 per cent, regard themselves as the 'better-off'. Only 6.8 per cent believe that they belong to the poverty group. Most (about 70 per cent) believe they are in the category of 'adequate' living conditions. Some caution is needed to interpret this. First, migrants generally have a lower expectation than that of permanent urban households. Secondly, migrants tend to compare their current living conditions with their previous position in the countryside. During the interviews, more than once migrants emphasized that 'there was simply no hope and no income at all in the rural area' and that they 'simply don't want to go back'. They think that even working as a rubbish collector in the neighbourhood is better than 'cultivating the land' (interviews, July 2004). Not all migrants are the poorest: they seek economic opportunities in the city and they deliberately live frugally in order to save money for sending back to the family in their home town. Figure 4.10 shows the living conditions of migrant housing in the Little Market.

The fact that a significant proportion of migrants believe their living standard to be adequate does not mean that they are living in comfortable conditions. The higher incomes of migrants compared with the poorest urban residents are due to the active job participation of the former. For example, a migrant family interviewed in Dongjingting has three family members. Both the husband and wife work as rubbish collector-cleaners for the neighbourhood. In the summer, they have to start work before 3

Figure 4.10   Conditions of migrants living in the Little Market

173

am in the morning and work again in the hottest time of the afternoon between 2 and 4 pm. They each receive 400 Yuan per month, giving a total family income of 800 Yuan per month. For this family, the income per capita is 266.7 Yuan per month, higher than the local MLSS line. This example clearly illustrates the harsh conditions accepted by migrants. Migrants who live like this are in fact the self-exploiting working poor.

In order to evaluate actual living conditions, the percentage of food expenditure in the total household expenditure is plotted into histograms for the three social groups (Figure 4.11). For permanent households, the proportion spending over 50 per cent of their income on food expenditure is lower than for the MLSS households. Migrants clearly have a better profile: their average food expenditure is 42.3 per cent, compared with the average percentages of 66.7 per cent for MLSS recipients and 55.7 per cent for permanent households. The standard deviation for migrants' food expenditure is 16.7 per cent, for MLSS households 18.3 per cent and for permanent households 19.1 per cent. Running an ANOVA gener- ates an F-test value of 40.904 with two degrees of freedom, significant at 0.0001, which suggests the mean of the percentage of food expenditure is significantly different across these three groups. This pattern is consistent with their self-evaluated standards, suggesting that migrants are not at all the economically poorest group, despite the discrimination imposed on them. Many migrants are economically active: for the population over 15 years old, job participation is as high as 75 per cent, while ordinary urban households have a rate of only 36.8 per cent. In this low-income community, retirement accounts for 42.8 per cent of the non-working population, a figure typical of industrial districts (see Y.P. Wang, 2004, for comparison). Many workers in this community were recruited in the 1960s and 1970s and are now reaching the age of retirement. In compari- son, laid-off workers plus the unemployed accounted for 66 per cent of the non-working population for MLSS households.

Although the non-poor permanent households have a lower ratio of food expenditure to total expenditure, it is still worth noting that a signifi- cant number of permanent urban households have a very high percentage of food expenditure, some even over 70 per cent. The ratio of 60 per cent can be regarded as the absolute poverty threshold, according to the usual international standard. The distribution is skewed towards the higher end (that is high percentage of food expenditure). Considering that the ques- tionnaire was also conducted among MLSS recipients and ordinary urban households, there is no reason to suggest why ordinary households should exaggerate their food expenditure ratio. The only explanation is that, although there is a high food expenditure ratio for these non-poor urban households, they manage to live on a very tight budget and thus avoid

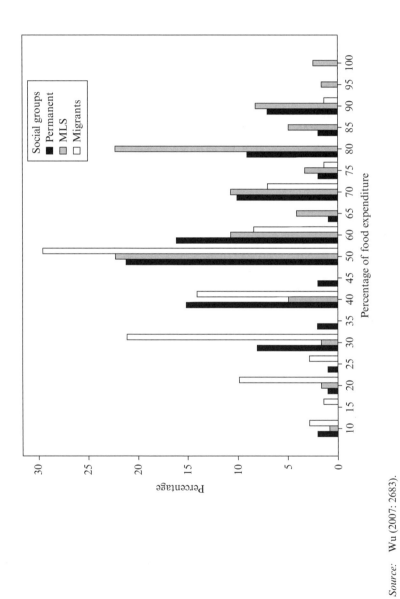

Source: Wu (2007: 2683).

Figure 4.11 Food expenditure as a percentage of total household expenditure in the surveyed Little Market

falling into the poverty group. This is a worrisome indicator, as a large number of urban households in this low-income community are poverty-*vulnerable*, living on the brink of poverty. Because of this near-poverty condition, any slight change in the environment (for example, a fee levied on what was previously a public good, such as medical and health care or schooling) or a crisis incident, such as illness, might easily drive them into the poverty trap.

The distribution of food expenditure clearly suggests that migrants have a relatively better profile of household expenditure. This is consistent with their self-evaluated living standards. To verify this further, income distribution is used. Figure 4.12 shows the distribution of per capita annual incomes among different social groups in the Little Market. The figure clearly reveals that the migrants do not have the worst income profile and indeed may have a better average income than the poorest urban households. The distribution of MLSS recipients is heavily concentrated around 1600 Yuan, probably due to the MLSS qualification criteria. The mean of per capita annual income for permanent households is 6732 Yuan, with a standard deviation of 5514 Yuan. For MLSS households it is 2216, with a standard deviation of 1273 Yuan; and for migrants it is 6680 Yuan, with a standard deviation of 9156 Yuan. This generates an F-test value of 22.386 in ANOVA, significant at 0.0001, which suggests a significant variation of income across the three social groups. The profile of the migrants is very similar to that of permanent urban households. Of course, pure income measurement may underestimate in-kind benefits and hidden subsidies for schooling and other services and facilities enjoyed by permanent residents.

Public Policy: Housing Privatization and the Formation of a Poverty Neighbourhood

The Little Market, as a low-income community, is affected by pervasive housing privatization policies. The housing system in China has experienced a significant shift from the system of collective consumption to the system of homeownership through increasing commodity housing (Huang, 2003; Li, 2000; Lee, 2000; Wang and Murie, 1999). However, the dominant theme in low-income communities is housing privatization rather than commodification, because the suburban industrial area is not a place for commodity housing construction.

Even in this low-income community, the rate of homeownership is as high as 83 per cent for permanent urban households (Table 4.3). For MLSS recipients, this figure is lower, but still about 53 per cent of MLSS households are homeowners. Homeownership provides housing security

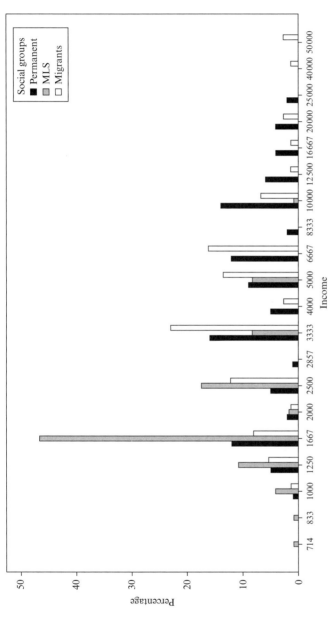

Note: Income is measured as Yuan per capita per year.

Source: Wu (2007: 2684).

Figure 4.12   The income profile of different social groups in the Little Market

*Table 4.3   Housing tenures by different social groups in the Little Market
          (in percentage)*

	Permanent urban households	MLSS households (*dibao hu*)	Migrants
Homeowners	83.0	52.7	4.2
1. Self-constructed or inherited private housing	9.0	19.7	1.4
2. Purchase of sitting public housing	68.0	29.9	1.4
3. Purchase of economic housing	6.0	3.1	0.0
4. Purchase of commodity housing	0.0	0.0	1.4
Rentals	17.0	47.3	95.8
1. Rental of work-unit housing	10.0	20.4	11.0
2. Rental of municipal public housing	3.0	14.2	19.2
3. Rental of private housing	4.0	3.9	64.4
4. Living with relatives	0.0	8.8	1.4

Source: Wu (2007: 2685).

to the urban poor, as they are not affected by the rent increases of private rentals. The relatively low rate of ownership among MLSS recipients compared with all permanent households can probably be partly explained by their lack of access to capital when it came to purchasing property rights over their homes. It is also partly explained by the fact that some of these households would not have been entitled to work-unit housing in the pre-reform era; that is, they were disadvantaged in the housing system prior to housing reform (see Logan et al., 1999, for divisions between households in the pre-reform era; Davis, 2003, for the comparison of working class with managerial; and Unger and Chan, 2004 for redistribution of housing in a state-owned factory). About 20 per cent of MLSS recipients still rent work-unit housing. In fact, the work unit is still an important source of provision for their housing needs. Further privatization or removal of work-unit housing stock from poor residents may have a negative impact on this remaining residual group of public housing occupants. They are not able to purchase their housing stock and are more likely to remain as public housing tenants in the near future.

The dominant source of homeownership has come from the purchase of public housing. About 68 per cent of public housing tenants have bought their housing and thus shifted their housing tenure from rental to home-ownership. For permanent, non-poor households, rental in municipal public housing is as low as 3 per cent, while rental in work-unit housing is

10 per cent. The percentage of rental in work-unit housing is much higher than for rental in municipal public housing, given the fact that most urban households are SOE employees and were entitled to work-unit housing before housing reform. For migrants, the percentage renting municipal public housing is 19 per cent. This is slightly unexpected but is explained by the fact that some neighbourhood organizations take migrants as tenants at a higher rent to help cover the cost of maintenance. Some local residents' committees even develop temporary housing for rural migrants who work for them in the neighbourhood.

None within the sampled urban households has purchased commodity housing. This is low compared with the city of Nanjing as a whole. According to the population census in 2000, commodity housing was owned by 3.4 per cent of the city population. The rate of ownership of 'economic housing' in the Little Market is as low as 6 per cent for ordinary permanent households and 3 per cent for MLSS households. These figures are not too low compared with the city as a whole (2.8 per cent, according to Nanjing Population Census Office, 2002). Housing privatization is mainly achieved through converting public housing tenants to homeowners.

The development of a private housing market, however, creates a space for rural migrants. About 64 per cent of migrants live in private rental housing. This is consistent with the findings from Shanghai and other cities (Wu, 2002; W.P. Wu, 2004; Ma and Xiang, 1998). The homeownership rate for migrants is extremely low, accounting for only 4.2 per cent. Migrants are not allowed to purchase subsidized 'economic housing' (a type of subsidized commodity housing, cheaper because the land leasing fee is waived by the municipality). Neither are they allowed to buy public housing, as they were not public housing tenants. The main reason for the low rate of migrant housing ownership is therefore institutional: migrants cannot access subsidized private housing and are not eligible to purchase public housing. Although the economic profile of migrants is not the lowest, migrants cannot generally afford commodity housing. Moreover, they have a strong cost-saving residential preference (Wu, 2002). Private rental is the only option for most migrants. As we have said before, a constrained housing supply combined with almost infinite demand means relatively high rents for migrants. This structural feature of local housing markets in China can clearly be seen in the rental differences faced by migrants and urban *hukou* holders in the Little Market. Monthly rent paid by migrants is as high as 405.6 Yuan, much higher than the average rent of 35.4 Yuan per month paid by poor urban households living in public housing. The Little Market is a peripheral industrial area and these rents are therefore not as high as those in comparable areas nearer the city centre.

In order to understand residential mobility between the poor and non-poor, the survey investigated residential relocation since 1980. Compared with ordinary urban households, MLSS households are more stable. About 60 per cent of MLSS recipients have not changed their residence in more than two decades, while 63 per cent of permanent residents have moved at least once. This suggests that the poverty in the neighbourhood is stable and spatially fixed in this industrial district.

In sum, the key process of housing change in this low-income community is housing privatization. Very few residents can afford commodity housing. Privatizing public housing insulates tenants from the risk of becoming homeless, thus maintaining some social stability in this community. As an organized industrial area, the local governing authorities do not allow spontaneous construction of private housing. The cost of private rental filters out non-working migrants in this industrial community. Diminishing public housing also means the reduction of cheaper housing sources. Therefore, newcomers may have to find housing from the market, which could be more expensive, given the same quality. This is the case for migrants who fall in the gap between the policy of commodity housing and the policy of public housing privatization. They become the working poor because, although they have a better income than the poorest local residents, the cost of housing is much higher. They are attracted by the relatively cheaper private rental in low-income communities on the periphery.

CONCLUSION

This chapter gives a detailed account of the formation of impoverished neighbourhoods in China using case material and survey data. We started by examining the distribution of the urban poor in selected cities such as Nanjing and Guangzhou, and observed that the poor are concentrated in particular locations. We then conceptualize the development of poor neighbourhoods and their types. We then tested this classification of poor neighbourhoods through a pilot study of three neighbourhoods in the city of Nanjing and then expanded our consideration to a study of 25 neighbourhoods in six cities. This descriptive and fine-grained analysis confirms observations made in the previous chapters of this book and deepens our understanding of the distinctive types of poverty found in different types of poor neighbourhoods. The principal distinction we draw from these narratives is the same as the one we draw from the quantitative analysis of Chapter 3: poor neighbourhoods have emerged as a function of their relation to the particular mode of development in socialist and reform periods.

Finally, we investigated a former industrial area, the Little Market, to study the dynamics of poverty formation at an even finer grain of analysis at the neighbourhood level.

In Chapter 5 we shift our focus back to an aggregated level of analysis. The conclusion offered here is drawn from this chapter's descriptive accounts of a set of very diverse poor neighbourhoods. We argue that the spatiality of new urban poverty is rooted in the specific history of recent urban development in China. Determined by the geography of poverty concentration, three types of poor neighbourhood can be identified. These are dilapidated inner neighbourhoods, degraded workers' villages, and poor urban villages for rural migrants. These neighbourhoods have been developed under specific socioeconomic conditions that were created by the interaction of the legacy of socialist development with the dynamics of market transition. We have described a number of impoverished neighbourhoods to illustrate the problems they are facing. Through these case studies, we can see the complexity of urban poverty: falling into poverty is very much conditioned by particular life history events, particular local policies, and path-dependent events including the allocation of workers to work units and the phasing of land requisition. Therefore poverty risks cannot be generalized into a model of individual demographic and socioeconomic attributes: the neighbourhood context has to be taken in consideration too.

At the neighbourhood level, some trend has been observed. Taking the Little Market industrial area as an example, as an original workers' community, it has now evolved into a mixed poverty neighbourhood of laid-off workers and migrants, with half of its population without the status of local household registration. This case provides a good opportunity to understand how low-income groups are being created in the aftermath of state-led industrialization. This traditional industrial area has been hit hard by economic restructuring and displays a high level of urban poverty. With the decline of state-owned enterprises, industrial workers and those who were at the periphery of the state sector, that is small and quasi-state (collectively owned) sectors, were the first to be driven out of the labour force. This process reveals the hidden marginality that existed under socialism, through which economic hardship in the pre-reform era is converted into a state of deprivation and poverty in the market era.

But the decline of state employment in the context of the fast-growing economy has created a new space for migrant workers, who are successfully converting themselves from peasants to employees in the booming non-state sector. Although they are subject to institutional and social discrimination (Chan, 1996; Solinger, 1999; Knight and Song, 1999), they survive under tough conditions and are becoming active workers in the labour market. They adopt cost-saving tactics, for example by living in poor housing conditions in low-income communities at peripheral locations. The retrenchment of job-based welfare is irrelevant to them as they have never been included in the state system. In fact, they are more likely to benefit from the expansion of informal spaces outside the state and to forge an enclave-like economic space (Xiang, 1999; Ma and Xiang, 1998). The influx of rural workers into poor neighbourhoods squeezes the survival space of the poor, permanent residents, as although both social groups share similar low educational attainment, the migrant workers are more tolerant of hard conditions, and they are numerous.

Different from the retrenchment of the Keynesian welfare state in the West (Mingione, 1996; Musterd and Ostendorf, 1998), social security is operating under an expansionist regime in urban China. Poverty generation thus cannot be simply understood as a retrenchment of the welfare state, because there was no universal 'citizenship' under state socialism (see Szelenyi, 1983 for the situation in Central and Eastern Europe). Rather, the delivery of welfare was organized through state-led industrial establishments. To borrow Polanyi's (1944) notion of the mode of integration, industrial workers were integrated through the mode of economic integration (job participation). Some laid-off workers changed their mode of integration into the state redistributive mode under the MLSS regime. In contrast, migrant workers are increasingly being absorbed into the system through the economic mode, but are denied the redistributive mode. To some extent, the replacement of permanent employment with flexible employment is a process of economizing labour. While the influx of migrants itself does not increase the poverty level, it does stretch the labour market and infrastructure provision. The result of this process is that there is a co-existence of working poor (migrants) and households made poor by redundancy.

The creation of impoverished neighbourhoods is facilitated by the new housing policy ethos. Post-reform housing commodification takes the shape of housing privatization in poor neighbourhoods, because peripherally located industrial areas are not the places to build commodity housing estates to attract the affluent. Large-scale industrialization left a stock of public housing for industrial workers. The policy of privatization has converted public tenants to homeowners. But it also serves to trap them within poor communities, because the value of their assets is so low that they cannot use them as a stepping-stone to the preferred location of commodity housing estates. Neither is there a well-developed market in second-hand privatized properties. And in any case, with strong local ties and social capital built up over decades, many low-income or poor owner-occupiers would have little reason to move. As a result, poor workers' neighbourhoods are very stable, without large-scale outflow. By contrast, old pre-1949 neighbourhoods have seen a significant filtering of population, with the better-off leaving and migrants and intra-urban movers moving in to take advantage of central locations. The changes in urban villages have been a result not so much of filtering as of an increase of low-rent housing, organized by villagers and village committees and joint stock companies.

Housing privatization in workers' villages is so pervasive that even in the low-income community of the Little Market, the homeownership rate is over 80 per cent for non-poor residents and over 50 per cent for MLSS recipients. The available housing stock prevents the emergence of large-scale homelessness in this kind of poor neighbourhood. This is very different from the situation in other developing countries, where the retreat of the public sector or the inability of the local state often results in the spread of extreme housing poverty (UNCHS, 2001).

Different too, is the housing poverty in urban villages. Urban villages, in fact, are the most similar to housing poverty areas in other developing countries. They are distinct, however, in their restricted spatial extent and property rights. As an anachronistic legacy of the collective era, these collectively owned territories within cities allow for the only informal spontaneous market response to the housing demand created by the vast armies of migrant workers. Villagers cannot sell-on their rights to a share in the collectively owned land and these islands in the city therefore become fixed locations of low-income tenants. The housing poverty is different from that in workers' villages. It is the poverty of unregulated, low-cost and overcrowded private construction rather than the poverty of underinvestment in publicly organized construction. This is different again from the housing poverty in pre-1949 neighbourhoods, where buildings and facilities are typically of even poorer quality than in urban villages. Underinvestment has gone on for longer than in workers' villages as have the social processes of filtering by income, rent and social exclusion.

The types of poor household found in these different types of neighbourhood are also quite distinct from each other. In urban villages, migrants predominate. Many do not consider themselves poor and objectively they are less prone to poverty than urban *hukou* holders in the other two types of poor neighbourhood. All but an unlucky few of the indigenous occupants of urban villages tend not to be poor. On the contrary, the capitalization of the property rights they have inherited from the socialist era has made them relatively well off. Very well off in some cases. In pre-1949 neighbourhoods, those unlucky enough to find themselves marginalized by allocation in the socialist era remain trapped. They find it difficult to compete with the migrants who increasingly look at these neighbourhoods as living places from which to gain access to city centre jobs. In workers' villages, a majority of the poor are owner-occupiers. They have inherited their homes from their former (or in fewer cases, current) work units. But they cannot do much with them apart from live at near subsistence levels. Their home ownership keeps them from a worse form of compounded poverty but most cannot afford to make the investments needed to upgrade these very basic and deteriorating properties. And their lifetime experience of depending on work units for welfare support and a job that offered reasonable employment conditions has become an immense barrier to doing what they must to get on: compete with rural migrants. In many ways, this kind of community of urban poor is to be pitied most.

5. Poverty dynamics: property rights perspective

After previous investigation of impoverished neighbourhoods, this chapter further examines the dynamics of urban poverty generation in China from the perspective of property rights. We explain the dynamics through changing property rights and entitlement failures, the insight of which is derived from new institutional economics. Urban poverty is generated through changing institutional arrangements in critical consumption areas (housing, education and health care) and the loss of rights to urban space during land appropriation. We treat property rights as the basis of entitlements and draw seminal insights from the Nobel Prize Laureate Amartya Sen (1981) on food entitlement failure to describe urban poverty as a series of entitlement failures to secure vital input to sustain urban living. We examine the impacts of service commodification on the urban poor and deprivation of land entitlement for landless farmers.

The first section of the chapter provides a brief review of theoretical property rights perspectives. Then we examine entitlement failure in the critical consumption areas of education, housing and health care and the deprivation of land and land-related entitlements. In the two sections following, we firstly examine the property rights issues facing the urban poor in China, and secondly discuss the plight of impoverished landless farmers using case studies of two villages.

ENTITLEMENT FAILURE: PROPERTY RIGHTS PERSPECTIVE TO URBAN POVERTY

The entitlement approach to economics in general and poverty studies in particular was developed by Sen (1981). The basic idea is that people's ability to command food rather than the availability of food per se, is the key to understanding the problems of poverty and starvation. Sen developed his idea through a historical study of famines, in which he noted that mass starvation was often experienced in countries where there was, in the aggregate, enough food to go round. Starvation typically occurs because of a dramatic decline in effective purchasing power, or more precisely, of exchange rates: particularly the exchange value of labour but also of other owned assets including land, domestic and draught animals and other durable property. The entitlement approach thus provides a theoretical account of a person's ability to command commodities – food in particular. Lack of food is viewed as a problem arising from a particular set of relations between the consumers of food and the owners of food. The approach views a famine-struck economy as a network of so-called 'entitlement relations'. Market economies typically include three kinds of entitlement relations: (i) trade-based entitlements; (ii) production or own-labour entitlements; and (iii) inheritance and other transfer entitlements. The concept of exchange entitlement is particularly important because few individuals live a purely subsistence life. Even in the most primitive economies, a person's entitlement to resources can be enhanced by trading as well as by investing labour in production processes that add new value to raw resources.

Sen's framework rests first on the idea of entitlements (or property rights) and second on the notion of the 'exchange entitlement mapping' (so-called *E-mapping*). A household is viewed as owning a bundle of rights (over land, labour, water and other potentially welfare-enhancing resources). The E-mapping is the relation that specifies the set of exchange entitlements effectively owned by a household given (a) its particular ownership bundle and (b) the prevailing 'rates of exchange'. The exchange rates are set by markets, governments and customary practices, and in a famine, they typically move in a direction that disadvantages the poor, the vulnerable and the starving.

A household entitlement set (the set of resources defined by its entitlement-mapping) therefore depends on the legal, political, economic and social characteristics of the society and the household's position within it. It depends on production opportunities, trade possibilities, social security provisions such as unemployment benefits and pensions, taxation liabilities, the prices of labour and other tradable property and the prices of food, production inputs, shelter, health services and other essential consumables (Sen, 1981: 46).

This framework allows a systematic analysis of the hypothesis that a decline in entitlement via a change in entitlement mapping – entitlement failure – can result in starvation and poverty even if there is enough food to go round. Food entitlement of a household may fall catastrophically either because it has produced less food for its own consumption (direct entitlement failure), or because the amount of food it can obtain through trade is reduced through the rate of exchange between buyers and sellers of food (trade entitlement failure) (Sen, 1981: 51). In reality, it is possible for a person to suffer both direct and trade entitlement failure. As famine deepens, draught animals may die, for example, reducing the labour and land productivity of a farm family – a direct entitlement failure. As the purchasing power of households in the region declines with their deepening poverty, the price of saleable assets goes down. A household that could have sold land or a draught animal to raise money for food, finds that the price is too low to cover even meagre quantities of food (the price of which is rising dramatically with its increasing scarcity). Similarly, the wage that could once have been expected from selling labour (as a farm labourer in the fields or a security guard in the town) has dropped because there are fewer people demanding those services. In these ways, the exchange price of owned property falls while the price of food rises, and the exchange mapping changes in a way that pushes households towards starvation.

Sen's entitlement approach is based upon the notion of property rights. It is helpful to elaborate this notion beyond the rather static interpretation in Sen's original formulation. Property rights – entitlements in Sen's terms – are static. In his analysis, a household faces a fixed bundle of entitlements and it is the exchange value of them that changes. Using ideas from the economic theory of property rights (Alchian and Demsetz, 1973) we can improve upon this.

Capitalist societies rely heavily on markets and private property rights to resolve conflicts over the use of scarce resources. Under a market economy, clearly defined property rights – land tenure security in the case of land rights – are generally believed to be an essential precondition for efficient economic outcomes (Coase, 1959). However, property rights are not static endowments: they are themselves dynamically created in relation to scarcity. To capture the variety and complexity of the ownership relationship, it is more appropriate to describe ownership as owning the socially recognized rights to use resources rather than owning resources per se. Demsetz (1967) defines property rights as a 'bundle of rights' or a 'social relation'. Hoebel (1966: 424) also suggests that property is not a thing, but 'a network of social relations that governs the conduct of people with respect to the use and disposition of things'. In saying this, he is equating property with rights, not physical assets. This idea leads to the notion that the rights over a resource can be partitioned among several parties (Alchian and Demsetz, 1973) – creating different properties owned or enjoyed by different agents. In reality, there are many properties of any physical resource, the rights to which can be separated and assigned to different parties. A resource may be owned in part by the state, one or many private individuals or by some kind of collective. This is a useful perspective for analysing poverty since under conditions of scarcity, rights over resources tend to be fragmented. For example, land scarcity in many poor cities drives poor people to exert a right to live on or trade from publicly owned land. The long established squatter neighbourhoods in Mexico City, for example, have, by force, effectively distributed land ownership rights from a single owner to very many. Poor people requiring access to jobs in high density cities induce the sub-division of land and buildings. They bid modest individual rents for very small amounts of space and land, and building owners fragment the rights over their land and buildings to accommodate this demand.

Demsetz developed a dynamic theory of property rights. His hypothesis (1967; 2002) states that property rights will emerge when the social benefits of establishing such rights exceed the social cost. They emerge, either as *de facto* rights protected by individual or group, or as *de jure* rights protected by formal law. The latter tend to follow (and formalize) the former. Property rights have the effect of reducing the cost of competition (conflict) over scarce resources. In poor communities all manner of informal rules emerge to allocate rights over scarce basic-needs resources such as land, water and housing. The scarcer water is, the finer the rules allocating rights to access – by time and quantity rationing, pricing and so on. Property rights are not static, therefore, but shifting. And they shift at many different levels concurrently and with complex interacting effects. Formal land market rules change to reflect increasing pressure on land, at the same time as informal rules adapt to cope with non-market competition or informal market competition on land with unclear property rights. China's urban villages are micro land economies within emerging formal land economies, the former governed by a mix of formal administrative allocation rules and informal practices. Within them, as our studies have shown, poverty is shaped for good or for ill as the changing property rights of farmers have an effect on their entitlement to basic urban goods and services.

While we agree with Alchian and Demsetz's basic proposition that in a society that upholds the rule of private property, property rights will tend to evolve in ways that reduce the overheads of economic and social cooperation, we do not think that this is an even-handed process. Anderson and Hill (2002) make the point that the entrepreneurial efforts of individuals capable of capturing economic benefits from the establishment of property rights are often the instigators of property institution changes. Similarly, Banner (2002) suggests that property rights emerge when powerful oligarchs control both the largest share of resources and the political system, that is the inequality of power and wealth is a premise of property rights formation. This is clearly the case with land reform in China at the present time. It is not the interests of farmer occupants of the suburban villages engulfed by successive waves of urban expansion that have shaped the rules governing that expansion.

We develop this approach to analysing property-right/entitlement failure in order to better understand the poverty risks faced by landless farmers deprived of their rights over land. For example, farmers who cultivated their own food are now required to buy food in the market. However, their skills are such that the best use of their labour is in agriculture production. In the new industrial and commercial environment their labour cannot be traded for the quantity of food and other consumption materials that they need if they are to keep out of poverty. In the case of landless farmers, however, some are in a better position than others with respect to their E-mapping because some are allowed to keep their housing plots. They subsequently develop rental apartments on this land and derive rental income that keeps them out of poverty. Before developing the analysis, we elaborate a set of theoretical propositions from the perspective of property rights. Institutions evolve to reduce the cost of competition over scare resources. For obvious reasons, rural areas on the edge of cities have increased in scarcity and are subject to intense competition from urban uses. Institutions work by assigning property rights to attributes of those resources subject to particular scarcity. Laws have developed over the past two decades to assign rights over contested peri-urban land, specifying particular rights to particular interests – for example, formal legal rights to urban conversion are owned by the state (municipality); farmers have rights to a variety of forms of compensation; in some cases, farmers retain the rights to village housing land; in law, they have a right to benefit from a percentage of the expropriated farmland (not upheld in practice); and so on. Institutions are designed by individuals representing groups with vested interests. In the re-allocation of peri-urban farm and village land in China, these laws principally benefit the state, whose interest is in rapid economic development. Institutions never completely allocate rights, however, which means that some valuable rights will remain in the public domain and subject to competition. Municipalities, village cadres and villagers themselves all attempt to capture value from property rights changes where legal or customary ambiguity (or lack of enforcement) allow this. Property rights changes governing the land once occupied by China's peri-urban villages have the effect of changing resource entitlements among villagers. Changes in the villagers' entitlement-mappings lead to increased vulnerability to food and other forms of poverty. The ability of villagers to capture public domain rights in land – notably the ability to turn village housing land into a rental business – determines the direction of change in their entitlement mappings following land restructuring.

Now to probe the role of property rights changes in poverty generation further, we examine two processes: commodification of consumption in housing, education and health care; and land acquisition in the peri-urban areas.

'THREE MOUNTAINS': ENTITLEMENT FAILURE IN HOUSING, EDUCATION AND HEALTH CARE

Mao Zedong once argued that before the Chinese Communist Party had established its regime, the old China had 'three mountains' that presented insurmountable obstacles to the common people. These were 'feudalism, bureaucrat-capitalism, and imperialism'. The Chinese have a saying that now there are 'new three mountains' that make people poor: education, health care and housing. The capacity to climb these mountains is unequally distributed. The wealth of cities is built upon them and together they elevate society and economy, accommodating and shaping the social infrastructure that makes life more than bearable. They reproduce and improve the human factor of production, releasing indigenous enterprise, innovation, improvement and economic development.

The city in modern China is the motor of growth and it draws its low-cost human inputs from two great reservoirs bequeathed by the centrally planned era: agricultural workers and urban industrial workers. Human capital now flows from the countryside to the cities to subsidize urban-based national enrichment. Although this is, from one point of view, an equalizing and equilibrating process (equalizing the demand for and supply of labour), from another, it is an 'unequalizing' process (wages and life-chances rapidly differentiate because of, for example, institutional, historical, educational and labour quality differences). China's version of the unequal growth problem has four unique twists arising from its recent history of entitlement redistribution. First, its cities contain millions of workers whose expectations of income, housing, education and health security were shaped within the state-organized work units (*danwei*), within which they worked. For many, these were like mini-states (production–consumption clubs), providing access to jobs, housing and necessary public goods and services. *Danwei* management was typically responsive to workers' needs, using its rights to the residual value of the unit's production to earn rent for the entire community. Work units were able to do this because they deducted costs of housing, education and so on along with production costs before returning revenue to higher government authorities. This partly explains the extensive swaths of worker housing built (or commissioned) by work units in the 1980s and 1990s and now occupying the inner cities. The vast population of former *danwei* employees have had removed from them many of the entitlements they enjoyed in the centrally planned era. Their world has changed and most find it very difficult to adapt.

Second, in the late 1990s, the state legislated for widespread redistribution of property rights in assets accumulated by the two types of collective at the heart of the communist economy: work units and village collectives. Here we use Alchian and Demsetz's (1973) and Demsetz's (1967, 2002) distinction between legal property rights and/or *de facto* property rights (exerted rights to derive benefit from a resource) either as sole consumer or as a joint consumer within a collective consumption arrangement. This redistribution has been driven by a policy to commodify the housing sector and by the privatization of village collectives. The majority of urban workers have received title deeds to their apartments, and villagers received collective title to their fields and *de facto* private title to the plots on which their houses stood. The housing plots of farmers are privately 'owned' under a complex administrative law that gives them what is effectively a 30-year lease allocated by the village collective. This is different from the land for urban housing and this legal development strengthened the ownership of farmers' housing land plots.

Third, unlike rural migrants in other developing countries, Chinese peasants are legally distinguished from urban workers by residence entitlement, defined by household registration (*hukou*). Urban residency gives rights to important scarce public goods within the city, including education, and puts migrants and competitor urban workers on an uneven footing. Urban *hukou* is still intact as an institution. The distinction in rights between official and unofficial urban residents is changing, however, both in response to changes in laws (for example a recent law that allows migrant workers greater access to municipal schools) and because of the private sector alternatives to municipal services – which are available to all residents who can afford them.

Fourth, in China, the state (municipal government) owns the freehold rights to all urban land. This has a consequence for the spontaneous organization of low-income housing and services, including informal schools and clinics. The municipality can use its land to build low-income housing. Or it can allocate land for low-income commodity housing. It could, in principle, allocate land for sites-and-services style housing projects. However, since land sales have comprised a significant part of municipal revenue from the time of the 1990s land reforms and since the performance of urban governors and their managers has been measured against local growth targets, municipalities have had few incentives to pursue such options. In the 1990s land sales constituted between 30 and 70 per cent of local revenue; from 2001 to 2003, land revenue amounted to 910 billion Yuan, accounting for 35 per cent of local revenue; and in 2004, land sales were valued at 589 billion Yuan, accounting for 47 per cent of local revenue (*21st Century Economic Herald*, 2 September 2006; see Wu et al., 2007 for the land system). This means that there is a high opportunity cost to providing public rental or subsidized commodity housing or leaving urban villages as islands of spontaneous housing. It is only very recently that a new (but numerically insignificant) wave of low-cost housing has started to emerge – under a revised set of municipal performance targets.

The municipal government's ownership of land also means that it can control the growth of spontaneous low-income housing more effectively than the governments of most other countries during similar phases of urbanization and economic growth and this has a major impact on the manifestation of urban poverty in China.

The story of contemporary Chinese urban poverty has therefore to be told with explicit reference to property rights. The distribution of property rights is now widely recognized as being a crucial factor in the pace and sustainability of national economic development. The same is true of the urban development that drives national growth. In many ways, the distribution of rights to land and housing is a fundamental influence on a household's poverty experience. From rights over land and buildings are derived productive entitlements (space for agriculture and petty industry), and exchange entitlements (through asset alienation, property-based income and capital borrowing). However, the distribution of property rights to the three mountains: housing, education and health and to the jobs that convert labour entitlements to income and wealth, is a crucial dimension to the urbanization and economic development story. It helps explain the patterns of enrichment and impoverishment found in cities.

Housing

In terms of housing, in a given social, economic and cultural context, the minimum level of consumption is defined according to acceptable limits to the normal way of living. In extreme conditions, it is startling to observe how low the norms can reach. In China, there is evidence that migrants seek to minimize housing cost and are therefore willing to accept severe deprivation in their housing consumption. In our study of six cities, migrant families share one room in an apartment and have to pay 150 to 200 Yuan per month per family while their average income ranges from 600 to 900 Yuan per month. One migrant family we interviewed comprised a married couple and two school-aged children. They lived with three other families on the tenth floor of an illegally built block of apartments in an urban village in Guangzhou. Their private space, created by roughly constructed hardwood partitions, was approximately 6 square metres, which was enough space for two beds and little else. This is beyond some notional minimum livable density defined by one bed space per person and required the household to time-share – at least one parent worked during the night when the children and the other parent used the beds. From our study, of the three types of poverty neighbourhood, the lowest minimum living space is found in the urban villages, at 1.33 square metres per capita, where 6.9 per cent occupy space less than 2 square metres per capita and almost 1 per cent occupy less than 2 square metres per capita. In the old neighbourhoods surveyed, the lowest mean living space was 13.43 square metres per capita. Of four categories of resident in these neighbourhoods, three (working local urban resident, unemployed urban resident, and migrant) all had a minimum of less than 2 square metres per capita. The lowest mean space per capita was among the unemployed.

For migrant workers the minimum level of housing consumption is more or less fixed by the market, which is a constrained market. Migrants have four basic choices of home and location. First, they can rent in an ex-*danwei* complex. This is relatively rare since the resale and rental market in these newly privatized properties is very much undeveloped. Second, they can rent in the old pre-1949 neighbourhoods. These have the benefit of being central and accessible to certain types of employment – especially service – but typically contain the poorest quality housing in Chinese cities. Third, migrants can rent from former farmers in urbanized villages. Fourth, migrants with capital or a good job can purchase – either in the privatized *danwei* sector or the newly built commodity housing estates. In all these markets, there are institutional constraints which tend to keep prices high. The privatized work-unit housing market is constrained because owner-occupiers are not generally moving. The market institutions (for example real estate agents and mortgage providers) that would facilitate exchange, movement, investment and differentiation in this sector, are undeveloped. Incumbent residents given the right to buy are typically middle-aged and over, many of them retired or laid-off and they cannot afford to buy into the commodity housing sector. Institutional deepening would allow the *danwei* sector to differentiate at a later stage but this has so far not happened. The pre-1949 sector is in diminishing supply as a result of active urban renewal projects. Urbanized villages are, in principle, in increasing supply as cities expand and engulf more villages, but in practice, they are static or diminishing as these too are subject to redevelopment.

The impact of restricted low-cost migrant housing supply is dependent upon entitlement. For a given income, a household facing higher rent, or more generally higher housing costs, has a more restrictive budget constraint. Higher housing prices result from a more constrained supply and this exerts a downward pressure on the real income of Chinese migrants. Migrants therefore have a relatively lower entitlement mapping between food and education compared to the mapping they would have if land rights were more widely distributed among individuals.

By contrast, urban *hukou* confers the right to compete with other low-income urban *hukou* holders for public rental housing and for economic (affordable) market housing (Y.P. Wang, 2004). For many over the past decade, it has also conferred the right to buy former state housing. The bundle of rights conferred by urban *hukou* therefore give official city residents housing opportunity advantages. Because cheaper housing increases their purchasing power more generally compared to migrants, it raises their entitlement mapping. In principle, for the same income, they can afford more of both basic goods and human capital development.

If housing consumption falls below some minimum level, migrants will no longer find it bearable to work in the city. Migrants in developing countries can generally be thought of as 'welfare takers' – they live in conditions dictated to them. Their only choice is not to live in that city. This is analogous to and consistent with the Lewis–Fei–Ranis (Fei and Ranis, 1964; Lewis, 1954) model of rural–urban migration which assumes that there is an endless supply of low-wage rural labour ready to move to marginally higher wage urban jobs, and that urban wages are kept to a minimum through competition. By analogy, living space is also kept to a minimum by competition among renters – which exerts particularly strong downward pressure on living conditions in Chinese cities because of the constraints on the low-cost housing sector.

Looking at the living space used by our survey respondents who categorized themselves as poor and non-poor, 1.5 per cent of the poor consume under 2 square metres per capita and 13.4 per cent consume under 4 square metres per capita. The minimum for the poor is only 1.33 square metres, and the mean is 14.05 square metres. In contrast, the non-poor have a mean living space of 19.6 square metres. If a household's entitlement mapping falls sufficiently, it may not be able to afford some necessary combinations of housing and food subsistence requirements and it becomes poor in these dimensions. If it cannot afford minimum housing and minimum food then it faces homelessness, starvation and destitution. The response to this situation depends on rights to welfare services. Rural migrants have few, if any, of such entitlements in the city, and since housing 'starvation' is not permitted in China (homelessness and squatting is forbidden), their only choice is to return to their rural home or move to a lower-cost town.

Education

Urban households with urban *hukou* have a right to public education in the catchment district in which they are registered. Until 2006, despite the state offering nine years' obligatory education (including 6 years' primary and three years' junior high education), parents still needed to pay a considerable amount of miscellaneous fees for their children. The revised Obligation Education Law in 2006 states that both tuition fees and miscellaneous fees should not be payable during the nine obligatory years of education. A total of 15 billion Yuan of miscellaneous fees per year have been cancelled in China's rural area (online news: http://edu.people.com. cn, accessed 14 May 2007). In principle, children should attend school in the district in which they are registered, that is the place of their *hukou* registration. Therefore, migrant children without urban *hukou* are denied entitlement to state-run schools in the city. According to statistical data, in 2006 there were more than 3 million migrant workers in Beijing, who have brought around 370,000 school-age children to the city. This creates congestion in schools. A common response in Chinese cities has been to impose both a quota and a price on school places for migrants. In order to attend those state-run schools which accept non-local-*hukou* students, migrants have to pay an extra fee – notwithstanding the 2006 law. For students undertaking nine years' obligatory education, the extra cost will normally be around 1000 Yuan per semester; while for students attending high school, the cost could be as high as 6000 Yuan per semester. Not surprisingly, most rural migrants choose to purchase private education in the low-cost, informal and typically low-quality education sector. To accommodate a huge number of children who cannot afford state-run schools, more than 200 informal schools have been established spontaneously in Beijing. The organization, scale and quality of these schools vary considerably.

Despite their low cost in comparison to state schools, informal schools cannot offer exemption from miscellaneous fees nor the other state subsidies enjoyed by students in the rural areas, since these schools are completely outside the state sector (apart from being loosely and often haphazardly regulated). The informal schools are run by organizations of varying permanency and professionalism. They are technically illegal and not protected by law, and constantly face the risk of demolition. Beijing and Shanghai have started to demolish a number of informal schools in pursuit of city beautification projects. After the publication of the revised Obligatory Education Law, more and more informal schools have been demolished in the name of providing quality education for migrant children. Hundreds of thousands of migrant children have lost a cheap and convenient source of education. Although many state-run schools have started to exempt or decrease their charges and are trying to absorb more migrants, many migrants still cannot afford to attend. Through demolishing informal schools, the state intends to offer better education for migrants, but it also forces more migrant children to leave school.

By comparison, laid-off workers have full rights to state education bundled into their urban *hukou*. It is free to them unless they wish to attend a better quality school located outside the district in which they were registered, in which case extra charges or so-called 'contributions' are applied.

The education opportunities for urban villagers depend on schools available to them and their *hukou* status. In cases where the original village school remains or new schools replacing the old ones are developed, urban villagers are entitled to state-subsidized education in these schools. When old schools are demolished without new schools being built, urban villagers have to look for education opportunities in the urban areas. In these cases, they have to pay extra money for school places, unless they have been allocated urban *hukou* in a new urban district. Compared with rural migrants, the advantage enjoyed by most urban villagers is that they do not need to spend money on renting, which means they can spend more money on education.

There are possibilities of 'education starvation' only among the migrants therefore because of an absence of entitlement to subsidized education. If the costs (economic and psychological) of sending children home are too high, then the household can be said to face education starvation, and its position in the urban labour market becomes untenable and unsustainable. It cannot reproduce itself as a unit of urban production. An equivalent laid-off worker household with the same money income but with entitlement to a home faces a budgetary advantage. Not only does such a household have entitlement to state education, but its relatively lower housing expenditure means it can better afford the additional expenses that inevitably come with education, subsidized or not.

Health Care and Public Services

Education, housing and health care in China have all undergone significant developments since the start of the reforms. The rate of higher education enrolment has reached a record high of 17 per cent (Yang, 2007). The number of university students in China is as high as 23 million. General public health has vastly improved as indicated by rising per capita housing space in cities and towns, which reached 25 square metres in 2004. Access to specialist medical services has improved in cities throughout China, and urban residents, in principle, have access to extensive advanced medical testing equipment such as colour sonar scanners and CT equipment. However, the cost and price of education, housing and health care have inflated rapidly, making affordability a big problem. Higher education costs have risen 25 times since 1997. Per capita medical costs inflated at 1.5 to 2.5 per cent along with every 1 per cent increase in income. House prices have increased in major cities at double-digit rates since 2000.

Adding to the problem of affordability is the issue of government policy of health care privatization. For example, medical costs in China rose from 3 per cent of GDP in 1978 to 5 per cent in 2005. However, the proportion of government expenditure on health care declined from 32 per cent to 15 per cent. The proportion of 'social expenditure', that is the proportion paid on insurance by work units, declined from 48 per cent to 25 per cent, whereas the proportion of medical cost born by individuals rose from 20 per cent to 60 per cent (Yang, 2007). In other words, the health system in China has become mainly a privately funded system, while public expenditure is only used to fill the gap (Wang, 2008). In advanced economies, private health care typically accounts for 27 per cent of the total medical care cost. In transitional economies this figure is nearer 30 per cent, and for the least developed countries it is 41 per cent. The Chinese health system is 'perhaps the most radically marketized system in the world' (Wang, 2008: 132).

ENTITLEMENT DEPRIVATION IN LAND ACQUISITION

The complex and diverse process of property rights reassignment between public and private agents is of essential significance in studying China's economy reform. Walder and Oi (1999) recognize that a more finely differentiated set of gradations from 'public' to 'private' is crucial to an understanding of property rights reform in the Chinese economy. Studies of changing property rights regimes in China, particularly the reform of public firms and the emergence of private firms, reveal the fuzziness, uncertainty, hybridness and incompleteness of the reform process (Oi and Walder, 1999; Nee, 1992). Along with property rights reforms in other domains of the Chinese economy, changes in land rights are a central concern of the Chinese government. Recognizing the importance of land, the government has endeavoured to develop landed property rights as part of its raft of reforms to create institutions suitable for a mixed market economy (Ho, 2005). These institutions have not, however, fully recognized the importance of land to the farmer household's well-being. In addition to labour, land is a farm household's most valuable asset – the essential source of its livelihood. To understand the impoverishment of landless peasants, we therefore examine the changing institution of land requisitions and the consequent property rights redistributions.

The Institution of Land Requisition

In China, the state, including state administrations and state agencies at all levels, is the absolute owner of urban land and of most natural resources. Parallel to the state's ownership, the collective is the owner of rural land, including peri-urban village land. However, the collective ownership is a less stable institution because the ownership of collective land can be transformed into state ownership if the needs are justified and proper procedures for land requisition are followed. Not only is it less stable but it is also less well defined since the exact processes of administrative control (of land and other assets) within the village unit are not always well prescribed, or not always adhered to where they are, because of lack of monitoring and accountable institutions. The establishment of a land leasing system in 1988 allowed the usufruct (use) right of state-owned land to be transferred for payment (Yeh and Wu, 1996). This opened opportunities for land market development and created a new revenue source for local government. In some places, land-related revenue can account for up to 60 per cent of total local fiscal income (Ding, 2007). The pursuit of revenue and rapid urbanization has dramatically increased the demand for land and has resulted in the relentless encroachment of peri-urban rural land. In order to make use of such land for non-agricultural purposes, the state first needs to acquire land ownership from the collective through land requisition, then to transfer land use rights to developers, firms or government organizations.

However, since the property rights of China's land have long lacked clarity of definition, ownership disputes occur among state institutions, between the state and the collective, and among the collectives (Ho, 2005; Zhu, 2004). For instance, the extent and nature of state ownership of land was not fully specified in the 1986 Land Administration Law (LAL). In particular, there was no specification of which level of the state or which state agency is the title holder. To address this, a revised LAL in 1998 specified that the central state is the ultimate owner of urban land. The municipal authorities no longer have the power to approve land requisition, no matter how small a parcel. Approval of the State Council (the central state) is now necessary for any transfer of agricultural land classified as being of highest fertility; for any transfer of 35 hectares or more of cultivated land classified as moderate fertility; and for any transfer of 70 hectares or more of any other rural land. The transfer of smaller tracts of land has to be approved by the provincial authorities under delegated competency. This amendment in the LAL was supposed to end the practice of immoderate and illegal land requisition by making the approval procedure stricter and costlier. However, the administrative and fiscal decentralization and the huge margins to be gained in land requisition and land leasing entice local authorities to bypass these restrictions by various means including subdividing big projects and bribery. A large amount of rural land has been converted to urban construction land before the proper procedures have been approved (Lin and Ho, 2005). Amongst the vast wave of university park and high technology park development, illegal land requisition and land transactions are rampant.

Since the local state needs to consider the trade-off effects between benefits and costs, the approach to property rights redistribution varies from case to case. In general, there are two major approaches to land requisition in urbanized villages. First, when the benefits generated from land requisition are much higher than the costs of compensating and relocating farmers from their farmland and housing plots – as is the case with a large volume of residential development or industrial park development – the village's entire stock of collective land is converted to urban land. Second, when the costs of compensating and relocating villagers are too high compared to the anticipated monetary gains, only the village farmland is converted to urban land. In such cases, ownership of villagers' housing plots remains unchanged. In principle, they remain under collective ownership. By administrative allocation and sometimes internal pricing as well, housing plots are distributed by the collective to villager families, who thus have the de facto right to use and profit from them (Zhang et al., 2003).

Although the revised LAL clarified some ownership problems, fundamentally, it still failed to clarify the ambiguity of collective ownership. The definition of the effective owner of the collective land in villages remains blurred and this proves to be crucial for the dynamics of impoverishment of urbanized villagers. In fact, the ownership rights of rural land are not in the hands of the basic rural organization – the natural village or villagers' group – but are vested in a higher level, the administrative village or the township (Ho, 2005). The legal rights of collective land are not clearly assigned between administrative villages and townships, and the villagers' groups. Cadres of the former often manage to 'sell' land to the city government to make profit for the higher level of administrative unit – and also to their own benefit. Once deals are set under the table between cadres of the collective, the city government and developers, collective land can be converted to urban construction land well before the proper procedures have been run and formal approval gained. Farmers' opinions are rarely sought before the land conversion. The natural villages or villagers' groups are in many cases not capable of protecting farmers' interests, because they are not defined as the legal owner of the collective land. Since the definition and initial assignment of property rights is crucial to the efficient and equitable use and transaction of land, the indeterminacy of property rights over China's peri-urban village land has provided opportunities for rent-seeking, unfair practice and corruption, and has resulted in socially and environmentally inefficient land transactions.

Strictly speaking, the conversion of rural land rights from the collective to the state is still deemed to be an administrative allocation rather than a market transaction. A one-off compensation is offered to the collective and to farmers, regardless of the 'real' market value of the land after conversion. Until now, the market-valued land use system (the land leasing system) is still restricted to state-owned urban land. A rural land market does not exist. Although land requisition is carried out in the name of public interest, city governments make huge profits by leasing land to developers and firms after converting farmland. The costs of transferring rural land to city governments are set by the state (via compensation formulaes), while the benefits are set by the market – the price of a land lease. The margin between the two is taken by the city government. Therefore, land requisition has become a low-cost and high-yielding revenue source for city governments. In less attractive cities and urban locations, city governments will share some of the betterment profit with developers – through negotiated lease price. At the same time, the compensation part of the land costs for a project is shared between the administrative village or township and farmers themselves and their villagers' groups, with the former generally having the greatest power to influence the size and nature of the compensation package. So there are two points at which ambiguous property rights permit rent to be extracted by agencies (the city government and the administrative village or township) other than farmers themselves. The dispossessed farmers often end up with a residual payment equal to or less than the statutory amount set in compensation formulaes.

The Dynamics of Property Rights Redistribution

Figure 5.1 shows the institution of land requisition and the dynamics of property rights redistribution between different stakeholders brought about by land leasing. The solid (anti-clockwise) arrows show the direction of property rights redistribution. Farmers have owned the *de facto* rights of rural land since farmland was contracted to individual households in the late 1970s. The collective owns the *de jure* rights under the LAL. This ownership is not clearly defined by law, but in practice the administrative village or the township holds the collective control of these rights. When land requisition occurs, both *de facto* rights and *de jure* rights of rural land are converted from the collective to the state. In the diagram, municipal authorities represent the state, since land requisition and land leasing are implemented at the municipal level, even though the central state is the

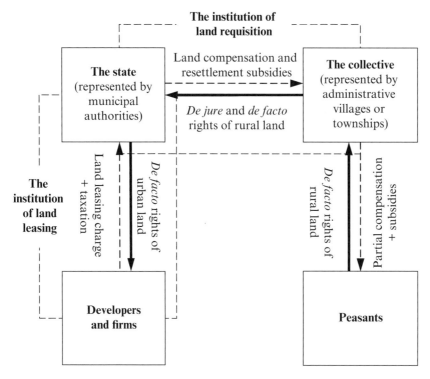

*Figure 5.1   The institution of land requisition and property rights
redistribution*

legal owner of urban land according to the LAL. The final step is transferring rights of land from the state to developers or directly to occupying firms through the land leasing institution. This is the only step that
introduces a market operation and also the only step that generates profits
and makes possible other steps. The process has the effect of transferring
farmers' *de facto* usufruct rights of land into *de jure* freehold rights owned
by the state and leasehold rights owned by developers and end-user firms.

The broken (clockwise) arrows show how profits generated from property rights conveyance are distributed among different stakeholders. The
municipal government acquires a considerable amount of land conveyance fee and revenue by transacting these rights. However, since land requisition is still deemed an administrative rather than market transaction,
the collective only receives, as we have described already, a fixed price
compensation related to agricultural productivity of the land rather than
the market value of the land. Finally, farmers end up receiving only partial

compensation from the collective authorities, since according to the LAL the collective should retain part of the compensation for future development. This leaves great scope for rent-seeking and corruption on the part of the collective officials. Cadres of the collective authorities often receive bribes from developers in attempts to persuade them to 'sell' their village land (Ho, 2005). It is also not uncommon that cadres deliberately hide the exact amount of compensation offered by the state and misappropriate the share meant for individual farmers. It is quite obvious that a great proportion of gains generated from property rights redistribution is routinely taken by municipal authorities and local village and township officials with impunity and without negotiation or local discussion.

The redistribution of land rights in China's urban villages clearly follows the distribution of bargaining power, with the municipal authorities being the most powerful by virtue of their ownership of land and their monopoly rights over land development permits. The developers have capital and knowledge, which puts them in a secondarily powerful position – having more power the less attractive the development site and the lower the competition from other developers. Collectives have power over the internal distribution of parts of the compensation package within the collective and in some cases, over the nature of that package. Village households themselves have the least power, since neither the initial distribution of rights within the collective, nor the reallocated rights give them control of a valuable asset in the land requisition process. They are reduced to an encumbrance on the land that needs to be removed.

The Compensation System of Land Requisition

To understand the impoverishment of landless farmers, we need to look at the entitlement change rendered by the compensation system. The compensation for land requisition is guided by the LAL, while detailed rules are set by individual provinces. Land acquisition compensation contains four main components: (a) land compensation; (b) resettlement subsidies; (c) compensation for young crops and attachments on land; and (d) labour resettlement. According to the LAL, compensation for young crops and land attachment should be given to farmers whereas land compensation and resettlement subsides should be retained by the collective to resettle and assist affected farmers. Compared with the 1986 LAL, the 1998 revision raised compensation levels. It stipulated that compensation for land should be 6–10 times the average annual output value of acquired land in the preceding three years; resettlement subsidies should normally be 4–6 times the average annual land productivity; and that in exceptional circumstances the latter may be raised to a maximum of 15 times the average annual land productivity. If it can be demonstrated that the total compensation still fails to maintain the living standard of affected farmers, the combined amount of land compensation and resettlement subsidies may be increased to 30 times the average annual land productivity at most, with the approval of the provincial authority. However, the revised LAL does not specify any requirement in respect of the resettlement of rural labour, except for encouraging the collective authorities to develop township and village enterprises (TVEs) to create job opportunities for landless farmers.

Land requisition without fully adequate compensation and resettlement has generated hundreds of thousands of impoverished landless farmers (Fan, 2004; Zhang, 2004). In acknowledgement of this, in 2004, the Ministry of Land and Resources published the Guidance on Consummating the Compensation and Resettlement System for Land Requisition. According to this document, local government should further subsidize affected farmers if the total compensation specified by law still fails to maintain living standards after offering the highest combined compensation standard. Funds for subsidies should be derived from local government's land leasing income. This effectively gives local governments the right to bargain over land profit sharing with farmers. The 'Guidance' also suggests strategies for resettling affected rural labour, for example, organizing cultivated land for affected farmers in other places; providing free professional training; giving priority to affected farmers on available job vacancies; giving priority to affected farmers to purchase stock shares offered by the new lessee of the expropriated village land. Such schemes have yet to take wide effect and there is no published evidence to show that they are significantly lessening the problem of impoverishment.

Having lost the most essential source of livelihood, landless farmers have to struggle to find a way of surviving in the city. However, most of them fail to do so due to a number of long-lasting disadvantages in education, skills, and information, which are all consequences of the principal institution governing the allocation of rights to the city in the centrally planned era, namely, the urban–rural *hukou* dichotomy. Although the power of this administratively assigned right is weakening and new institutions designed to oil the wheels of the market economy are constantly being developed and refined, farmers continue to receive an unequal distribution of the profits generated from reforms. For example, the requirement to 'maintain the living standard for landless farmers' in the revised LAL and the 2004 'Guidance' is too vague. It does not specify a time period over which living standards should be maintained and fails to consider changes in the acceptable standard over time. Although farmers are offered compensation and subsidies for their lost farmland, they are left puzzling over

the question of what they are going to live on after spending the compensation money within a few years. There is no published research on how
farmers make use of these funds.

Furthermore, the compensation is set by the value of lost agricultural
income in the past. This ignores the problem of differential entitlement
mappings in rural and urban livelihoods. Urban living has a different
set of overheads from village living. Financial compensation for lost
agricultural production capacity does not necessarily translate into an
equivalent value of urban purchasing power as the case study further on
in this chapter shows. It is difficult to survive without farmland, even with
the highest level of compensation – which is still a one-off payment, rarely
accompanied by alternative employment opportunities or entitlements to
social security.

Several summary points may be made about farmer compensation.
First, being an administratively set price/cost (price of lost assets, cost of
un-encumbering land), compensation standards are inevitably inaccurate.
In a market, price reflects the value of property rights given up (cost of
production or the opportunity costs of securing alternative rights) and the
value of property rights acquired. It reflects the benefit of the purchaser
and the costs of the producer and seller. The true value of land given up
by farmers equals the true cost of re-establishing a viable livelihood in the
city. The true value of land acquired by the government is the leasehold
price developers are willing to pay for it. If the former is greater than the
latter, then the change to a new urbanized use is technically inefficient in
an economic sense. However, this is unlikely to be the case. There is more
likely to be a net gain to society through urbanizing peri-urban land,
meaning that net financial gains to development could be positive even
after compensating farmers for the loss of land to a level that is sufficient
to set them up in an alternative livelihood. If farmers could negotiate a
price in the market, the true price would be revealed – based on their local
and subjective knowledge and preference for alternative occupations,
locations and living conditions. So, in principle, it is possible to find a price
that more accurately reflects the true cost faced by farmers in transferring
their assets. The administratively set compensation mechanism is incapa-
ble of identifying such a price, however, since the central administrators
lack the local knowledge that farmers have.

Second, not only is the administratively devised pricing system incapa-
ble of reflecting the true costs borne by farmers, but it is unwilling to do
so. The state's priority is to promote urban-based industrial and tertiary
growth. If it set compensation to reflect the true social cost of land reform,
some of its economic goals would be sacrificed. If the administratively
set price was high enough to cover most farmers' readjustment costs then

cities would deprive themselves of some of the land revenue they currently use to finance local government. If the price was set by negotiation, involving farmers, then development would be slowed down in many cases. The artificially low compensation price is the hidden subsidy that makes fast urban growth possible in China.

Third, being a politically controlled price, compensation standards are inconsistent both across different regions and over time (Ding, 2007). There will inevitably be a systematic allocation of land profits in favour of local governments, who have the upper hand in the development process, but this will vary over space and time according to different development pressure, local politics, and so on.

Fourth, a further consequence of an administratively set price is that unjust practices and corruption are inevitable. These include exploitative practices by local government, aiming to reduce compensation payments, and illegal appropriation by village cadres of compensation meant for farmers.

MEASURING DIFFERENT FORMS OF POVERTY/ STARVATION

Continuing our focus on the 'three mountains', we turn again to measuring poverty in our sample households, and in particular, to measuring specific poverty experiences. First we asked respondents if housing, education and health care expenditure had ever affected their ability to secure basic necessities including food. Reversing this, we also asked if expenditure on housing, education and health care had ever been delayed or forgone for the sake of securing basic necessities including food. This gives six indicators of poverty experience (Table 5.1).

Respondents are broken down into groups characterized by different bundles of rights to key urban resources. Urban residents, with local urban *hukou*, have rights to state welfare services including health, school and social rental housing. Many also have ownership of their own home. Landless farmers are of two types – those who retain ownership of their urbanized village housing land (partial village redevelopment) and those who were evicted from both productive and housing village land (total redevelopment of the village). The latter have urban *hukou* rights but no land rights and the former have land rights but may not have urban *hukou* rights. Rural migrants, the third group, typically have *de facto* ownership of a house and farmland back in their village but live without citizenship rights in the city in which they work. Urban residents generally have better access to public housing and *danwei* housing, therefore housing

Table 5.1 *Poverty experiences for groups with different bundles of property rights*

	(%)	Following expenditures affected life necessities			Delay/cancel following expenditures		
		Housing	Education	Health care	Housing	Education	Health care
Urban residents	65.0	7.8	13.1	13.4	5.5	7.5	10.8
Landless farmers	8.0	13.2	13.8	8.3	9.7	8.3	6.9
Rural migrants	27.0	13.7	12.7	13.7	11.3	7.8	9.6
Total	100	9.8	13.0	13.1	7.4	7.6	10.2

expenditure rarely affected their life necessities, and vice versa. They rarely delay or cancel housing expenditure. Landless farmers are deprived of use rights to their productive land and sometimes housing land as well. The first type of landless farmer invests heavily in building houses to make a living. Some even get into debt. The second type have to pay a price difference to move into a new home offered by the city government or developer as part of a compensation package (see He et al., 2009).

Commercialized social services impose heavy burdens on rural migrants. Migrants have to pay for everything: housing, education and health care. In many cases migrants report that they have had to delay or cancel housing expenditure to save for other expenses. Cancelling might mean living with friends or relatives in the city for a while or may mean returning to the rural village for a while. The poverty experiences of the three groups with respect to education expenditure are quite similar. In terms of health care expenditure, landless farmers seem to be the better-off group. This is mainly because some landless farmers have been offered a comprehensive social security insurance package, including pension, unemployment and health care insurance, as part of the compensation package for land loss. By contrast, a great proportion of urban residents and rural migrants are not covered by health care insurance, and experience degrees of health care 'starvation'. The percentage of urban residents reporting that they have delayed or cancelled health care expenditure was highest among urban residents. This is probably related to the fact that many urban residents are much older than rural migrants and are more likely to suffer from bad health.

To empirically test the implication of 'the three mountains' on suppressing the welfare of the poor and their association with various predictors, we run two models for each 'mountain'. The first estimates the influences on the probability that expenditure on this 'mountain' pushes a household into basic needs starvation. This assumes that expenditure on housing, education or health care has at some stage affected the ability to purchase other basic needs, including food. In this logistic regression model, we include independent variables which are relevant to respondents' housing, education and health care consumption ability and patterns. They are categorized as: household characteristics, household-head human capital, property rights and other predictors. The second model estimates the influence of these variables on the probability of delaying or forgoing expenditure on each 'mountain' in order to secure other basic needs, including food. Together these two models show what kinds of households are liable to be pushed and entrapped into basic needs starvation or other forms of poverty/starvation by 'the three mountains' (see Tables 5.2, 5.3 and 5.4).

The Housing 'Mountain'

Table 5.2 shows the results of two logistic regression models of the housing 'mountain'. They measure the probability of falling into the category of households who: a) have experienced deprivation of basic necessities because of housing expenditure; b) have had the experience of having to delay/forgo housing expenditure. In terms of household characteristics, the number of unemployed household members, the number of dependent children, and household savings are three variables showing statistical significance in both models. Larger numbers of unemployed household members and dependent children suggest a higher probability of being oppressed by the 'mountain' of housing expenditure, that is either basic necessities have been forgone in order to meet housing expenditure or housing expenditure has been delayed in order to secure basic necessities. Higher household savings on the other hand, reduce the burden of the 'housing mountain' since savings help a household avoid a trade-off between two types of basic need.

In the category of household-head human capital, party membership surprisingly turns out to increase the probability of being pushed towards basic needs starvation by the housing mountain. One possible explanation is that party members tend to have better access to private homeownership, including privatized *danwei* housing, subsidized housing and commodity housing, which require instalment payments. It may be that they have a heavier than usual housing burden because of present or previous privileged access to housing. Greater assets under the pre-reform period may convert to greater liabilities when jobs have gone (for example, larger apartments that cost more to purchase).

Household head's health condition also shows statistical significance in both housing mountain models. As expected, chronic illness is a huge disadvantage leading either to occasional basic needs poverty resulting from excessive housing expenditure or to housing starvation. Household head's schooling years, work experience in SOE/COE, and job contract show no statistical significance in either models.

Although weekly working hours, working years and part-time job do not seem to matter in the housing mountain models, unemployed years does show significant connection with the two types of housing-related hardships. Long periods of unemployment are a huge disadvantage, which jeopardizes laid-off workers' life prospects, in this case their ability to climb the housing mountain. With 'informal sector' set as the reference, 'public sector' only shows statistical significance in the first model, while SOE/COE is significant in both models. The finding suggests that people employed by SOE/COE are less likely to suffer from occasional

Table 5.2   The model of housing-related poverty experience

	Housing expenditure affected basic necessities		Delayed/forgone housing expenditure	
	B	SE	B	SE
Household (HH) characteristics				
Household size	.011	.055	−.013	.069
No. of unemployed	.177*	.103	.057	.122
No. of dependent children	.285**	.120	.320**	.135
Household income	.000	.000	.000	.000
Household saving	−.716***	.157	−1.111***	.227
HH human capital				
Schooling years	.002	.028	.045	.033
Party membership	.655**	.304	.068	.397
Working experience in SOE/ COE	.401	.222	.364	.250
More than 30 days' sick leave per year	.790**	.378	.875**	.416
Job contract (reference: no contract-temporary job)				
Permanent job	−.438	.555	.113	.540
Long-term contract (more than 3 years)	−.141	.662	.007	.687
Medium-term contract (1–3 years)	.453	.477	−.161	.552
Short-term contract (less than 1 year)	−.249	.622	−.716	.716
No contract-private business owner	.302	.331	−.209	.382
No contract-no job	.477	.446	−.311	.528
Work experience				
Weekly working hours	.005	.004	.005	.004
Working years	.003	.006	.002	.007
Unemployed years	.069***	.016	.041**	.019
Part-time job	−18.404	6003.500	−18.007	5963.475
HH employer type (reference: informal sector)				
Public sector (CCP organization education, research, health care etc.)	−.997*	.572	−.696	.592
SOE/COE	−.908***	.318	−1.074***	.377
Private enterprise	−.167	.289	−.020	.330

Table 5.2   (continued)

	Housing expenditure affected basic necessities		Delayed/forgone housing expenditure	
	B	SE	B	SE
Joint venture/foreign enterprise	−1.113	.798	−.589	.819
Self-employed/Small business owner	−.395	.370	−.141	.434
PROPERTY RIGHTS				
Hukou (1 = rural; 0=urban)	.476*	.257	.593**	.292
MLSS Recipient	.693**	.272	.936***	.305
Housing tenure (reference: private rental)				
Public rental	−.850**	.376	−.820**	.400
Self-built housing	−.480	.361	−.779*	.406
Inherited housing	−.529	.384	−.790*	.437
Privatized public housing	−.692**	.352	−1.401***	.420
Subsidized/welfare housing	−.620	.411	−1.221**	.481
Commodity housing	−.591	.782	−1.597	1.065
Second homeownership	−.002	.294	−.395	.369
OTHER PREDICTORS				
Housing conditions				
Housing provident fund	−.387	.560	.192	.536
Housing area	−.002	.003	−.001	.003
Housing quality index	.304	.394	.767	.440
Constant	−1.726***	.500	−1.475**	.591
Model chi-square		214.550***		185.196***
−2 Log likelihood		757.026		757.026

Notes: * p < 0.1; ** p < 0.05; ***p < 0.01. B = coefficient; SE = standard error.

basic necessity starvation caused by housing expenditure or suffer from housing starvation. Even after the radical SOE/COE reform and housing reform, legacy housing benefits from the centrally planned system (access to low-rent *danwei* housing and rights to purchase privatized *danwei* housing at a deeply discounted price) remain as huge advantages for public sector and SOE/COE employees in keeping them from this kind of poverty.

In the category of property rights, *hukou* remains an important predictor of housing hardships. Rural *hukou* is significantly related to both basic needs starvation caused by housing expenditure and housing starvation.

Although rural migrants are allowed to work and live in the city, they are still suffering from institutional discrimination which imposes additional pressure on top of the three mountains. Meanwhile, MLSS recipients also tend to suffer from both types of housing-related hardship.

As for housing tenure predictors of housing poverty, in the first model, only public rental housing and privatized public housing show statistical significance, with private rental housing set as a reference. In the second model, all types of housing tenure except for commodity housing are significantly related to lower possibility of delayed/forgone housing expenditure (the number of commodity housing is comparatively small). Among all types of housing tenure, privatized public housing shows the strongest effect in reducing the probability of housing starvation, holding other variables constant. This further confirms the finding that legacy housing benefits from the former *danwei* system effectively protect people from housing starvation.

Overall, these housing mountain models suggest that housing hardships are still closely related to various institutional factors, especially the legacies from the centrally planned system and the *danwei* housing welfare system.

The Education 'Mountain'

Table 5.3 shows the results of the two regression models of the 'education mountain'. For the variables in the category 'household characteristics', similar results are found to those in Table 5.2. In the first model, the number of unemployed family members and the number of dependent children are significantly related to the probability of basic needs deprivation related to the education mountain, while in the second model, only the number of dependent children affects education poverty. In both models, household savings help lessen the impoverishing effects of the education mountain.

In terms of human capital, surprisingly, more years of household head's schooling is associated with a higher probability of education-related hardships. This suggests that higher educational attainments are not always able to be converted into better economic returns, under the particular institutional setting prevailing in urban China. For instance, rural migrants with higher educational attainments are not exempted from being charged extra costs for sending their children to local public school. Type of job contract does not seem to matter in the first model, but it shows statistical significance in the second model. With 'temporary job' (without contract) set as a reference, people with a short-term contract and those without jobs are less likely to delay or cancel their education

Table 5.3   The model of education-related poverty experience

	Education expenditure affected life necessities		Delayed/cancelled education expenditure	
	B	SE	B	SE
Household (HH) characteristics				
Household size	.020	.047	.074	.048
No. of unemployed	.193**	.089	.121	.108
No. of dependent children	.659***	.119	.477***	.141
Household income	.000	.000	.000	.000
Household saving	−.499***	.117	−.455***	.147
HH human capital				
Schooling years	.060**	.025	.054*	.031
Party membership	−.159	.276	−.539	.377
Working experience in SOE/ COE	.239	.202	.143	.247
More than 30 days' sick leave per year	.464	.356	.637	.394
Job contract (reference: no contract-temporary job)				
Permanent job	−.158	.354	.403	.381
Long-term contract (more than 3 years)	−.142	.499	.120	.546
Medium-term contract (1–3 years)	−.305	.470	−.677	.576
Short-term contract (less than 1 year)	.036	.473	−1.327*	.798
No contract-private business owner	.288	.281	−.378	.355
No contract-no job	−.122	.411	−1.441***	.530
Work experience				
Weekly working hours	.005	.004	.005	.004
Working years	.003	.006	−.005	.008
Unemployed years	.026	.016	.016	.019
Part-time job	−1.623	1.109	−.990	1.094
HH employer type (reference: informal sector)				
Public sector (CCP organization education, research, health care etc.)	−.543	.418	−.276	.481
SOE/COE	−.200	.249	−.417	.314
Private enterprise	−.888***	.277	−.250	.335

Table 5.3 (continued)

	Education expenditure affected life necessities		Delayed/cancelled education expenditure	
	B ·	SE	B	SE
Joint venture/foreign enterprise	−.252	.566	−.360	.803
Self-employed/Small business owner	−.149	.349	.861**	.431
PROPERTY RIGHTS				
Hukou (1=rural; 2=urban)	.233	.240	−.027	.283
MLSS Recipient	.548**	.227	.079	.291
Housing tenure (reference: private rental)				
Public rental	.158	.300	−.682	.414
Self-built housing	−.174	.283	−.160	.329
Inherited housing	.188	.327	−.189	.401
Privatized public housing	−.018	.289	−.219	.343
Subsidized/welfare housing	.450	.329	−.056	.409
Commodity housing	−.327	.589	−.938	.787
Second homeownership	.201	.276	.060	.356
OTHER PREDICTORS				
School Type				
Local public school	.509***	.177	.280	.215
Local private school	.328	.511	−.405	.777
Local migrant school	−.088	.679	−.975	1.059
Village school in home town	−.035	.332	−.296	.416
Constant	−2.519***	.444	−2.098***	.544
Model chi-square		234.504***		122.872
−2 Log likelihood		1164.915		851.593

Notes: * p < 0.1; ** p < 0.05; *** p < 0.01. B= coefficient; SE = standard error.

expenditure. This can be explained by the fact that most migrants and re-employed laid-off workers only manage to get jobs with short-term contracts, and landless farmers who belong to the comparatively privileged group in the urban villages are usually jobless. Compared with those people who get temporary jobs and without contract, these two groups are relatively better off, and therefore are less likely to delay or forgo their children's education expenditure.

None of the four indicators of work experience show statistical significance in either model. In terms of employer types, 'private enterprise employer' seems to be associated with less probability of basic needs poverty related to educational expenditure; while in the second model, 'self-employed' or 'small business owner' is associated with delayed/forgone education expenditure. This will be because of the special occupation composition in poor neighbourhoods. In our survey, 'self-employed or small business owners' mainly refers to those who engage in family-run low-profile businesses, and these households are generally too busy to pay much attention to their children's' education. In many cases, their children drop out of school at an early age and help run the family business.

Hukou has no statistical significance in either model, while MLSS recipients tend to suffer from basic needs deprivation linked to the education mountain. All other property rights indicators are insignificant in both models. When we compare the different types of school that children are sent to, those attending public school (compared with low-quality migrant or informal schools), are more likely to impose a burden of educational cost-related basic needs deprivation. This is particularly true for rural migrants. Overall, the hardships imposed by the education mountain are mainly associated with household characteristics, household head's job contract, employer's type, and type of school.

The Health Care Mountain

Table 5.4 examines the correlates of health-care-related poverty. Household size is a significant indicator for both basic needs deprivation caused by the health care mountain and health care starvation. More unemployed household members also increases the risk of poverty caused by excessive health care expenditure. Again, household savings significantly reduce the exposure to hardships imposed by the mountain of health care. As expected, adverse health conditions, that is more than 30 days' sick leave per year, significantly increases the risk of suffering from the negative consequences of the health care mountain.

Although job contract does not show statistical significance in the first model, in the second, private business owners are less vulnerable to health care starvation, when compared with no contract-temporary workers. This is likely to be because those who manage to run a small business are comparatively better off, and therefore are less likely to be as vulnerable to the tragic consequences imposed by the health care mountain. The number of unemployed years is another significant indicator for health-care-related basic needs deprivation, but not for health care starvation. One possible reason is that some laid-off workers were offered an initial package of health care insurance by their former employers, so they are in

Table 5.4   The model of health-care-related poverty experience

	Health care expenditure affected basic necessities		Delayed/cancelled health care expenditure	
	B	SE	B	SE
Household (HH) characteristics				
Household size	.093***	.035	.113***	.037
No. of unemployed	.148*	.082	.074	.093
No. of dependent children	.062	.107	.013	.120
Household income	.000	.000	.000	.000
Household saving	−.682***	.129	−.821***	.164
HH human capital				
Schooling years	−.008	.023	−.022	.025
Party membership	−.178	.256	−.258	.302
Working experience in SOE/COE	.311	.200	.150	.218
More than 30 days' sick leave per year	.691**	.335	.726**	.357
Job contract (reference: no contract-temporary job)				
Permanent job	−.470	.354	−.041	.381
Long-term contract (more than 3 years)	.354	.444	1.084	.447
Medium-term contract (1-3 years)	.112	.443	.679	.478
Short-term contract (less than 1 year)	−.904	.649	−1.408	1.049
No contract-private business owner	.232	.278	.549*	.305
No contract-no job	.533	.409	.052	.457
Working experience				
Weekly working hours	−.005	.004	−.004	.004
Working years	.009	.006	.005	.006
Unemployed years	.031**	.015	.014	.017
Part-time job	−1.354	1.093	−1.138	1.091
HH employer type (reference: informal sector)				
Public sector (CCP organization education, research, health care etc.)	−.183	.411	−.165	.425

Table 5.4   (continued)

	Health care expenditure affected basic necessities		Delayed/cancelled health care expenditure	
	B	SE	B	SE
SOE/COE	.231	.243	−.033	.267
Private enterprise	−.010	.275	−.442	.301
Joint venture/foreign enterprise	.226	.604	−1.403	1.061
Self-employed/Small business owner	−.100	.362	.319	.385
PROPERTY RIGHTS				
Hukou (1 = rural; 2=urban)	.585**	.238	.228	.260
MLSS Recipient	.597***	.220	.874***	.232
Housing tenure (reference: private rental)				
Public rental	.126	.304	.018	.333
Self-built housing	.024	.273	.155	.294
Inherited housing	.456	.316	.123	.355
Privatized public housing	.360	.280	.093	.312
Subsidized/welfare housing	.048	.356	.197	.371
Commodity housing	−.026	.592	.533	.560
Second homeownership	.234	.278	−.290	.363
Constant	−1.760***	.435	−1.373***	.464
Model chi-square		191.417		183.244
−2 Log likelihood		1211.783		1005.181

Notes: * $p < 0.1$; ** $p < 0.05$; *** $p < 0.01$. B= coefficient; SE = standard error.

a better position to maintain health care insurance even though they have to squeeze their expenditure on other basic necessities.

Hukou remains a huge constraint for rural migrants and is predictably significantly correlated to basic needs poverty related to health care. Again, MLSS recipients are more likely to be exposed to health-care-related hardships. Housing tenure and ownership of a second home do not seem to matter in either model.Overall, families with large household size, more unemployed members, chronic illness, and rural *hukou* are more likely to experience hardships imposed by the mountain of health care. This is mainly the result of the commodification of health care services and institutional deficiency and discrimination against rural migrants.

Income Poverty and the Sense of Deprivation

After examining these three different forms of poverty vulnerability we now test the association between the same sets of independent variables and another two poverty measures: income poverty and sense of deprivation. The results of logistic regression models are shown in Table 5.5.

Household size, number of unemployed household members, and number of dependent children are all significantly associated with income poverty. In the second model, households with a large number of unemployed members tend to have a stronger sense of deprivation; while households with more savings tend to have less sense of deprivation. Although working experience in a SOE/COE and health condition do not significantly affect income poverty, they do affect people's sense of deprivation. People having working experience in a SOE/COE tend to have less sense of deprivation. This is likely to be because they enjoyed, or still enjoy, various forms of social welfare offered by their employers. Unsurprisingly, household heads with more than 30 days sick leave tend to be pessimistic about their lives.

Again, job contract is not significantly related to income poverty, while having a long-term or medium-term contract are significantly associated with feeling deprived, (with 'no contract-temporary workers' set as a reference). One possible reason for this counter-intuitive finding is that people with long or medium-term contracts are mainly manual workers or low-profile employees working in SOEs/COEs. They generally have comparatively little salary compared to those in higher positions and those working for private enterprises, and are without social welfare packages offered by employers. They tend to have a strong sense of deprivation due to the contrast in their situation before and after SOE/COE reform.

In terms of work experience, more unemployed years are related to a stronger sense of deprivation, while having a part-time job is significantly related to income poverty. This suggests that people having part-time jobs have become the working poor. Employer type does not show statistical significance in the income poverty model, but people working in the public sector are less likely to have a sense of deprivation, with 'informal sector' set as a reference. By comparison, public sector employers usually provide a more stable income source and better social security. As expected, MLSS recipients tend to have a strong sense of deprivation.

Housing tenure is not significant in either model, but second-home ownership helps reduce a sense of deprivation. Finally when we compare different social groups and neighbourhoods, unemployed urban residents are more likely to feel deprived than rural migrants (reference group). This is likely to be because the laid-off/unemployed are in a worse-off situation when they make comparison with their own past under the *danwei* welfare

Table 5.5 Income poverty and the sense of deprivation

	Income poverty		Sense of deprivation	
	B	SE	B	SE
Household (HH) characteristics				
Household size	.608***	.076	.001	.041
No. of unemployed	.580***	.132	.248***	.080
No. of dependent children	.714***	.161	.101	.103
Household income	−.005***	.000	−.001***	.000
Household saving	−.085	.163	−.619***	.116
HH human capital				
Schooling years	−.011	.036	−.027	.022
Party membership	−.005	.432	−.231	.256
Working experience in SOE/ COE	−.303	.322	−.423**	.192
More than 30 days' sick leave per year	.367	.491	.589*	.330
Job contract (reference: no contract-temporary job)				
Permanent job	−.053	.494	.229	.322
Long-term contract (more than 3 years)	−18.470	4493.784	.703*	.425
Medium-term contract (1–3 years)	.350	.716	.710*	.393
Short-term contract (less than 1 year)	.116	.650	−.032	.451
No contract-private business owner	−.576	.424	.302	.261
No contract-no job	−.589	.628	.190	.383
Work experience				
Weekly working hours	.003	.005	.001	.003
Working years	.008	.011	.006	.006
Unemployed years	.011	.027	.064***	.016
Part-time job	4.066***	.892	.280	.609
HH employer type (reference: informal sector)				
Public sector (CCP organization education, research, health care etc.)	.673	.577	−.678*	.377
SOE/COE	.177	.426	.035	.247
Private enterprise	.061	.389	−.198	.246
Joint venture/foreign enterprise	−1.196	1.449	−.505	.559

Table 5.5 (continued)

	Income poverty		Sense of deprivation	
	B	SE	B	SE
Self-employed/Small business owner	−.395	.534	−.453	.333
PROPERTY RIGHTS				
Hukou (1 = rural; 2=urban)	.981	.622	.343	.418
MLSS Recipient	73.872	280770795.545	1.039***	.218
Housing tenure (reference: private rental)				
Public rental	.681	.477	.137	.282
Self-built housing	−.145	.394	.049	.249
Inherited housing	−.649	.517	.174	.301
Privatized public housing	−.173	.453	−.115	.287
Subsidized/welfare housing	.109	.567	−.206	.344
Commodity housing	−.930	.752	.459	.464
Second homeownership	.365	.426	−.555*	.292
Social groups (reference: rural migrants)				
Working urban residents	1.154	.701	.089	.460
Unemployed urban residents	.366	.685	.789*	.447
Retirees	.011	.775	.223	.500
Neighbourhoods (reference: urban villages)				
Old urban neighbourhood	.063	.329	.266	.203
Workers' village	.025	.436	−.163	.267
Constant	.189	.842	−.087	.549
Model chi-square		1373.589***		546.823***
−2 Log likelihood		542.360		1351.535

Notes: * $p < 0.1$; ** $p < 0.05$; *** $p < 0.01$. B= coefficient; SE = standard error.

system. This sense of deprivation is compounded by the fierce competition they face from rural migrants.

In general, income poverty is mainly related to household characteristics and work experience, while a sense of deprivation is more related to respondents' unemployment experience. This reflects the negative consequences of redundancy policy and SOE/COE reform, and more generally, the consequences of entitlement decline.

To sum up this chapter so far, we have examined the entitlement arrangements that affect the livelihoods of the poor and argue, borrowing from Sen's tradition, that the poor suffer from a relative depreciation in the value of their resources in exchange. They are deprived of exchanged-based entitlement and this compounds their deprivation resulting from a fall in transfer-entitlements. We go further than this and examine how the entitlement mappings facing the urban poor have been affected by entitlement changes during the reform period. Notwithstanding the widespread redistribution of assets to the low-income sector, the reform and commodification of housing, health care, schooling and other public services exacerbates the poverty situation in ways that we describe. The various groups occupying China's poorest urban neighbourhoods do not face a single uniform kind of poverty. The variation in entitlements they possess – a pattern broadly hanging over from the socialist era – leads to a variety of poverty experiences.

This chapter tries to understand why the poor (industrial and migrant workers) have become poor after having gained property rights to their own labour (all groups), land (right-to-buy urban workers) and capital (all, but urban villagers in particular). Migrant workers cannot sell their labour for a good price, because the price is depressed by the low cost of labour reproduction in rural areas. Rural to urban migration introduces rural poverty into the city. For industrial workers, they are facing increasing competition from migrant workers, especially in the informal sector. Both groups are disadvantaged by their property arrangements. Migrant workers are deprived of the rights to access public services and have to rely on commoditized services at a higher price. Farmers who have lost their land rights on the fringe of cities become landless. For industrial workers, although some have managed to purchase heavily discounted housing, they cannot capitalize on their assets. Those who live in public and private rental accommodation are more disadvantaged in comparison with home-owners, as the former cannot benefit from property appreciation. They are becoming relatively poor in terms of wealth. For many of the poor, the exchange value of their labour has not been appreciating at the same pace as commoditized services. As a consequence, many experience service 'starvation'. This is not due to lack of services or the lack of labouring capacity. But rather, as with famine in Sen's classic work, it is the relative market-based exchange mechanism that fails the poor and drives them further into a multi-dimensional poverty trap.

IMPACT OF LAND ENTITLEMENT FAILURE ON DISPOSSESSED FARMERS

In order to provide a deeper understanding of the impoverishment of landless farmers, we investigate two rural villages that have been affected differently by land requisition in the city of Xi'an. We focus on property rights redistribution during land requisition and see how this redistribution affects landless farmers' entitlements, which led to their impoverishment. These two villages have experienced different land arrangements. The first village, Dengdian, lost both farmland and land for housing, while the second village, Renyi, only lost its farmland. This difference turned out to be critical, as the village that kept its land for housing has developed rental housing through which villagers have drawn a steady income.

Known as one of the Four Great Ancient Capitals of China, Xi'an has more than 3100 years of history and was the capital city of China for 13 dynasties. In the post-reform period, the city has seen rapid economic and urban growth. It is the capital city of Shaanxi province and the largest and most developed city of north-west China. Since the late 1980s, farmland surrounding the urban built-up area has been requisitioned in large quantities by the city government to construct urban roads, factories, commodity housing, offices and so on. A recent wave of university parks and high-tech industry parks has further intruded into the collective land of the suburban areas.

Entitlement Failure: Farmland plus Housing Land

Dengdian New Village is a newly developed residential complex for farmers relocated to make way for the development of Chang'an Technology Park. The village is located at Guodu Town, just off the south-west corner of the city ring road. In December 1999, the construction of Chang'an Technology Park was approved by the Xi'an municipal government. In making the land requisition case to the central government, the municipality requested permission to expropriate 1500 *mu* (15 *mu* =1 hectare). On the ground, however, nearly 7000 *mu* of rural land was converted (interview with the former Chinese Communist Party (CCP) secretary in the village on 1 January 2007). Only 20 days after permission was granted to the municipality, the management office of Chang'an Technology Park, a semi-public organization affiliated to Xi'an National Hi-tech Industrial Development Zone, signed a land requisition agreement with Guodu Town government to relocate four villages. In June 2001, the demolition and relocation of South and North Dengdian Village and East and West Wuqiao Village was completed. In November 2001, all villagers moved to their new houses in Dengdian New Village, 1.5 kilometres away from the old villages. In total more than 1100 households, amounting to about 5500 farmers, lost their farmland and moved away from their homes to make room for the urban construction project. By the time of our survey in December 2006, a commodity housing project – Ziwei City Pastoral – and several high-tech firms had occupied the land vacated by farmers.

According to the land requisition agreement, the land compensation standard for the collective was set at 3900 Yuan per *mu*. The actual compensation received by farmers was 2550 Yuan per *mu*. The residual 1350 Yuan per *mu* still remains in the hands of the collective authorities (township and administrative village), which has claimed that the money was used to resettle and assist landless farmers according to the requirement of the LAL. The village was also offered more than 1.6 million Yuan for resettlement subsidies – including the costs of removing village assets. Only 0.6 million Yuan was spent on demolition and site clearance, leaving a surplus of 1 million Yuan. This was intended, according to the compensation settlement, to be used for improving the built environment of the new residential area. However, the amount, as well as the residual land compensation, was retained by the collective authorities without account and without giving a clear explanation to the farmers. Five years on, it is not clear what the money has been spent on, since the money is controlled by the cadres of the village.

Landless farmers were resettled to a modern residential complex with semi-detached houses (see Figure 5.2). However, they needed to pay the price difference between their old and new houses. The price of their old houses was calculated at the rate of 247 Yuan per square metre, while the price for new houses was set at 465 Yuan per square metre. The cost of the latter relates to the cost of construction, while the cost of the former was claimed to be related to its value on the market. This meant that farmers needed to pay a considerable amount to purchase their upgraded homes. The typical shortfall that had to be found by a farmer household was 50 000 to 70 000 Yuan, which often took up a great proportion of their cash compensation.

The story of a poor farmer in Dengdian New Village illustrates how land requisition results in a direct entitlement failure and eventually leads to impoverished landlessness. Mr Li, 52 years old, was educated to junior secondary school level. Before land requisition he planted wheat and corn on his 2.6 *mu* farmland. He also did some temporary work in his spare time. His annual income was 1862 Yuan plus 50 kilograms of wheat (apart from a self-consumed portion of his harvest) and some money earned from temporary work. His 21-years-old son has left home and now works in Shenzhen after he graduated from a technology school in 2004. In 2001 Mr Li was offered a one-off compensation of 69,600 Yuan for his lost farmland. However he needed to pay a price difference of 54,300 Yuan for his new house, leaving him with 15,300 Yuan. In 2005, the last remaining wheat harvested from Li's farmland – 600 kilograms – had been consumed

Figure 5.2   Resettlement housing for the Dengdian village in the City of Xi'an

and he had to start buying wheat from the market for the first time in his life. After losing his farmland he has made a living picking up rubbish, supplemented by temporary work when he can find it. His two-storey semi-detached house is now full of rubbish collected from the field. The house is the only land he has to enhance the value of his labour and he has turned it into a refuse processing plant. Mr Li's health condition and his age have been great hurdles for him finding a proper job. He has had an injured back since 1978 and needs to see a doctor often. Without a secure livelihood he has had to count on the residual from his land compensation – which did not last very long. His monthly expenditure has been squeezed to only 300 Yuan including 75 Yuan health care cost and his basic living security has been threatened. All he owns is a two-storey house full of rubbish. He told us:

> On average, I can earn 150 Yuan per month by picking up rubbish. Occasionally, I work for the construction company. They pay me as little as 7 Yuan per day. Even so, the payment is often delayed. My income hardly sustains my everyday expenses. Moreover, it has been more and more difficult to pick up valuable rubbish from the field. I have nobody to support me. My son has not sent me any money yet. The village does not offer any social welfare or living subsidy. . .Sometimes, I think I would rather have remained a farmer. At least I didn't need to spend money on food, and didn't have to worry about tomorrow. I could support myself. (Interview on 1 January 2007)

Before land requisition, his entitlement to land and his own labour secured his family a livelihood. Immediately after land requisition, Mr Li still managed to maintain a living above the minimum subsistence line, with his entitlement being shifted to rubbish collection plus money compensation. Since he could neither sell his own labour at a rate that would buy him the amount of food he once produced with it, nor sell or rent his new house, his entitlement set has been in constant decline. He used to produce enough food for his family and earn 155 Yuan per month, but now he can only earn 150 Yuan per month, approximately equivalent to the price of 50 kilograms of flour or rice. The lack of social security provisions further pushes Mr Li into the trap of impoverishment. Although Mr Li's story may be an extreme case, he is not the only one threatened by a direct entitlement failure after land requisition. His story is that of many landless farmers facing deteriorating entitlement.

As we have already implied, the local cadres – fellow villagers in control of negotiating and administering the compensation deal at the village end – are not neutral in this loss of entitlement. Many clearly act opportunistically to secure personal gain. To persuade farmers to move from their homes to make room for the technology park, the local government used the slogan 'sacrifice personal interests for the sake of public interests'. It turns out that the public interest of landless farmers was sacrificed in part for the personal interests of government officers and cadres of the collective authority. As an example of the petty rent-seeking made possible by the rights ambiguity within the collective, township and village cadres decided that small households with less than three persons should be charged 10 000 to 30 000 Yuan by the Guodu Town government and the collective authorities for extra infrastructure expenses – rather like a vacant room surcharge in a hotel. The charge was eventually deemed to be illegal and was refunded in 2003 after farmers faced the cost of appealing to the central government several times (interview with villagers on 1 January 2007).

A further opportunity for rent-seeking came at the construction stage. The contract for building the resettlement houses in Dengdian New Village was awarded to a firm in which local government officers and their relatives had an interest. Villagers allege that the contractor deliberately squeezed the investment in infrastructure and housing construction to increase its margin (interview with villagers on 1 January 2007). This resulted in very low quality houses and a poor standard of infrastructure in the new village. Although the new houses look modern and spacious from the outside, there have been many problems with cracking and leaking inside. The houses were not fitted with modern facilities such as piped gas, central heating and telephone cables.

There were no direct employment opportunities offered to villagers from this redevelopment project and no additional interest was offered in the economic activities developed on the land that was once theirs. Quite the reverse – after land requisition, two small TVEs, brick factories in the village, were closed down. According to the land requisition policy published by the central state, the developer should offer the collective a plot of industrial/commercial land equivalent to 4 per cent of the original rural land area. This concession was not made in Dengdian village, since the village authority and the city government had reached a mutual agreement not to follow the policy. In fact this policy has rarely been properly implemented anywhere in China. With the removal of agriculture land and the brick kilns, the collective economy disappeared. Farmers had to make a living on their own. However, by the time of our survey, 80 per cent of farmers over 30 years old were chronically unemployed (interview with villagers on 1 January 2007).

Compounding their situation, by 2007 the villagers still remained classified as peasants with rural *hukou*, and were not entitled to an urban package of social security rights. Furthermore, they still had not received title deeds to their houses, meaning that selling a house is not possible.

This has meant that villagers are unable to relocate to find jobs elsewhere and are unable to raise capital on the basis of their housing equity. The constraint on relocation is a problem since the new village is located in a comparatively isolated part of the city at the time of survey, and it was not easy for villagers to rent out their houses given the small number of rural migrants in this part of the city. The development of the technology park brings neither job opportunities nor many potential tenants to the village, since there is a mismatch between available jobs and the skills of villagers and migrant workers.

Entitlement Failure: Farmland Only

We use the village of Renyi to illustrate the problem of entitlement failure. The basic information about Renyi is provided in Chapter 4 (see the urban village section). In 1993 when the local city government acquired 60 *mu* of land from one of the village's production teams at a one-off compensation of 9.7 million Yuan, the land was quickly developed and leased to a developer for the price of more than 66 million Yuan. The developer quickly made a profit of 24 million Yuan by transferring its land use rights to another firm. The local state and land lessees both harvested windfall profits, which the collective and landless farmers had no share in. The 'price' they received for their land was set administratively while the prices the local government and the on-selling developer received were negotiated in the market (see Yeh and Wu 1996; Wu et al., 2007).

As part of the compensation deal, farmers were offered the right to urban *hukou*. But in Renyi villagers managed to develop a business of rental housing. In the urbanized village, all villagers are entitled to an equal share of the collective land with unrestricted tenure and have been allowed to build houses when their needs have been approved by the collective (Zhang et al., 2003). Land for housing is allocated by the collective authorities to every household free of charge or for a nominal fee. Since renting houses has become the most effective income resource for villagers after losing their farmland, they try to build as much rentable floor area as possible and the collective authorities acquiesce in this maximizing behavior, the collective cadres themselves being petty developers and renters as well. Inevitably, the collective village land has soon filled up with high density, poor quality and disorderly houses. The low price and convenient access to the city has meant that the village currently provides accommodation for more than 6000 migrant workers. This is a pattern found in many Chinese cities (see Gu and Liu, 2002; Liu and Wu, 2006b; Ma and Xiang, 1998; Wu, 2002; Zhang et al., 2003).

An informal housing rental market has therefore developed in the village. Most houses are rented on the basis of informal bilateral (written or verbal) agreement between landlords and tenants. With this influx of migrants, Renyi Village has developed into a mini town that provides not only housing, but also a range of other neighbourhood facilities such as open markets, restaurants, convenience shops, barbershops and so on. The population density in the village is higher than in many other places in the city. The ratio of migrants to local villagers is as high as three to one, which means on average that every villager lives with three migrants and that every villager on average has a rental income from three people. In reality, rental income is not as evenly distributed as this. Some households with more resources, such as families of village cadres, manage to build more houses and thus have higher rental income, while other households with few resources cannot afford to invest in their share of the village land.

Although urban villages are well known for their disorder and unruliness, they help to reduce poverty and provide shelter for migrant workers. Free from state regulation on housing construction (because this is collectively owned land in the city), landless farmers build as many houses as possible on their plots to create a ready source of income. The formation of dense rental properties in urban villages bears witness to landless farmers' ability to develop anti-poverty solutions through making use of whatever assets they have at their disposal – in this case, their *de facto* right to housing land. They have succeeded, for a while at least, in raising their entitlement-set by investing in the only productive assets they have left – village housing plots plus their entrepreneurial skills.

Landless farmers in Renyi adopted a rational tactic: they invested heavily in building bigger and higher houses to increase their rental income, while also establishing a position from which to bargain for higher compensation when redevelopment finally came. For Renyi village, the collective authorities, the state and developers have already proposed a redevelopment plan. According to village cadres, the whole village will be redeveloped into a high-end commodity housing complex, suited to its central location. This plan is a cooperative venture by the collective, the state and the developer: the collective agrees to offer land for a negotiated compensation package; the state offers preferential policies and some infrastructure investment; while the developer offers capital and development knowledge. Villagers are relocated on-site to new houses equivalent to their current housing area.

The state response to the game being played is also rational, from its perspective. The housing area above the second floor will not be counted when calculating the equivalent new housing area offered to households. To do so would make the compensation package too expensive for the city government and would share too much of the development gain with the villagers. Only construction costs of the upper floors will be offered. In principle, this makes the villagers' economic calculation in respect to the densification of their plots cost-neutral. So long as they can make rental income, even in the short term, that covers their expenses including loans, then it is worth continuing to invest even as redevelopment looms. The cost-replacing compensation rule is in this sense a progressive policy, permitting landless farmers to extract maximum value from their temporarily retained *de facto* land rights and expand their entitlement set via trade.

The redevelopment of Renyi nationalized the residual collective land in the village and transfered land rights via a lease and then via property sales, to a population of relatively well-off commodity home buyers. This eventually took away the landless farmers' final residual asset. Without the income from renting, villagers who own little equity in their rental properties in principle become vulnerable to impoverishment.

Mr. Shan, a 46-year-old single parent, is one of those facing the risk of impoverishment. He was divorced by his wife 20 years ago and has a son with a learning disability, who receives a monthly subsidy of 136 Yuan from the collective authority. From the late 1980s to 1993, Mr Shan was offered a total cash compensation of 54000 Yuan for his lost farmland. This is rather a large amount of money as on average a university lecturer earned about 100 Yuan at that time. Before 1985, Mr Shan earned 30 Yuan a month by planting vegetables, which made his family better off at that time compared with most farmers. From 1985 to 1997, after losing his farmland Mr Shan made a living by transporting customers using a tricycle, from which he could earn up to 60 Yuan per day – which he considered to be not a bad income. However, the competition from taxis and his unfavourable health forced him to stop cycling. After that, he could not find a job since he was only educated to junior secondary school level and had no skills matching the needs of the new industry in Xi'an. Mr. Shan then took out a loan to build a two-storey house and open a tiny grocery shop, managing to pay off the debt in 2005. The monthly income from the shop is around 500 Yuan, and the monthly rental income is only 480 Yuan for three rooms. The total income only covers the family's basic living. But this steady income prevented his family from falling into poverty.

When talking about the redevelopment scheme of the village, Mr Shan showed his worries:

> I really wish they [the collective authorities and city government] wouldn't rebuild the village, because that will take away my final straw. After moving to the new apartment, I won't be able to run my shop and rent out rooms any more. These are my only income sources. . . Not like many other people in the

village, I didn't earn much money from renting my house, and I don't have much deposit. I really don't see a future for my poor son and myself. (Interview on 3 January 2007).

Mr Shan represents one side of a rapidly differentiating economic class divide in the village based on initial endowment at the time of fast development of the collective land. Similar to Mr Li, Mr Shan's entitlement was changed to a housing plot after losing his farmland. Mr Shan managed to sell his own labour by transporting customers for a while. This helped provide capital and entrepreneurial know-how to invest in and run the small grocery shop and rental business. Mr Shan then has a more favourable set of entitlement than Mr Li, who lost all entitlements of farmland and housing land. However, he will eventually lose his entitlement when his housing land plot is acquired.

Other villagers enjoy a continuing increase in their entitlement sets through a virtuous cycle of investment–income–reinvestment. In this dynamic, timing, connections, knowledge, power and foresight are everything. In principle, the petty developer and renter stage of the urban village's life cycle could provide a capital resource to subsidize villagers' integration into the modern urban economy.

CONCLUSION

In this chapter we have used notions of entitlement and property rights to explore the patterns and correlates of impoverishment under China's unique institutional arrangements. The distribution of property rights tends to change when the anticipated profits yielded from the change exceed the transaction costs of making the change. In the two village case studies considered in this chapter, property rights to collective land were redistributed to maximize the interests of the politically and economically powerful agents, that is the state, developers and the collective authorities; while the less powerful players – villagers – bore the costs of land requisition. In particular, villagers having all their landed entitlements removed are not given a sufficient share in rural–urban land value uplift to cover the costs of redeploying their labour entitlement in the urban economy. This outcome is very much related to the power structure of land requisition institutions and of modern Chinese society in general. Stronger collective governance (stronger 'local state corporatism' in the terms of writers such as Lin, 1995; Oi, 1992; Walder, 1995) with better organization, clearer division of labour and clarified property rights, could have helped the collective and villagers to negotiate property rights changes more beneficial for themselves. However, in the two villages a weak collective economy and village organization gave village cadres an opportunity for rent-seeking and corruption. Villagers remained in a passive and disadvantageous position. This is very common in most underdeveloped inland regions of China as some of the other stories of the 25 neighbourhoods sketched in Chapter 4 reveal.

Displaced villagers face adverse changes in their exchange entitlement mappings as the regression analysis in the first part of this chapter illustrates. For example, in the case of Dengdian New Village, a large proportion of the cash compensation had to be used to purchase a house in the relocation village, and villagers' capital is therefore locked up and cannot be converted into food or other non-housing essentials. In the case of Renyi village, social security provision – an important parameter of exchange entitlement mapping – is lacking, which leaves less capable villagers unprotected and particularly vulnerable when the last phase of village redevelopment finally happens. Entitlement failure has become and will be the direct cause of the impoverishment of villagers like Mr Li and Mr Shan. Impoverished landless farmers have faced a combination of direct entitlement failure and trade entitlement failure. They have been deprived of food production land without the offer of equivalent compensation to develop viable livelihoods that can cope with the different entitlement mappings of the urban economy.

The relentless pursuit of urban economic growth has led to the redistribution of land-based property rights from farmers to governments and from governments to developers and then end-users. Large-scale urban redevelopment has now occurred at the place where Renyi village used to be located. The village has been replaced with a large shopping mall, called 'Times Square' (Figure 5.3). On the face of it, such redevelopment programmes eliminate poverty from the organized city. Poor people are removed from city centre locations, and islands of informal economy within the city are regularized. Petty landlords renting self-organized low quality housing at excessive densities are paid off. The future of many is not bright, however. Some – the better connected cadres in the main – will have made sufficient surplus that can be re-invested elsewhere. For many, however, it is likely that the brief period of renting will have been a pause in the process of impoverishment. In villages like Renyi, the ex-agriculturalists turned ex-rentiers will eventually leave their village land with a package that includes alternative accommodation. This will give them an advantage in terms of real income and exchange entitlements, as the regression models and stories show. But many, if not most, will be left with skills that cannot immediately be redeployed: farming and renting. The picture is not entirey bleak, although it is a harrowing one. The story

Figure 5.3   Newly built 'Times Square' shopping mall near the former site of Renyi Village

of villagers who became a petty property developer and rentier class for a while shows the resilience of the marginalized peoples of urban China. Hundreds of thousands of farmers quickly developed the new skills necessary to take advantage of residual assets left them by the half-completed redevelopment process. They are not flotsam drifting helplessly in the currents of urban expansion and economic development. If sufficient numbers have managed to convert some of the surplus from renting into capital that can be reinvested – educating their children, purchasing a small business that can survive the demolition of their rental properties, investing in the stock market and so on – then there will be positive stories to be told in the future, about how villagers who became renters then became something else. No doubt the future economy of Chinese cities will contain some success stories. For those who have not been able to accrue sufficient surplus, however, they are likely to share the trajectory of the other poverty groups that feature in the analysis of this book: farmers fully dispossessed of their land at the time of urbanization; laid-off workers and rural migrants. All need to start again. They find themselves climbing the rungs of the urban economy in pursuit not only of the goal of security and prosperity but, more often than not, in search of subsistence strategies.

As the Chinese urban economy moves through successive phases of transition, those with claims over the assets once owned collectively attempt to do what they can to capture any rights that lie ambiguously in the public domain.

Farmers now in possession of the right to deploy their own labour, the right to enjoy the fruit of their own labour and the right to relocate at will, flock to the cities to try and capture an urban job. Jobs are not allocated any more and the liberalized labour markets mean that job opportunities are in the public domain. Given the volume of rural–urban migrants, the jobs have to be competed for through selling one's labour very cheaply and through being willing to live in inhuman housing conditions. Some have other assets that help in this competition – Communist Party membership, experience working in a state-owned enterprise and so on. Our regression models show that the various assets owned by poor households influence their vulnerability to poverty as they join in the mass competition for urban-based enrichment.

Local governments, not unlike the rural migrants, seem to act as revenue maximizers and/or cost minimizers, though at a completely different scale, of course. They expropriate, develop and sell rural land with the land acquisition (compensation) costs fixed but the sale price negotiated in the market.

Village cadres have to acquiesce but have scope in their administrative allocation of compensation payments to secure their own as well as their fellow villagers' interests. In urban villages located in the developed south coastal areas, especially in Guangdong province where demand for migrant housing is enormous, some villagers have made a great fortune through renting to migrant workers and renting factory space. They have become a privileged rentier class. It has also been shown that well-established village organizations fostered by dynamic collective enterprises or lineage/kinship traditions have a strong and positive impact on rent redistribution outcomes among villagers (Mei, 2004; Tsai, 2002; Unger and Chan, 1999; Webster et al., 2006). Elsewhere, notably in places where dynamic industries are lacking and lineage/kinship organizations are weak, the outcomes of property rights changes incurred by land requisition are often negative and even lethal to landless farmers' livelihoods. This is particularly true in those less-developed areas in inland China, especially the western region, an area that remains comparatively under-researched and less familiar to non-Chinese specialists. Our study in Xi'an, for example, tells a less optimistic story that will be common to most of the cities in the vast inland region of China.

The dynamics of impoverishment faced by landless farmers is closely related to the institution of land requisition and the poorly defined property rights over collective land. Since land requisition is not treated as a market transaction but rather controlled by the local state, unjust and illegal transactions become unavoidable and endemic. Our case studies suggest that clearly defined property rights for individual farmer households, not just for the village collectives, would help improve the prospects of landless farmers. Were peasants to have clearer property rights over their shared village land, they could make much better deals with the city government and developers over land transaction. The reassignment of property rights would mean that urban projects would be more costly and urban development would proceed more slowly. But it would proceed with farmers having better land entitlement mappings; able to make better choices about their own future; and having a clearer and longer-term stake in the urban economy.

We do not suggest that a clearly defined bundle of property rights would, of itself, automatically remove the risk of poverty or poverty vulnerability. In fact, if villagers were given full property rights over their agricultural or housing land, the rapid economic growth experienced by Chinese cities would slow down and there would be fewer new jobs and fewer enrichment opportunities. Any clarification of property rights issues in urban villages therefore needs to include a fair and efficient distribution of rights between individuals and the collective and between the collective and the state. The state clearly needs to be able to make investments that are of strategic importance to the city. But mechanisms should be found that give villagers a greater proportion of the proceeds from government-generated land value increase. Currently, too much of this ends up as windfall profit for developers and general local government income. As our case studies show – and as our analytical models illustrate – the imperfect implementation of the compensation institutions (and possibly their imperfect design) means that the sums do not stack up for many dispossessed urban villagers. Bearing privately a significant proportion of the costs of urban expansion, they become vulnerable to poverty. The essential problem is that the compensation aims to subsidize the transaction costs of converting land from rural to urban use. In fact, it established quite clear property rights over this to transfer income. What it plainly does not do is to adequately subsidize the costs of transferring labour from rural to urban production.

In this book we have studied in great depth the patterns of poverty found in a sample of the poorest neighbourhood in six Chinese cities. Urban poverty in China is not homogenous. It is experienced by different types of individuals for different reasons. It is, however, concentrated, and concentrated in a predictable way. Our purpose in undertaking this study is to reveal the commonalities and the differences: to profile China's emerging urban poverty systematically and comprehensively. As a result of the study we have found evidence that there is a neighbourhood effect in the way poverty dynamics operates in the Chinese city. Controlling for other determinants, the probability of being poor is affected by living in a poor neighbourhood. We have also found that the chances of being poor and the chances of being vulnerable to different kinds of poverty are firmly rooted in the socialist era. The patterns of urban poverty in China are both a new and a historical phenomenon. For many, the line between poverty and wealth in the market economy was drawn under the centrally planned era. Relative and absolute poverty is highly correlated with the entitlements allocated by administrative fiat under socialism. In the gaps that have emerged during transition – opportunities to exploit legacy ownership entitlements – vast fortunes have been amassed, not the least by local governments. The benefits have trickled down unevenly. This unevenness has a spatial dimension as a new socio-spatial geography emerges at all scales. Poor neighbourhoods are one feature of this. Some of the neighbourhoods we have studied will not be there in ten, or even two years' time. Their disadvantaged populations will have been displaced, however, and by the nature of urban dynamics, will inevitably cluster in other new, poor neighbourhoods. Our prediction would be that the poverty in many of the disappearing urban villages will eventually end up in the least accessible and currently poorest urban worker villages, which, without reinvestment, are China's slums of tomorrow. Many rural migrants are currently returning home as the urban jobs dry up. This will be a temporary pause in the kind of processes we have documented in this book. The 'fundamentals' of China's spatial economy will not change for decades. When the global economy recovers, the migrants will flood back. Some of the pre-1949 neighbourhoods we have studied will be gone as well as some of the urban villages. There will be fewer new urban villages as the pace of urban expansion slows. Many of the poor worker villages will become more unstable than they are at the moment. With their elderly residents entering very old age or dying off and with their children (a much more heterogeneous group than their parents) making individual decisions to sell, rent or live in their parents' decaying homes, these neighbourhoods will rapidly differentiate in the coming years. Some will undoubtedly 'tip' and become the migrant neighbourhoods of the future. As a second-hand and rental market develops, some will upgrade, and some will continue to deteriorate through lack of investment. There is, in principle, scope for a much greater supply of poor neighbourhoods via this source than via urban villages. This could work in favour of migrants' living conditions. A release of low-income homes will relieve the pressure on space and conditions. When the next round of rural migration hits Chinese cities, migrants may have slightly better renting options. Many of the poor worker villages still retain a rich stock of social capital – a legacy of the state-owned enterprise culture. As the reality and memory of legacy institutions fades, these places will become more subject to market sorting processes, and the dynamics of neighbourhood poverty is likely to become rather more familiar to those familiar with urban poverty in the West.

References

Alchian, A.A. and H. Demsetz (1973), 'Property rights paradigm', *The Journal of Economic History*, **33**(1), 16–27.

Anderson, T.L. and P.J. Hill (2002), 'Cowboys and contracts', *Journal of Legal Studies*, **31**(2), 489–514.

Appleton, S. and L. Song (2007), 'The myth of the "new urban poverty"? Trends in urban poverty in China, 1988–2002', in J.R. Logan (ed.), *Urban China in Transition*, Oxford: Blackwell, pp. 64–85.

Appleton, S., J. Knight, L. Song and Q.J. Xia (2002), 'Labor retrenchment in China – Determinants and consequences', *China Economic Review*, **13**(2–3), 252–75.

Appleton, S., J. Knight, L. Song and Q. Xia (2006), 'Labour retrenchment in China: determinants and consequences', in S. Li and H. Sato (eds), *Unemployment, Inequality and Poverty in Urban China*, Abingdon: Routledge, pp. 19–42.

Asian Development Bank (ADB) (ed.) (2004), *Poverty Profile of the People's Republic of China*, Manila: Asian Development Bank.

Badcock, B. (1997), 'Restructuring and spatial polarization in cities', *Progress in Human Geography*, **21**(2), 251–62.

Banner, S. (2002), 'Transitions between property regimes', *Journal of Legal Studies*, **31**(2), 359–72.

Bian, Y. and J.R. Logan (1996), 'Market transition and the persistence of power: the changing stratification system in China', *American Sociological Review*, **61**, 739–58.

Blecher, M.J. (2002), 'Hegemony and workers' politics in China', *The China Quarterly*, **170**, 283–303.

Burrows, R. (1999), 'Residential mobility and residualization in social housing in England', *Journal of Social Policy*, **28**, 27–52.

Cai, F. (2003), *Green Book of Population and Labour No.4*, Beijing: Social Science Documentary Press.

Cai, F., Y. Du and M. Wang (2002), 'What determine hukou system reform?', available at http://www.cass.net.cn/chinese/so6_rks/chrrsite/paper/working%20paper%2015.pdf.

Chan, K.W. (1994), *Cities with Invisible Walls*, Hong Kong: Oxford University Press.

Chan, K.W. (1996), 'Post-Mao China: a two-class urban society in the making', *International Journal of Urban and Regional Research*, **20**, 134–50.

Chan, K.W. and L. Zhang (1999), 'The hukou system and rural–urban migration: processes and changes', *China Quarterly*, **160**, 818–55.

Chen, C.Y. and Y.Y. Yang (eds) (2005), 'Education, living costs and housing limit the expenses of rural migrants', ('Zilv Jiaoyu, Dagong Shenghuo chengben he Zhufang Zhiyue Nongmingong Xiaofei'), available at http://news.sina.com.cn/c/2005-05-18/13255922175s.shtml (accessed at 18 May 2005).

Chen, F. (2000), 'The re-employment project in Shanghai: institutional workings and consequences for workers', *China Information*, **XIV**(2), 169–93.

Chen, G., C.L. Gu and F.L. Wu (2006), 'Urban poverty in the transitional economy: a case of Nanjing, China', *Habitat International*, **30**(1), 1–26.

China's State Council Information Office (CSCIO) (2004), 'Chinese Social Security and Policy', available at http://news.xinhuanet.com/zhengfu/2004-09/07/content_1952488.htm.

Coase, R. (1959), 'The federal communications commission', *Journal of Law and Economics*, **2**(2), 1–40.

Colasanto, D., A. Kapteyn and J. van der Gaag (1984), 'Two subjective definitions of poverty: results from the Wisconsin Basic Needs Study', *Journal of Human Resources*, **19**, 127–38.

Crump, J. (2002), 'Deconcentration by demolition: public housing, poverty, and urban policy', *Environment and Planning D*, **20**, 581–96.

Davis, D.S. (2003), 'From welfare benefit to capitalized asset: the re-commodification of residential space in urban China', in R. Forrest and J. Lee (eds), *Housing and Social Change: East–west Perspectives*, London: Routledge, pp. 183–98.

Demsetz, H. (1967), 'Towards a theory of property rights', *The American Economic Review*, **57**(2), 347–59.

Demsetz, H. (2002), 'Toward a theory of property rights II: The competition between private and collective ownership', *Journal of Legal Studies*, **31**(2), 653–72.

Ding, C.R. (2007), 'Policy and praxis of land acquisition in China', *Land Use Policy*, **24**(1), 1–13.

Dorling, D. and R. Woodward (1996), 'Social polarisation 1971–91: a micro-geography analysis of Britain', *Progress in Planning*, **45**, 1–66.

Duckett, J. (2004), 'State, collectivism and worker privilege: A study of urban health insurance reform', *The China Quarterly*, **177**, 155–73.

Fan, C.C. (2002), 'The elite, the natives, and the outsiders: migration and labour market segregation in urban China', *Annals of the Association of American Geographers*, **92**(1), 103–24.

Fan, C.C. (2004), 'The state, the migrant labor regime, and maiden workers in China', *Political Geography*, **23**(3), 283–305.

Fang, C., X. Zhang and S. Fan (2002), 'Emergence of urban poverty and inequality in China: evidence from household survey', *China Economic Review*, **13**(4), 430–43.

Fei, J.C.H. and G. Ranis (1964), *Development of the Labor Surplus Economy*, Homewood, IL: Irwin.

Forrest, R. and A. Murie (1990), *Selling the Welfare State*, London: Routledge.

Foster, J., J. Greer and E. Thorbecke (1984), 'A class of decomposable poverty measures', *Econometrica*, **52**, 761–5.

Friedrichs, J., G.C. Galster and S. Musterd (2003), 'Neighbourhood effects on social opportunities: the European and American research and policy context', *Housing Studies*, **18**(6), 797–806.

Friedrichs, J.R. and J.R. Blasius (2003), 'Social norms in distressed neighborhoods: testing the Wilson hypothesis', *Housing Studies*, **18**(6), 807–26.

Galster, G. and A. Zobel (1998), 'Will dispersed housing programmes reduce social problems in the US?', *Housing Studies*, **13**(5), 605–22.

Gans, H.J. (1993), 'From "underclass" to "undercaste": some observations about the future of the post-industrial economy and its major victims', *International Journal of Urban and Region Research*, **17**, 327–35.

Gilbert, A. (1997), 'Employment and poverty during economic restructuring: the case of Bogota, Colombia', *Urban Studies*, **34**(7), 1047–70.

Giles, J., A. Park and F. Cai (2006), 'Reemployment of dislocated workers in urban China: the roles of information and incentives', *Journal of Comparative Economics*, **34**(3), 582–607.

Greenstone, J.D. (1991), 'Culture, rationality, and the underclass', in C. Jencks and P.E. Peterson (eds), *The Urban Underclass*, Washington, DC: The Brookings Institution.

Gu, C.L. and H.Y. Liu (2002), 'Social polarization and segregation in Beijing', in J.R. Logan (ed.), *The New Chinese City: Globalization and Market Reform*, Oxford: Blackwell Publishers, pp. 198–211.

Guan, X. (2000), 'China's social policy: reform and development in the context of marketization and globalization', *Social Policy & Administration*, **34**(1), 115–30.

Guan, X. (2001), 'Globalization, inequality and social policy: China on the threshold of entry into the World Trade Organization', *Social Policy & Administration*, **35**(3), 242–57.

Gustafsson, B. and S. Li (2001), 'The effects of transition on the distribution of income in China: a study decomposing the GINI coefficient for 1988 and 1995', *Economics of Transition*, **9**(3), 593–617.

Gustafsson, B. and L. Shi (2004), 'Expenditures on education and health care and poverty in rural China', *China Economic Review*, **15**(3), 292–301.

Gustafsson, B. and W. Zhong (2000), 'How and why has poverty in China changed? A study based on microdata for 1988 and 1995', *China Quarterly*, **164**, 983–1006.

Gustafsson, B., S. Li and H. Sato (2006), 'Can a subjective poverty line be applied to China?' in S. Li and H. Sato (eds), *Unemployment, Inequality and Poverty in Urban China*, Abingdon: Routledge, pp. 152–72.

Hamnett, C. (1991), 'The relationship between residential migration and housing tenure in London, 1971–1981: a longitudinal analysis', *Environment and Planning A*, **23**, 1147–62.

Hamnett, C. (1996), 'Social polarization, economic restructuring and welfare state regimes', *Urban Studies*, **33**(8), 1407–30.

Hamnett, C. (2001), 'Social segregation and social polarization', in R. Paddison (ed.), *Handbook of Urban Studies*, London: Sage Publications, pp. 162–176.

He, S., Y. Liu, C. Webster and F. Wu (2009), 'Property rights redistribution, entitlement failure and the impoverishment of landless farmers in China', *Urban Studies*, **46**(9), 1925–49.

He, S., C. Webster, F. Wu and Y. Liu (2008), 'Profile the poor in a Chinese city: a case study of Nanjing', *Applied Spatial Analysis and Policy*, **1**(1), 193–214.

Ho, P. (2005), *Institutions in Transition: Land Ownership, Property Rights and Social Conflict in China*, Oxford: Oxford University Press.

Hoebel, E.A. (1966), *Anthropology: The Study of Man*, New York: McGraw-Hill.

Hong, D.Y. (2003), 'Shilun gaige yilai de zhongguo chengshi fupin' ['Reducing the urban poverty in China since reformation'], *Zhongguo Renmin Daxue Xuebao [Journal of Renmin University of China]*, **1**, 9–16.

Hu, A.G. (1999), *Zhongguo Fazhan Qianjing [China's Development Prospects]*, Hangzhou: Zhejiang Peoples Publisher.

Huang, Y. (2003), 'A room of one's own: housing consumption and residential crowding in transitional urban China', *Environment and Planning A*, **35**, 591–614.

Huang, Y. (2005), 'From work-unit compounds to gated communities: Housing inequality and residential segregation in transitional Beijing', in L.J.C. Ma and F. Wu (eds), *Restructuring the Chinese City: Changing Society, Economy and Space*, London and New York: Routledge, pp. 192–221.

Hussain, A. (2003), *Urban Poverty in China: Measurement, Patterns and Policies*, Geneva, Switzerland: International Labour Office.

The Investigating Group of Chinese Migrant Workers' Problems (2006), 'Reporting on the problems of Chinese farmer-turned workers', ['Zhongguo Nongmingong Wenti Yanjiu Zong Baogao'], *Reform [Gaige]*, **5**, 5–30.

Jargowsky, P.A. (1997), *Poverty and Place: Ghettos, Barrios, and the American City*, New York: Russell Sage Foundation.

Jencks, C. (1992), *Rethinking Social Policy: Race, Poverty, and the Underclass*, Cambridge, MA: Harvard University Press.

Jencks, C. and S.E. Mayer (1990), 'The social consequences of growing up in a poor neighborhood', in M.G.H. McGeary and E.L. Lawrence (eds), *Inner City Poverty in the United States*, Washington, DC: National University Press, pp. 111–86.

Khan, A.R. and C. Riskin (eds) (2001), *Inequality and Poverty in China in the Age of Globalization*, New York: Oxford University Press.

Knight, J. and L. Song (1999), *The Rural–urban Divide: Economic Disparities and Interactions in China*, Oxford: Oxford University Press.

Lee, G.O.M. (2001), 'Labour policy reform', in L. Wong and N. Flynn (eds), *The Market in Chinese Social Policy*, London: Palgrave Macmillan, pp. 12-37.

Lee, G.O.M. and M. Warner (2004), 'The Shanghai re-employment model: from local experiment to nation-wide labour market policy', *The China Quarterly*, **177**, 174–89.

Lee, J. (2000), 'From welfare housing to home ownership: the dilemma of China's housing reform', *Housing Studies*, **15**(1), 61–76.

Lewis, O. (1969), 'The culture of poverty', in D. P. Moynihan (ed.),*On Understanding Poverty: Perspectives from the Social Sciences*, New York: Basic Books, pp. 187–200.

Lewis, W.A. (1954), 'Economic development with unlimited supply of labour', *The Manchester School of Economic and Social Studies*, **22**(5), 139–91.

Li, B.Q. (2004), 'Social policy reform in China: views from home and abroad', *Journal of Social Policy*, **33**, 674–75.

Li, B.Q. (2006), 'Floating population or urban citizens? Status, social provision and circumstances of rural-urban migrants in China', *Social Policy & Administration*, **40**(2), 174–95.

Li, Q. (2002), *Social Stratum Structure under Market Transition in China* [in Chinese], Harbin: Heilongjiang People's Press.

Li, S. (2006), 'Rising poverty and its causes in urban China', in S. Li and H. Sato (eds), *Unemployment, Inequality and Poverty in Urban China*, Abingdon: Routledge, pp. 128–51.

Li, S. and H. Sato (eds) (2006), *Unemployment, Inequality and Poverty in Urban China*, Abingdon: Routledge.

Li, S.M. (2000), 'Housing consumption in urban China: a comparative study of Beijing and Guangzhou', *Environment and Planning A*, **32**(6), 1115–34.

Li, S.M. and L. Li (2006), 'Life course and housing tenure change in urban China: a study of Guangzhou', *Housing Studies*, **21**(5), 655–72.

Li, Z. and F. Wu (2008), 'Tenure-based residential segregation in post-reform Chinese cities: a case study of Shanghai', *Transactions of the Institute of British Geographers*, **33**(3), 404–19.

Lin, G.C.S. and S.P.S. Ho (2005), 'China's land resources and land use change', in C.R. Ding and Y. Song (eds), *Emerging Land and Housing Markets in China*, Cambridge, MA: Lincoln Institute of Land Policy, pp. 89–123.

Lin, N. (1995), 'Local market socialism: Local corporatism in action in rural China ', *Theory and Society*, **24**(3), 301–14.

Liu, F.R. and J.H. Pan (2007), *China Urban Development Report*, Beijing: Social Science Documentation Press.

Liu, Y.T. and F. Wu (2006a), 'The state, institutional transition and the creation of new urban poverty in China', *Social Policy & Administration*, **40**(2), 121–37.

Liu, Y.T. and F. Wu (2006b), 'Urban poverty neighbourhoods: typology and spatial concentration under China's market transition, a case study of Nanjing', *Geoforum*, **37**(4), 610–26.

Liu, Y.T., S.J. He and F. Wu (2008), 'Urban pauperization under China's social exclusion: a case study of Nanjing', *Journal of Urban Affairs*, **30**(1), 21–36.

Logan, J.R., Y.J. Bian and F.Q. Bian (1999), 'Housing inequality in urban China in the 1990s', *International Journal of Urban and Regional Research*, **23**(1), 7–25.

Lu, Z. and S. Song (2006), 'Rural–urban migration and wage determination: the case of Tianjin, China', *China Economic Review*, **17**(3), 337–45.

Ma, L.J.C. (2002), 'Urban transformation in China, 1949–2000: a review and research agenda', *Environment and Planning A*, **34**(9), 1545–69.

Ma, L.J.C. and B. Xiang (1998), 'Native place, migration and the emergence of peasant enclaves in Beijing', *China Quarterly*, **155**, 546–81.

MacDonald, H. (1997), 'Comment on Sandra J. Newman and Ann B. Schnare's "And a suitable living environment": the failure of housing programs to deliver on neighbourhood quality', *Housing Policy Debate*, **8**, 755–62.

Marcuse, P. (1996), 'Space and race in the post-Fordist city', in E. Mingione (ed.), *Urban Poverty and the Underclass*, Oxford: Blackwell, pp. 176–216.

Massey, D.S., A.B. Gross and K. Shibuya (1994), 'Migration, segregation, and the geographic concentration of poverty', *American Sociological Review*, **59**, 425–45.

McCulloch, A. (2001), 'Ward-level deprivation and individual social and economic outcomes in the British Household Panel Study', *Environment and Planning A*, **33**, 667–84.

Mei, F.Q. (2004), 'Report on power structures in Mingxing Village, Shenzhen City, Guangdong Province', *Chinese Sociology & Anthropology*, **36**(4), 44–65.

Meng, X., R. Gregory and G. Wan (2006), 'China Urban poverty and its contributing factors, 1986–2000', Research Paper No. 2006/133, Helsinki: UNU-WIDER.

Mingione, E. (1993), 'The new urban poverty and the underclass: introduction', *International Journal of Urban and Regional Research*, **17**, 324–26.

Mingione, E. (ed.) (1996), *Urban Poverty and the Underclass: A Reader*, Oxford: Blackwell.

Ministry of Civil Affairs (various years), 'The Statistical Report of Civil Affairs 2003–2007', available at http://www.mca.gov.cn/article/zwgk/tjsj/, accessed 15 January 2009.

Mohan, J. (2000), 'Geographies of welfare and social exclusion', *Progress in Human Geography*, **24**(2), 291–300.

Morris, L.D. (1993), 'Is there a British underclass?', *International Journal of Urban and Regional Research*, **17**, 404–12.

MoSS and SSB (2001), *Laodong yu Shehui Baozhang Fazhan de Tongji Baogao [Statistical Report of Labour and Social Security Development 2000]*, Beijing: MoSS and SSB.

Musterd, S. and A. Murie (2006), 'The spatial dimensions of urban social exclusion and integration', in S. Musterd, A. Murie and C. Kesteloot (eds), *Neighbourhoods of Poverty: Urban Social Exclusion and Integration in Europe*, Basingstoke: Palgrave, pp. 1–16.

Musterd, S. and W. Ostendorf (1998), *Urban Segregation and the Welfare State: Inequality and Exclusion in Western Cities*, London: Routledge.

Musterd, S., H. Priemus and R. Van Kempen (1999), 'Towards undivided cities: the potential of economic revitalisation and housing redifferentiation', *Housing Studies*, **14**(5), 573–84.

Nanjing Census Office (NCO) (2002), *Population of Nanjing at the Turn of the Century*, Beijing: China Statistics Press.

Nanjing Statistical Bureau (NSB) (2003, 2004), *Nanjing Statistical Yearbook 2003, 2004*, Beijing: China Statistics Press.

Nee, V. (1989), 'A theory of market transition: from redistribution to markets in state socialism', *American Sociological Review*, **54**, 663–81.

Nee, V. (1992), 'Organizational dynamics of market transition: hybrid forms, property rights, and mixed economy in China', *Administrative Science Quarterly*, **37**, 1–27.

Neef, N. (1992), 'The new poverty and local government social policies: a West German perspective', *International Journal of Urban and Regional Research*, **16**, 202–21.

Oi, J. (1992), 'Fiscal reform and the economic foundations of local state corporatism in China', *World Politics*, **45**(1), 99–126.

Oi, J. and A. Walder (eds) (1999), *Property Rights and Economic Reform in China*, Stanford, CA: Stanford University Press.

Orfield, M. (1998), *Metropolitics: A Regional Agenda for Community and Stability*, Washington, DC: The Brookings Institution and the Lincoln Institute of Land Policy.

Peck, J. (2001), 'Neoliberalizing states: thin policies/hard outcomes', *Progress in Human Geography*, **25**(3), 445–55.

Polanyi, K. (1944), *The Great Transformation*, New York: Rinehart.

Pradhan, M. and M. Ravallion (2000), 'Measuring poverty using qualitative perceptions of consmer adequacy', *The Review of Economics and Statistics*, **82**(3), 462–71.

Ravallion, M. and S. Chen (2007), 'China's (uneven) progress against poverty', *Journal of Development Economics*, **82**, 1–42.

Riskin, C. (1987), *China's Political Economy: The Quest for Development since 1949*, Oxford: Oxford University Press.

Sassen, S. (1991), *The Global City: New York, London, Tokyo*, Princeton, NJ: Princeton University Press.

Sato, H. (2006), 'Housing inequality and housing poverty in urban China in the late 1990s', *China Economic Review*, **17**(1), 37–50.

Sen, A. (1981), *Poverty and Famines: An Essay on Entitlement and Famines*, Oxford: Clarendon Press.

Shen, J.F. (2002), 'A study of the temporary population in Chinese cities', *Habitat International*, **26**(3), 363–77.

Silver, H. (1993), 'National concept of the new urban poverty: social structure change in Britain, France and the United States', *International Journal of Urban and Regional Research*, **17**, 336–54.

Small, M.L. and K. Newman (2001), 'Urban poverty after the truly disadvantaged: the rediscovery of the family, the neighborhood, and culture', *Annual Review of Sociology*, **27**, 23–45.

Solinger, D.J. (1999), *Contesting Citizenship in Urban China: Peasant Migrants, the State, and the Logic of the Market*, Berkeley: University of California Press.

Solinger, D.J. (2001), 'Why we cannot count the "unemployed"', *China Quarterly*, **167**, 671–88.

Solinger, D.J. (2002), 'Labour market reform and the plight of the laid-off proletariat', *China Quarterly*, **170**, 304–26.

Solinger, D.J. (2006), 'The creation of a new underclass in China and its implications', *Environment and Urbanization*, **18**(1), 177–93.

State Statistics Bureau (SSB) (2000, 2002, 2004, 2007), *China Statistical Yearbook 2000, 2002, 2004, 2007*, Beijing: China Statistics Press.

State Statistics Bureau (SSB) (2006), *China Labour Statistical Yearbook 2005*, Beijing: China Statistics Press.

Steinfeld, E.S. (1998), *Forging Reform in China: the Fate of State-owned Industry*, Cambridge: Cambridge University Press.

Sun, L.P. (2002), 'Ziyuan chongxin jilei beijing xia de dicing shehui xingcheng' ['Coming into being of grass-root class against the background of capital reaccumulation'], *Zhanlue yu guanli [Strategy and Management]*, **1**, 18–26.

Szelenyi, I. (1983), *Urban Inequality under State Socialism*, New York: Oxford University Press.

Tang, J. (2003), 'Zhongguo Chengshi Juming Zuidi Shenghuo Baozhang Zhidude Tiaoyueshi Fazhan' ['China's urban MLSS leapfrogging development'], in X. Ru (ed.), *Zhongguo Shehui Xingshi Fengxi yu Yuche 2003 [The Analysis and Forecast of China's Social Development Trend]*, Beijing: Shehui kexue wenxian chubanshe (Social Science Press), pp. 192–202.

Tang, W.F. and W.L. Parish (2000), *Chinese Urban Life under Reform: The Changing Social Contract*, Cambridge: Cambridge University Press.

Todaro, M.P. (1969), 'A model of labour migration and urban unemployment in less developed countries', *The American Economic Review*, **59**, 138–48.

Tsai, L.L. (2002), 'Cadres, temple and lineage institutions, and governance in rural China', *The China Journal*, **48**, 1–27.

UN-Habitat (2003), *The Challenge of Slums: Global Report on Human Settlements* London: Earthscan.

UNCHS (United Nations Centre for Human Settlements) (Habitat) (2001), *Cities in a Globalizing World: Global Report on Human Settlements 2001*, London: Earthscan.

UNDP (2000), *Policies for Poverty Reduction in China*, Beijing: UNDP China Office.

Unger, J. and A. Chan (1999), 'Inheritors of the boom: private enterprise and the role of local government in a rural south China township', *The China Journal*, **42**, 44–74.

Unger, J. and A. Chan (2004), 'The internal politics of an urban Chinese work community: a case study of employee influence on decision-making at a state-owned factory', *The China Journal*, **52** (July), 1–24.

Van Kempen, E.T. (1994), 'The dual city and the poor: social polarisation, social segregation and life chances', *Urban Studies*, **31**(7), 995–1015.

Van Praag, B.M.S., A.J.M. Hagenaars and H. van Weeren (1982), 'Poverty in Europe', *Review of Income and Wealth*, **28**, 345–59.

Wacquant, L. (2008), *Urban Outcasts: A Comparative Sociology of Advanced Marginality*, Cambridge: Polity Press.

Wacquant, L.J.D. (1993), 'Urban outcasts: stigma and division in the black American ghetto and the French urban periphery', *International Journal of Urban and Region Research*, **17**, 365–83.

Walder, A. (1995), 'Local governments as industrial firms: an organizational analysis of China's transitional economy', *American Journal of Sociology*, **101**(2), 263–301.

Walder, A. and J. Oi (1999), 'Property rights in the Chinese economy: contours of the process of change', in J. Oi and A. Walder (eds), *Property Rights and Economic Reform in China*, Stanford, CA: Stanford University Press, pp. 1–24.

Walder, A.G. (ed.) (1996), *China's Transitional Economy*, Oxford: Oxford University Press.

Walks, R.A. (2001), 'The social ecology of the post-Fordist/global city? Economic restructuring and socio-spatial polarisation in the Toronto urban region', *Urban Studies*, **38**(3), 407–77.

Wang, M. (2004), 'New urban poverty in China: disadvantaged retrenched workers', *International Development Planning Review*, **26**(2), 117–39.

Wang, S. (2008), 'Great transformation: the double movement in China since the 1980s', *China Social Science*, **1**(1), 129–207 [in Chinese].

Wang, Y.P. (2000), 'Housing reform and its impacts on the urban poor', *Housing Studies*, **15**(6), 845–64.

Wang, Y.J. (2002), 'Dui muqian woguo chengshi pinkun zhuangkuang de panduan fenxi' ['Assessment and analysis of urban poverty in China'], *Shichang yu renkou fenxi [Market and Population Analysis]*, **6**, 14–18.

Wang, Y.P. (2004), *Urban Poverty, Housing, and Social Change in China*, London: Routledge.

Wang, Y.P. (2005), 'Low-income communities and urban poverty in China', *Urban Geography*, **26**(3), 222–42.

Wang, Y.P. and A. Murie (1999), *Housing Policy and Practice in China*, Basingstoke: Macmillan Press.

Wang, Y.P. and A. Murie (2000), 'Social and spatial implications of housing reform in China', *International Journal of Urban and Regional Research*, **24**(2), 397–417.

Webster, C., F.L. Wu and Y.J. Zhao (2006), 'China's modern gated cities', in G. Glasze, C. Webster and K. Frantz (eds), *Private Cities: Global and Local Perspectives*, Abingdon: Routledge, pp. 153–69.

Wessel, T. (2000), 'Social polarisation and socioeconomic segregation in a welfare state: the case of Oslo', *Urban Studies*, **37**(11), 1947–67.

White, P.E. (1998), 'Ideologies, social exclusion and spatial segregation in Paris', in S. Musterd and W. Ostendorf (eds), *Urban Segregation and the Welfare State: Inequality and Exclusion in Western Cities*, London: Routledge, pp. 148–67.

Whyte, M.K. and W.L. Parish (1984), *Urban Life in Contemporary China*, Chicago, IL: University of Chicago Press.

Wilson, W.J. (1987), *The Truly Disadvantaged: The Inner City, the Underclass and Public Policy*, Chicago: Chicago University Press.

Wilson, W.J. (1996), *When Work Disappears: The World of the New Urban Poor*, New York: Random House.

Wong, C.K. (1995), 'Measuring third world poverty by the international poverty line – the case of reform China', *Social Policy & Administration*, **29**(3), 189–203.

Wong, C.K. (1997), 'How many poor people in Shanghai today? The question of poverty and poverty measure', *Issues & Studies*, **33**(12), 32–49.

Wong, L. and K. Ngok (2006), 'Social policy between plan and market: Xiagang (off-duty employment) and the policy of the re-employment service centres in China', *Social Policy & Administration*, **40**(2), 158–73.

World Bank (1993), *The East Asian Miracle: Economic Growth and Public Policy*, Oxford: Oxford University Press.

World Bank (2007), PovcalNet, available at http://iresearch.worldbank.org/PovcalNet, accessed December 2007.

Wu, F. (2004), 'Urban poverty and marginalization under market transition: the case of Chinese cities', *International Journal of Urban and Regional Research*, **28**(2), 401–23.

Wu, F. (2007), 'The poverty of transition: from industrial district to poor neighbourhood in the city of Nanjing, China', *Urban Studies*, **44**(13), 2673–94.

Wu, F., J. Xu and A.G.-O. Yeh (2007), *Urban Development in Post-reform China: State, Market and Space*, London: Routledge.

Wu, F.L. and N.Y. Huang (2007), 'New urban poverty in China: economic restructuring and transformation of welfare provision', *Asia Pacific Viewpoint*, **48**(2), 168–85.

Wu, W.P. (2002), 'Migrant housing in urban China: Choices and constraints', *Urban Affairs Review*, **38**(1), 90–119.

Wu, W.P. (2004), 'Sources of migrant housing disadvantage in urban China', *Environment and Planning A*, **36**(7), 1285–304.

Xiang, B. (1999), 'Zhejiang village in Beijing: creating a visible non-state space through migration and marketized networks', in F.N. Pieke and H. Mallee (eds), *Internal and International Migration: Chinese Perspectives*, Surrey: Curzon.

Xinhua News Agency. (2002), News report on poverty, 21 March 2002.

Yang, G. (2007), 'Reform creating new three mountains: the current situation and causes of education, healthcare and housing problems', *Contemporary China Studies*, available at http://www.chinayj.net/, in Chinese, accessed 10 October 2008.

Yao, S.J. (2004), 'Unemployment and urban poverty in China: a case study of Guangzhou and Tianjin', *Journal of International Development*, **16**, 171–88.

Yeh, A.G.O. and F. Wu (1996), 'The new land development process and urban development in Chinese cities', *International Journal of Urban and Regional Research*, **20**(2), 330–53.

Yin, Z.G. (2002), 'Beijing chengshi jumin pinkun wenti diaocha baogao' ['Survey report of urban poverty in Beijing'], *Xin Shiye [New Horizon]*, **1**, 47–51.

Yuan, Y., X.Q. Xu (2008), 'Geography of urban deprivation in transitional China: a case study of Guangzhou city', *Scientia Geographica Sinica*, **28**(4), 457–63.

Zhang, L., S.X.B. Zhao and J.P. Tian (2003), 'Self-help in housing and Chengzhongcun in China's urbanization', *International Journal of Urban and Regional Research*, **27**(4), 912–37.

Zhang, L.Y. (2003), 'Economic development in Shanghai and the role of the state', *Urban Studies*, **40**(8), 1549–72.

Zhang, S.F. (2004), *Make the Landless Farmers' Living Sustainable* [in Chinese], Beijing: Centre of Social Policy Studies Chinese Academy of Social Sciences.

Zhu, J.M. (2004), 'From land use right to land development right: institutional change in China's urban development', *Urban Studies*, **41**(7), 1249–67.

Zhu, L. (2002), *The Tide of Peasant Workers in China [Zhongguo Mingongchao]*, Fujian: Fujian Renmin Press.

Index